THE OLD
REVOLUTIONARIES

Also by Pauline Maier

FROM RESISTANCE TO REVOLUTION
*Colonial Radicals and the Development of
American Opposition to Britain, 1765–1776*
(1972)

THE OLD REVOLUTIONARIES

*Political Lives in the Age
of Samuel Adams*

by PAULINE MAIER

W.W. NORTON & COMPANY
New York • London

This book

is for my children.

An earlier version of this book
was presented as the
ANSON G. PHELPS LECTURES
at New York University for 1976.

Copyright © 1980 by Pauline Maier
Introduction © copyright 1990 by Pauline Maier
First published as a Norton paperback 1990 by arrangement with
Alfred A. Knopf, Inc.

Library of Congress Cataloging in Publication Data
Maier, Pauline [date], The old revolutionaries.
Includes bibliographical references and index.
1. United States—History—Revolution, 1775–1783—
Biography.   2. Revolutionists—United States—
Biography.   3. United States—Biography.
I. Title.
E302.5.M23   1980   973.3′092′2 [B]   80-7624

ISBN 0-393-30663-1

W. W. Norton & Company, Inc., 500 Fifth Avenue, New York, N. Y. 10110
W. W. Norton & Company Ltd., 37 Great Russell Street, London WC1B 3NU

1 2 3 4 5 6 7 8 9 10

INTRODUCTION

to the Norton Paperback Edition

I AM STRUCK, now, ten years later almost to the day, by the confession in the original preface to *The Old Revolutionaries* that the book was not undertaken to answer "questions of the sort historians are trained to ask." It emerged instead from a sense of personal discontent at having earlier written a book about American opposition to Britain between 1765 and 1776 without coming to know in a humanly satisfying way the Americans of whom I wrote. And so, where once I had read their papers to understand the course of the Independence movement, I went back to try instead to understand individuals caught up in that event.

Since my subjects were practitioners of politics, *The Old Revolutionaries* took up several political issues. It discussed the nature of revolutionary politics and examined the personal needs and experiences that prepared certain individuals to accept revolution and the changes it implied. The book also reported a few unanticipated discoveries—about the varied sources of what John Adams called the "sternness of stuff" necessary to sustain revolutionaries through trying times, and the different shades of meaning that common beliefs and commitments assumed for different individuals in different places. But the greatest discovery lay in uncovering the reasons for my earlier discontent. In short, what I felt compelled to understand before I could "know" men of the eighteenth century was different from what they thought important to reveal. Americans of the revolutionary era spoke readily of their causes, not themselves; for Americans of the twentieth century, however, the self had become primary. Suddenly, as I noted in the first preface, even the apparently wooden quality of Samuel Adams's family correspondence became a revelation not just of Adams, but of what made life in the eighteenth century different, and so of what is distinctive (and even parochial) about life in the twentieth century.

But even when the historian strives primarily to understand the people of another time and to illuminate their world, the work bears on the more focused questions raised by professional scholars. *The Old Revolutionaries*, I now realize, includes considerable material relevant to a controversy that has come to dominate debate over the American Revolution, a controversy that concerns nothing less than the place of that event in American history.

At the center of the dispute is a body of writings that associate the American Revolution with a "civic humanist" or "classical republican" tradition in western thought described by J.G.A. Pocock. According to that tradition, republics, including the one founded in 1776, could survive only if their citizens were "virtuous," that is, if they were willing to sacrifice their private interests to serve the larger public good. But virtue, so the argument goes, had profoundly conservative implications. It demanded that the mass of the people subordinate their own ambitions and defer for leadership to a handful of "gentlemen" identified by their wealth, education, and leisure. Virtue also militated against capitalistic development because the expansion of a market economy implied a striving for private profit and a growth of luxury that would undermine both the civic commitment and the Spartan austerity essential to a republic.[1]

In short, according to those who associate Independence with "classical republicanism" or "civic humanism," the ideas that dominated the American Revolution and, by implication, the event itself, were "premodern" and even "antimodern," dedicated to the realization of nostalgic, backward-looking ideals that implied stasis, not progressive change. The socially fluid, democratic, entrepreneurial, materialistic world of the early nineteenth century depended, the argument continues, upon the acceptance of an alternative set of "liberal" ideas that laid aside the notion of virtue and legitimized the pursuit of individual self-interest. Although isolated groups within revolutionary America are identified as proponents or precursers of "liberal" ideas, in general the triumph of liberalism in the United States is said to have occurred sometime after 1789, the conventional closing date of the Revolution, and is frequently associated with the Jeffersonian Republicans.

It is, of course, dangerous to summarize briefly and still more to question a complex argument that has taken slightly different forms and emphases in books and articles by different authors, and even in different works by the same authors. Parts of the interpretation are, in any case, well founded. *The Old Revolutionaries* and other books provide abundant evidence that virtue had an important place in the republican creed of prominent American leaders of 1776. In fact, the concept of virtue confirmed and helps explain the revolutionaries' insistence upon discussing the public cause rather than their private selves, which makes them so elusive and difficult for the modern historian to "know." Nonetheless, for me the lives and convictions of the people examined here, all of whom were primary figures in the Independence movement, call into question descriptions of the Revolution as socially and economically conservative, and, moreover, the wisdom of efforts to impose upon individuals or political groups rigid, mutually exclusive ideological categories defined by historians of two centuries later.

Start with Samuel Adams, whom contemporaries considered the quintessential *"Man of the Revolution"* because, *The Old Revolutionaries* argues, his disregard for wealth and family honor, his wholehearted commitment to the public cause, even his literary and personal style, made him an incarnation of the virtuous man. Like Virginia's Richard Henry Lee, Adams was described as "one of Plutarch's men," that is, a republican of the classical model. He was, however, also a radical social equalitarian who went so far as to condemn deference to the rich as dangerous and demeaning and to suggest that it would be better to prefer men in need for public office.

Nor were Adams's equalitarian convictions his alone. For others, too, the Revolution warred against rule by a handful of rich, educated, leisured men. Rank in the American republic was to reflect virtue and ability. Wealth—as even the wealthy Charles Carroll of Carrollton once confessed—was an imperfect index of those attributes. If Carroll thought that propertied men were nonetheless more often virtuous than the poor, others insisted that modest means and dedicated patriotism went together. The pride Adams and Thomas Young took in their poverty is extremely important here because it shows that the concept of virtue, associated in the "classical" way with personal austerity, could carry socially radical implications. Leisure, on the other hand, became an unambiguous source of not honor but suspicion, a sign of aristocratic decadence in a new nation that valued industry and condemned idleness. Education and knowledge remained worthy of respect, but were no longer to be confined to the few because, as Adams noted, ability was distributed through the population unpredictably: "a cottager may beget a wise son; the noble, a fool."

There were some within the revolutionary movement like Lee, who assumed that the new values of the republic would sustain the rank of financially hard-pressed old elite families such as his own, or Carroll, who tried to limit the extent of social change once Catholics were granted civil status in Maryland. The Old Revolutionary who most closely approximated the social conservatism described by historians committed to the classical republican/liberal dichotomy was perhaps Christopher Gadsden, who in 1784 told the politically assertive mechanics and lesser merchants of Charleston's Marine Anti-Britannic Society that *"true genuine Republicanism"* demanded that every man, even if he had held a respectable station during the revolutionary war, fall "cheerfully into the ranks again," sacrificing "all his resentments and private feelings, to the good of the State." But Gadsden has been included among upwardly mobile Americans of the 1760s and 1770s who were supposedly drawn toward a "liberal view of society" because he endorsed free trade. Lee also argued that "the free nature and genius of commerce" abhorred restraint.[2] Such occasional "liberal" convictions did not, it seems, correlate reliably with social radicalism.

Similarly, some Old Revolutionaries such as Lee saw in virtue an imperative to self-denial that was necessarily at odds with commerce and the avarice that supported it. Americans of 1776 were, however, rarely so unrealistic as to tie the success of the Revolution to the denial of self-interest: note the calmness with which Adams conceded in 1778—without, however, abandoning faith in the Revolution—that human nature precluded his dream of an age when men would have no passion but love of their country, or Mary Bartlett's almost casual observation that "People You Know will Take Care of Self first."

Nor was it difficult for revolutionaries to reconcile republicanism with economic ambition. Even the New York Sons of Liberty, who "talked less of virtue than of interest" and aggressively sought material betterment, condemned corruption in the classic "civic humanist" manner and took care that their own conduct conformed to the standard of virtue. That standard precluded seeking private benefits at the cost of the public good—which was the essence of corruption—, but imposed no restriction upon enterprise where self-interest and the community's good coincided, as in privateering. A certain practical common sense lay behind the *New York Journal*'s conclusion that "no man is to be supposed so disinterested, as not to include his own interest, in all his endeavours to promote that of others." Note, too, that for Charles Carroll of Annapolis, money—not just landed property—could make a man independent, that is, free from a servile dependence on others, which was a classic attribute of the republican citizen.

More important, Americans of the 1770s almost universally associated liberty with prosperity and economic growth. One powerful source of that faith was John Trenchard and Thomas Gordon's *Cato's Letters*, which were probably more often reprinted in the colonial press and more frequently cited by colonists than any other single piece of English political writing, and which were within the allegedly regressive classical republican tradition. (Gordon was in fact a classicist who also published translations of Sallust and Tacitus with extensive introductions that drew out their meaning for the eighteenth century.) Trenchard and Gordon's "Whig economics" was based not upon an analysis of market mechanisms but an appreciation for the role of secure property rights in sustaining industry and initiative: men would not venture their time and capital on profitable ventures if arbitrary power could simply confiscate the fruits of their efforts. At times, however, "Cato" drew conclusions much like those of that prototypical "liberal" economist of a later day, Adam Smith. "Let the people alone," "Cato" wrote, "and they will take care of themselves and do it best."[3]

All this suggests that the classical republican/liberal dichotomy has misconstrued not just the role of European ideas in American politics, but the impact of the American Revolution. The revolutionaries of 1776 uniformly associated Independence and the foundation of a republic less with restoration or stasis than with change; the Revolution began a "novus ordo seclorum," a new order of the ages. Essential to that new order was the establishment of a meritocratic basis of rank and the abandonment of legal privilege, an enhanced respect and opportunity for individuals of humble origin, and a new and more broad-based prosperity, which would itself be the natural fruit of freedom. Those ideals, alive and well in the Age of Jackson, were understood correctly as a heritage from the Age of Samuel Adams.

Historians who hold different views can, however, still find evidence in *The Old Revolutionaries* to support their arguments. Lives are rich, full of complications and contradictions; they comprise part of the refractory, tangled substance of the past which historical interpretations must somehow accommodate and elucidate. When historical debate on the Revolution shifts, the lives of the Old Revolutionaries, including Samuel Adams, Isaac Sears, Thomas Young, Richard Henry Lee, the Charles Carrolls, Mary and Josiah Bartlett, will remain to test and judge new hypotheses. One of the greatest strengths of the biographical approach to history lies precisely in its capacity to undercut the distorting reductionism to which more abstract arguments are prey. For now, however, the new Norton paperback edition of *The Old Revolutionaries* will allow more readers to share what was once my private adventure, to come to know those earlier Americans and to glimpse through them the familiar and the unfamiliar in the distant worlds of eighteenth-century America.

Pauline Maier

Cambridge, Massachusetts
August 1989

CONTENTS

ILLUSTRATIONS

———••◦◦◦◦◦•••———

Insert following page 104.

PREFACE

LET ME CONFESS at the outset that this book, though it answers some questions of the sort historians are trained to ask, has also been—and was meant from the outset to be—a personal adventure. I wanted to know better what it was to be an American of the late eighteenth century and to live through the American Revolution. The project began eight years ago when I completed a book on the radicals of 1765–1776, those colonists who were in the vanguard of what became the American revolutionary movement. I was confident that I knew the revolutionaries' politics well, yet I had only a very limited sense of them as people—for reasons that are now far clearer to me than they were then. My interest in the colonists' "struggle for liberty" would have been considered appropriate two centuries earlier, but curiosity about the men involved in that struggle was alien to the culture of mid-eighteenth-century America. If we live in a culture of narcissism, theirs was the opposite. Self-indulgence was condemned as a form of "corruption," and self-indulgence often seemed to include that very concern with individuals, their needs and emotions that became a part of the modern sensibility with the rise of romanticism in the late eighteenth and early nineteenth centuries.

The great cultural transformation that divides us from the revolutionaries can perhaps be seen more clearly in English letters. The young James Boswell, born in 1740, was part of a new mentality in his obsession with individuals and subjective emotion. So different were the objects of his curiosity from those native to his subject, Samuel Johnson, who was born in 1709, that one of Johnson's recent biographers describes their dialogues as between two epochs as well as two men.* The Revolutionaries of 1776 belonged, like Johnson, to an earlier world concerned with men less in their separate and private capacities than as parts of some larger human enterprise. The Americans believed above all that good or "virtuous" men would subordinate personal considerations to the good of their communities—to the commonweal or *res publica*—which was a more proper object of their thoughts and efforts. It was therefore characteristic of the time that Charles Thomson, the Philadelphia patriot, scrupulously removed the names of Pennsylvania revolutionaries from David Ramsay's manuscript history of the Revolution. To emphasize who did what, it seemed, was to detract attention from their common public mission.

Americans of the mid-eighteenth century in general wrote more easily about causes than about themselves. Benjamin Franklin, the best-known American of that day, could write about himself only by making himself into a cause, a model to show younger Americans how personal ambition and public service could be reconciled. John Adams's diary, like the letters of Mary and Josiah Bartlett or the correspondence of Charles Carroll of Carrollton, reveal private feelings and needs in a more straightforward way. Those are, of course, personal documents, written for the author's own use or for the information of close relatives, and so one would expect them to include private information. But in an extreme case such as that of Samuel Adams, even family correspondence was by our standards highly impersonal, shaped above all by public commitments. Once I understood why, Adams's apparently wooden letters began to say something very important about him, and I could understand more of what made life in the eighteenth century different (or, which is the same thing, what is distinctive about life in the twentieth century). It is important to realize, however, that

* John Wain, *Samuel Johnson, A Biography* (New York, 1975), pp. 229-30.

when we push beyond the surface of most eighteenth-century sources and ask questions about the character of individuals' lives, we are often asking what our subjects had no intention of telling us, and even what those private provincial people would have said (perhaps properly, as I sometimes felt in reading the Carroll papers) was none of our business.

Visual expectations also interfere with our easy understanding of revolutionary Americans. We are accustomed to photographs and moving pictures. Instead, we have for the eighteenth century etchings or woodcuts that are often stiff (literally "wooden") and awkward to our eye. We also have posed portraits, which are sometimes wonderfully evocative of their subjects' characters as well as their physical appearances. But only a small part of the population had portraits painted—those who were wealthy enough to afford an artist's services, or who participated in some public event that was worth memorializing (signing the Declaration of Independence, for example). We have portraits of Samuel Adams, of Richard Henry Lee, of Charles Carroll of Carrollton—but not of Isaac Sears and Thomas Young, whose importance to the cause was more local than national, and who were involved in no events that caught the attention of wealthy patrons or of artists who recorded moments in the revolutionary struggle for the inspiration of later Americans. Similarly, we have portraits of Dr. Josiah Bartlett, a prominent New Hampshire statesman and a member of the Continental Congress—but none of his wife, Mary, whose life was also changed by the American Revolution.

Like my interest in the people of the revolutionary era, another more formal historical question arose out of my earlier work on the Revolution. In *From Resistance to Revolution: Colonial Radicals and the Development of American Opposition to Britain, 1765–1776,* which was published in 1972, I traced the process by which loyal colonists became revolutionaries. Given their political assumptions, and given the events that occurred in the previous decade, their decision of 1776 made great sense. British action not just in America but also in Ireland, Corsica, the West Indies, and in England itself contributed to the colonists' conclusion that they had no future as "free Britons" within the empire, that to remain under the Crown would be to accept for themselves and their children the status of the oppressed Irish. Instead they chose to become an independent nation; and to protect their freedom further, they founded a republic, eliminating from American institutions all traces of that hereditary power which was, they decided, the fatal flaw in Britain's constitution. The pieces fit in place nicely, adding up to a revolutionary argument that was "rational and compelling." But then why were some convinced and not others?

The answer to that question, I concluded, would require a far different study from the one I had just completed, and its approach should be that of collective biography. I never intended, however, to do collective biography in the quantitative sense. Statistical analyses of the persons involved in the revolutionary movement can be very instructive, particularly for a single community. But even the best of such analyses have difficulty moving from the characteristics of political activists to explaining why they did what they did. To understand the foundations of political commitment, it seemed to me equally valid to look at the lives of committed individuals in a variety of different places. I hoped to learn, as I suggested should be done in the preface of *From Resistance to Revolution,* how political ambitions, economic interests, or any other relevant considerations "encouraged, permitted, or retarded adherence" to the argument for revolution. Certainly there remain strong historiographical reasons for looking at the subject in so broad a perspective. For almost three-quarters of a century now, some historians have continued to debate whether socioeconomic or intellectual forces lay behind the Revolution without reaching any very satisfactory conclusion—time enough to indicate that the question is flawed, that human action is far more complicated than the question assumes. And so, appropriately, historians have in recent years attempted to see how the various determinants of politics coincided rather than to weigh their importance against each other.

The Revolution of 1776 was the single most important public event in the lives of the people I studied; it was a consuming cause that focused their energies and talents. So intense a commitment must have coincided with more private and local considerations. As a result I tried to discover what needs or aspirations individuals seized upon to give their lives meaning and consistency, and what if anything those demands and dreams had to do with their politics. All the persons I studied, except perhaps Carroll, were provincials; their lives and politics were formed within separate colonies that were linked only through London. They became nationalists in that they came to advocate American independence and, in their efforts to organize intercolonial cooperation against Britain, they served as architects of the United States. But the idea of the republic—as I explain in the final chapter—may well have been of greater importance to them and their politics than that of the nation, as was appropriate to their place in time. The nation, after all, is a concept that took on great emotional force in the more romantic politics of the nineteenth century. The republic, by contrast, was inextricably bound up with a belief in reason, which was a revolutionary creed of the 1700s. The Old Revolutionaries' republicanism built upon experiences that were widely different and even contradictory. But everyone recognized that the republic would eliminate much of the familiar past, that it would confirm and extend parts of the colonial experience, yet create a new world distinct from the old. In that sense they knew the founding of a republic for what it was in the eighteenth century, a revolutionary event.

The persons I have studied were radicals in the context of 1765–1776 but were not necessarily in the vanguard of change thereafter. I call them the "Old Revolutionaries" here because they were—as I explain in greater detail in the last chapter—a generation distinct from the younger and far more familiar "Founding Fathers." The latter term is sometimes used very broadly, to include everyone who served at the Philadelphia convention of 1787 or in important positions in the first national administrations under the new federal constitution. More often the emphasis is put on those who were most responsible for designing the constitution and getting it adopted. The Old Revolutionaries—men like Samuel Adams, Isaac Sears, Dr. Thomas Young, and Rich-

ard Henry Lee, along with Philadelphia's Charles Thomson,
North Carolina's Cornelius Harnett, and South Carolina's
Christopher Gadsden—were part of a nucleus of colonists
who promoted resistance to Britain from the Stamp Act
crisis on through independence. Historians sometimes incorrectly refer to them as "secondary figures of the Revolution."
They were more exactly primary figures of a distinct and
early part of the Revolution, and have become relatively obscure—as I suggest in the chapter on Adams—for reasons
that have little to do with their objective historical importance.

The five men I have chosen to study were selected for a
variety of reasons, all of which determined that each of the
biographical chapters would be distinct in character. I
needed adequate source material to sustain analysis. The
sources for a businessman like Isaac Sears, whose life is
memorialized in actions more than in words, supported a
different type of essay than those for people given to writing
and reflection. I also wanted geographical spread so that the
separate studies could go beyond politicians and explore the
different political cultures within eighteenth-century America. And then I adopted a method of proceeding by opposites.
That is, once I felt I had "explained" a person, I sought out
someone different and even contradictory in character to explore the outer limits of my subject. I started with Samuel
Adams and found that his New England identity was critical to him and to his politics, then took up Sears, a native
New Englander to whom the traditions of that section apparently meant very little, since he made his home in New
York. Adams and Sears were closely identified with specific
communities, so I turned next to Young, who moved around
in a way that seemed puzzling until I reflected upon his Irish
background. Young had little good to say about the landed
aristocracy of New York, so it seemed sensible to turn thereafter to Richard Henry Lee, a Virginia landlord who might
seem to embody everything Young disliked, but who shared
his commitment to the revolutionary cause. Lee was very
alienated from Virginia. By contrast, Charles Carroll of Carrollton was highly committed to neighboring Maryland, for
reasons that were not immediately obvious.

In truth, Carroll is somewhat out of place in the book. He was not a grass-roots organizer of the Revolution like the others. His papers, however, were rich and allowed a kind of treatment impossible for the others; and I had long wondered how a Catholic could participate in a revolution so intensely Protestant as that of 1776. Were I to continue, I would probably turn next to Thomson, whose interest in the classics is fascinating, and Gadsden, who would allow consideration of the different world of the most southern colonies. Five persons are, however, perhaps enough to ask a reader to remember, and enough to demonstrate what variety the Revolution encompassed. In a final chapter I draw some general conclusions, suggesting the importance of republicanism in explaining why the Old Revolutionaries could accept the "revolutionary argument" and the Loyalists could not, and also explore the difference between the politics of the Old Revolutionaries and those of the Founding Fathers. Because it is concerned with lives rather than simply with careers, the book has inevitably asked not just why Americans made the Revolution, but what the Revolution did to them.

Within the text I often quote from original manuscript sources. I would like to be able to say that I have transcribed all quotations according to the standard rules of modern editorial practice, but not quite enough to make me do it. The fact is, I have been in some measure inconsistent. I began by regularly spelling out the ampersands, writing "the" where the text said "ye," and eliminating the strange punctuation and irregular capitalization of eighteenth-century writers—all of which seemed a commonsensical way to make the meaning of passages clear to modern readers. But the practice increasingly bothered me. The meaning of course remained the same, but sentences and phrases sometimes looked disturbingly different when transcribed. Language is part of culture. My purpose in part was to convey the character of an eighteenth-century American culture, but in changing the language of that time I seemed to be making it ours instead of theirs. As a result I came increasingly to reproduce the texts as they stood. In particular I have left in the misspellings and eliminated the patronizing *sic* (if a word is spelled incorrectly in a quotation, the reader should assume it was misspelled in the original), and, in the case of the Bartlett correspondence, have left the prose as close to its original form as possible. I assumed the poetical form in the "Interlude," which is constructed from that correspondence, in part because it separates out sentences without the capitalization and punctuation we have come to expect. The Bartletts also seemed to write each other in a kind of prose poetry ("warm Rains & Shines by turns") and to reveal their experience of life and the Revolution with a direct emotional force that would only be lost if I were to describe what they said. I have, of course, intervened in selecting from and arranging their letters, but a historian cannot be expected to abandon all of her old habits at once.

An earlier incarnation of the first four biographical portraits as well as a truncated version of the book's introduction and conclusion were presented in 1976 as the Anson G. Phelps Lectures at New York University. The invitation to present those lectures was a great honor for which I am profoundly grateful. I appreciate also the graciousness of Carl Prince, Patricia Bonomi, and the Phelps Lectures Committee in not insisting that the lectures be printed as they were presented orally, and for allowing me to work out my thoughts and publish them in a form more akin to the monograph I had originally planned to write. Chapter 1 is an expanded and recast version of an article, "Coming to Terms with Samuel Adams," which appeared in the *American Historical Review* for February 1976. A less-developed version of Chapter 3 was published in the *American Quarterly* for the summer of 1976 as "Reason and Revolution: the Radicalism of Dr. Thomas Young." Research and writing were supported by a faculty growth grant from the University of Massachusetts, Boston; a Younger Humanist Award from the National Endowment for the Humanities; a research fund annexed to the Robinson-Edwards professorship at the University of Wisconsin, Madison, and by the help of the Charles Warren Center at Harvard University, where I was a fellow in 1974–75.

I am grateful to John F. Page and Frank C. Mevers of the New Hampshire Historical Society for permission to reprint large sections from the Bartlett papers, and to the Massachusetts Historical Society, the Connecticut State Library, the New York Public Library, the New York Historical Society, the Historical Society of Pennsylvania, the Maryland Historical Society, the University of Virginia Library, and the Huntington Library for permission within the limits of their rights to quote from their manuscript sources. Georgia B. Bumgardner, Curator of Graphic Arts at the American Antiquarian Society, taught me about "reading" prints while helping assemble pictorial materials for the book. The cost of illustrations has been met in part with the help of I. Austin Kelly III, a longtime supporter of humanistic scholarship at the Massachusetts Institute of Technology. Charles Montalbano has for years facilitated my continued and continual use of Widener Library. For that privilege I am grateful as well to Harvard University and to the financial assistance of M.I.T.

Sinclair Hitchings, now curator of prints at the Boston Public Library, will no doubt be surprised to see his name here. Perhaps twenty years ago, when we both worked for the Quincy, Massachusetts, *Patriot Ledger,* he told me he had conducted a rather extensive study of a nineteenth-century adventurer so he might "know better that generation of Americans." The phrase struck me, and it seems worth acknowledging that this book is in part its fruit. Over the years, several friends have offered comments on various parts of my manuscript, for which I am thankful; and Mary Beth Norton kindly took the whole in hand once it was completed. My husband, Charles S. Maier, has long been a patient and supportive reader as well as a good editor. His knowledge of European history and historical literature has also been an invaluable resource; he has often helped me see my material in a broader context than I would have done without his creative prodding. No doubt the book contains many ideas that were once those of Jack N. Rakove, who used to give me tantalizing bits of documentary material while working nearby in Widener. Several students from my days at the University of Massachusetts, Boston, also helped me understand the Old Revolutionaries through their comments and their own research. I would particularly like to thank Corinne Atkins, Marilyn Baseler, Linda Upham-Bornstein, and Henry Kasten (who once asked me if Samuel Adams had any faults). Brad Pines and Osa Fitch at M.I.T. educated me about privateers, and so explained much about Isaac Sears. My friend Susan Strang, a psychiatric social worker who considers human understanding an exercise less in science than of art and experience, was very helpful in unraveling the psychology of Charles Carroll. But to Thomas N. Brown, a longtime colleague and friend, was reserved the peculiar bad fortune of hearing me talk out most of the arguments that are printed here and several that got rejected along the way. He then read the manuscript at various stages, making splendid suggestions as to both substance and form. Whatever is best in the book owes much to his sensitivity and intelligence.

Andrea, Nicholas, and Jessica seem to take curious pride in a mother who chooses to spend long hours in a research library. The book is dedicated to them with good reason. May it contribute to their education as richly as it has to mine.

Pauline Maier

Cambridge, Massachusetts
August 1979

THE OLD
REVOLUTIONARIES

CHAPTER ONE

A NEW ENGLANDER
AS REVOLUTIONARY:
SAMUEL ADAMS

AMONG THE OLD REVOLUTIONARIES, one man stood out. More than any other American of his time, Samuel Adams became the quintessential member of that generation. He was hated by enemies who saw in him all the evils of Revolution, but was admired in equal measure by others, who used him as a standard to identify the most active friends of the colonial cause. Dr. Thomas Young referred to him in the late 1760s as "the Great Mr. Adams" and cited his approval of the New York radicals as an ultimate accolade, a mark of acceptance by the supreme arbiter of revolutionary politics. Josiah Quincy, Jr., another Boston Son of Liberty, identified Cornelius Harnett as "the Samuel Adams of North Carolina," and Charles Thomson was called "the Samuel Adams of Philadelphia." When John Adams first took up his diplomatic duties in France, he found himself (to his profound embarrassment) constantly confounded with "le fameux Adams," the famous Adams—cousin Samuel. "Everybody in Europe knows he was one of the prime movers of the late Revolution," the marquis de Chastellux noted in 1780.[1]

---

[1] Young to Quincy in Josiah Quincy, *Memoirs of the Life of Josiah Quincy, Junior, of Massachusetts, 1774–1775* (2nd ed., Boston, 1874), p. 92;

Yet today Adams remains remote. Even in his lifetime a certain mystery surrounded him. On October 3, 1803, the day after Adams's death, a Salem clergyman recalled that there had been "an impenetrable secrecy" about him. Adams was "feared by his enemies," the Rev. William Bentley confided to his diary, yet remained "too secret to be loved by his friends." Bentley was no expert on the affections of Adams's friends; but even cousin John noted how difficult it had been to know Samuel Adams, and what obstacles his distance would pose for future historians. Samuel Adams's character "will never be accurately known to posterity," he wrote, "as it was never sufficiently known to its own age."[2]

Where contemporaries saw elusiveness, however, biographers of later times found certainty. Too prominent to be forgotten or placed with the justly obscure, Adams has been well remembered, but remembered badly, which itself has served to hide the historical person. As the nation moved further from Samuel Adams's lifetime, portraits of him became increasingly confident, even stereotypic, and hostile: he became a man long and maliciously devoted to independence and so a subversive, a manipulator of the masses, a demagogue, an advocate of mob violence. All of this says less of Adams than of an effort, nearly two centuries in duration, to redefine or mythologize, to explain away, or simply to reject the Revolution of 1776, whose ethic is uncomfortable and whose doctrine remains unsettling in any established nation, including that which it founded. To understand the Revolution requires that these barriers of time and past histories be overcome. To comprehend the man demands still more—an understanding of why Samuel Adams took on such importance, both real and symbolic, for his contemporaries, and of how he defined himself.

John Adams diary for February 11, 1779, in Charles F. Adams, ed., *The Works of John Adams* III (Boston, 1850–56), 189–90; François-Jean, marquis de Chastellux, *Travels in North America in the Years 1780, 1781, and 1782,* ed. Howard C. Rice, Jr. (Chapel Hill, 1963), I, 142.

[2] John Adams to Thomas Jefferson, Quincy, May 27, 1819, in Lester J. Cappon, ed., *The Adams-Jefferson Letters,* II, *1812–1826* (Chapel Hill, 1959), 541; Bentley, entry for October 3, 1803, in *The Diary of William Bentley, D.D.* (Salem, 1911), III, 49.

All studies of Samuel Adams turn about one central observation: that his career climaxed in 1776. The son of a
Boston maltster, Samuel followed his father into the politics
of his town and province. He was a leader of the Boston
Town Meeting, a member (1765) and soon clerk (1766) of
the Massachusetts assembly, and a central figure in the extralegal politics of the decade before independence. A friend
if not a member of the Loyal Nine, a club that became Boston's Sons of Liberty in the Stamp Act crisis, he went on
to act as a leading supporter of the nonimportation effort
that opposed the Townshend duties, a spokesman for the
town in its effort to expel royal troops after the "Massacre,"
the organizer of Boston's committee of correspondence, and
a director of the province's transition from regular to revolutionary government. He served as a delegate to the Continental Congress and signed the Declaration of Independence. During these years, both in guiding Massachusetts
through the decade before independence and in forging a
durable intercolonial union, his importance was of the first
rank. Thomas Jefferson called him "truly the *Man of the
Revolution*"; John Adams said he was "born and tempered
a wedge of steel to split the knot of *lignum vitae*" that tied
North America to Great Britain.[3]

Considering his age when independence was declared,
Samuel Adams might well have played a less critical role in
the Revolution thereafter. He was fifty-four in 1776—that is,
ten years the senior of George Washington, thirteen of John
Adams; he was twenty-one years older than Thomas Jefferson, twenty-nine than James Madison, thirty-three than
Alexander Hamilton. Yet he served tirelessly on committees
of the Continental Congress from its outset until 1781, a period in which the administrative as well as legislative burden
of the new nation was borne by a handful of hard-worked
delegates. He then returned to Massachusetts, never to leave

[3] Jefferson quoted in John C. Miller, *Sam Adams: Pioneer in Propaganda*
(Boston, 1936), p. 343; John Adams to William Tudor, Quincy, June 5,
1817, in Adams, ed., *Works of John Adams*, X, 263.

again. He was chosen president of the state senate, lieutenant governor, then governor, an office to which he first succeeded on the death of John Hancock in 1793 and then was himself elected in 1794, 1795, and 1796. These latter offices were, however, granted him partly in recognition of earlier services, which were acknowledged by his current political opponents. Even those who refused to vote for Adams as governor, John Eliot testified in 1809, thought "he did worthily in those times, when instead of building up a government suited to the condition of a people, we had only to pull down a government becoming every day more tyrannical." Yet "from his age, habits, and local prejudice," Samuel Adams seemed to many unsuited "to mingle with the politicians of a later period, whose views must necessarily be more comprehensive, and whose object was to restrain rather than give a loose to popular feelings."[4]

Samuel Adams's image as a troublemaker, which later generations would develop—a master at pulling down government, at loosing the passions of the people—already existed when Eliot wrote. But another theme was equally, and perhaps more, persistent in the early nineteenth century: Adams was "austere . . . rigid . . . opinionated." "His conversation was in praise of old times, his manners were austere, his remarks never favourable to the rising generation." He belonged to another era, continuing to wear the tricornered hat of revolutionary days, convinced that "the Puritans of New England were the men to set an example to the world." Eliot's observations were seconded by William Tudor, who was born in 1779, fifty-seven years after Adams, and found that revolutionary leader a man of "too much sternness and pious bigotry." He was "a strict Calvinist," Tudor wrote, "and probably, no individual of his day had so much the feelings of the ancient puritans." And so Samuel Adams was excluded from the pantheon of revolutionary leaders around which Americans were asked to rally in the early nineteenth century. His first full biography, by William V. Wells, a descendant, was published only in 1865, more than a half-century after John Marshall's

---

[4] John Eliot, *A Biographical Dictionary* (Salem, 1807), p. 7.

Life of George Washington went to press and Mason Weems began producing his popular panegyrics to Washington and other Revolutionary heroes.[5]

John Adams noted this neglect with disapproval. "If the American Revolution was a blessing, and not a curse," he wrote in 1819, "the name and character of Samuel Adams ought to be preserved. It will bear a strict and critical examination even by the inveterate malice of his enemies. A systematic course has been pursued for thirty years to run him down." Constantly John defended Samuel, in conversations with the Englishman Richard Oswald against extravagant tales of "trouble-making"—"You may have been taught to believe . . . that he eats little children; but I assure you he is a man of humanity and candor as well as integrity"—and later against the more personal charges of William Tudor. If Samuel was stern, "a man in his situation and circumstances must possess a large fund of sternness of stuff, or he will soon be annihilated." As for bigotry, "he certainly had not more than Governor Hutchinson and Secretary Oliver," his old opponents, but "lived and conversed freely with all sectarians," never seeking to proselytize. Samuel was of course a Calvinist; "a Calvinist he had been educated, and so had been all his ancestors for two hundred years."[6] Already, it seemed, interpretations of Samuel Adams were being distorted because a younger generation had lost touch with a world so soon gone and imposed upon the dead its own, more modern expectations. Yet John himself was responding to an issue that had only recently taken on importance: was Samuel Adams a suitable national hero, or was he not? To a large extent that problem remains central in writings about him, and so historians have had to con-

[5] Ibid., pp. 6, 16; Stewart Beach, *Samuel Adams: The Fateful Years, 1764–1776* (New York, 1965), p. 310; John Adams to William Tudor, Quincy, June 5, 1817, in Adams, ed., *Works of John Adams*, X, 262; William Tudor, *The Life of James Otis* (Boston, 1823), pp. 274–75; William V. Wells, *The Life and Public Services of Samuel Adams* (Boston, 1865); John Marshall, *The Life of George Washington* (Philadelphia, 1804–07); Mason Weems, *The Life of Washington*, ed. Marcus Cunliffe (Cambridge, 1962; original 1808).

[6] John Adams quoted in Wells, *Samuel Adams,* I, v; John Adams diary, November 15, 1782; and Adams to Tudor, Quincy, June 5, 1817, in Adams, ed., *Works of John Adams,* III, 310; X, 262.

sider not only the human reality of their subject, but also his appropriateness as a model for modern Americans.

When Wells finally wrote Samuel Adams's biography, he tried to undo the damage of neglect, to restore Adams's name as "a necessity to those who revere virtue and exalted patriotism." For Wells's generation, "the righteous principle of the Revolution" was assumed. It remained only to stress Adams's role. And so Wells accepted uncritically George Bancroft's assertion that Samuel was an early advocate of separation from Britain. Adams "knew no political creed but absolute, unconditional independence," Wells claimed. " 'He hungered and thirsted after it' as an object of priceless attainment, in comparison to which all else on earth was of secondary importance," and in this he was distinguished from his colleagues in the revolutionary movement who sought to avert separation on into the 1770s. For Wells this was the stuff of heroism, and so he readily conceded that Samuel Adams was the "Arch Manager" of the revolutionary movement, the "Chief Incendiary."

But did "all contemporary evidence" show that Adams deserved those titles, as Wells suggested? Royal officials and loyalist writers had long ascribed the responsibility for colonial discontent to a faction of disaffected troublemakers, but Samuel Adams was only one of several Americans they singled out for condemnation. When in 1766 Lieutenant Governor (later Governor) Thomas Hutchinson wrote of "our grand incendiary," he was referring to James Otis, Jr. Two years later, Governor Francis Bernard suggested that nine local politicians be disqualified from office for their role in convening the convention of towns, which had been called in 1768 to decide how the province would respond to the imminent arrival of British troops. Samuel Adams was last on Bernard's list. As late as 1773, Adams's name appeared in Hutchinson's correspondence only as one member of a political faction supposedly disloyal to Britain. His subsequent reputation owed much to his exclusion, with John Hancock, from General Thomas Gage's Proclamation of Amnesty in 1774, to the explicit accusations of a few Loyalists (although it seems Loyalists frequently mentioned not Adams but Benjamin Franklin as the American arch-conspirator), and to his Federalist opponents of the 1790s who found his sympathy for the French Revolution and Jeffersonianism in keeping with an earlier identity as "grand mob-leader during the Revolution." Wells shared the Federalists' distaste for contemporary upheaval: despite his toleration of colonial insurgency, he was anxious to dissociate Samuel Adams from the Southern Confederate "revolutionaries" of the mid-nineteenth century, which he accomplished by stressing Adams's understanding of federalism.[7]

James K. Hosmer's *Samuel Adams* (1885) remained in the nineteenth-century tradition of filiopietistic biographies: the author noted that his great-great-grandfather had served with Samuel Adams in the revolutionary struggle. Adams remained a hero of sorts, but Hosmer was disturbed by the means Adams used to convert his countrymen to independence, which, Hosmer wrote, he had "begun to cherish" in the 1760s. The charge of the Loyalist James Rivington that Adams had a "Machiavellian streak in his character" seemed too strong, but like all New Englanders, Hosmer said, Adams "stooped now and then to a piece of sharp practice." This was "never for himself, but always for what he believed the public good." Still, it was a defect. The publication in 1773 of private letters by Governor Thomas Hutchinson, Lieutenant Governor Andrew Oliver, Charles Paxton, and others was particularly cited as "the least defensible proceeding in which the patriots of New England were concerned during the Revolutionary struggle." "Nothing," Hosmer claimed, "can be more sly than the maneuvering

[7] Wells, *Samuel Adams,* I, v, vi; II, 302–03. Cf. George Bancroft, *A History of the United States,* VI (10th ed., Boston, 1859). Hutchinson to Richard Jackson, Boston, November 16, 1766, and to Dartmouth, October 9, 1773, Massachusetts Archives, State House, Boston, XXVI, 253; XXVII, 549–50; Bernard letter, Boston, December 23, 1768, in Edward Channing and Archibald C. Coolidge, eds., *The Barrington-Bernard Correspondence . . . 1760–1770* (Cambridge, 1912), p. 255. For Loyalist accusations of Samuel Adams, see particularly *Peter Oliver's Origin and Progress of the American Rebellion: A Tory View,* Douglass Adair and John Schutz, eds. (Stanford, 1961), pp. 39–41; and Joseph Galloway, *Historical and Political Reflections on the Rise and Progress of the American Rebellion* (London, 1780), pp. 67–68. Professor Mary Beth Norton of Cornell provided the information on Loyalist accusations of Franklin. Wells, *Samuel Adams,* III, 274–76, 351n.

throughout." He in fact found it much easier to admire
Hutchinson, whose biography he subsequently wrote.[8]

From Hosmer's impatience with Yankee trickery, biographers became increasingly hostile toward Adams. His
still-unquestioned early commitment to independence rapidly lost any heroic qualities. For Ralph Volney Harlow,
whose *Samuel Adams: Promotor of the American Revolution* was published in 1923, all of Adams's actions seemed
irrational, the effusions of a psyche described as neurotic,
even psychotic. Before 1764, Harlow claimed, Adams had
failed in all he tried, which produced "a pronounced conviction of inadequacy, or an 'inferiority complex.'" Then he
drafted Boston's instructions to her legislative representatives
and suddenly found a cause in the Anglo-American controversy. His "extraordinary activity after 1765" was explained "as the result of his unconscious efforts to satisfy
his hunger for compensation, and to bring about a better
adjustment to his environment." By implication, the Revolution was attributed entirely to Adams's derangement—
there were no real problems to account for that event. "It
was something inside, rather than outside which drove him
on, something in the field of the unconscious." Adams
turned to politics only to find "relief from his tiresome mental problems." Often, Harlow suggested, followers see their

---

[8] James I. Hosmer, *Samuel Adams* (Boston, 1896; original 1885), pp.
viii–ix, 68, 368–69, 229. See also Hosmer, *The Life of Thomas Hutchinson*
(Boston, 1896). For a full account of the affair of the Hutchinson letters,
see Bernard Bailyn, *The Ordeal of Thomas Hutchinson* (Cambridge, 1974),
pp. 223–57. In short, the letters were received from Benjamin Franklin with
the stipulation that they not be published. On June 2, 1773, Adams read
them to the assembly, which condemned them as an effort to overthrow
the colony's constitution and introduce arbitrary rule. Exaggerated rumors
of their contents circulated until even Andrew Oliver believed they should
be published. Then on June 10 Adams reported to the legislature that a
separate set of letters had appeared in Boston. His announcement was
clearly a ruse to bypass Franklin's restriction and to permit the publication
of the letters, which was finally ordered on June 15. The published letters
distorted Hutchinson's position, Bailyn suggests, because those letters that
reached Boston had been selected *in England* several years earlier to but-
tress a political argument at odds with Hutchinson's views. The standard
assumption of historians before Bailyn was that the letters had been doc-
tored by Hutchinson's enemies in Boston so as to cast discredit upon him.
It now seems that Hutchinson's enemies were themselves misled in part
by a prior censorship.

leader "as a heroic patriot, when he may be only a neurotic crank," one who, in this case, found it "easy . . . to manufacture public opinion with a pen."[9]

The notion that Samuel Adams somehow "manufactured" the Revolution by manipulating others appeared again four years later in Vernon Parrington's *Colonial Mind*. Parrington found Adams a "professional agitator," "an intriguing rebel against every ambition of the regnant order," but could condone those roles since he believed Adams sought not only independence but, beyond that, a democratic republic. Doubts that ends could justify means soon reappeared, however. Manipulation was a central theme of John C. Miller's *Sam Adams: Pioneer in Propaganda* (1936), which remains the most scholarly of modern biographies. Miller wrote of Adams "transforming American discontent into revolutionary fervor." He was the puppeteer who "brought the people to approve his schemes and pulled the wires that set the Boston town meeting in motion against royal government," who created the convention of towns in 1768 "as a stepping-stone to a later usurpation of governmental power," and then "deliberately set out to provoke crises that would lead to the separation of mother country and colonies." Finally, "by transplanting the caucus from Faneuil Hall to Philadelphia," Adams, working behind the scenes, "directed every step toward independence." This interpretation was reduced to stereotype in the portrait of Samuel Adams prepared for *Sibley's Harvard Graduates* (1958) by Clifford Shipton, who accepted uncritically the accounts by Harlow and Miller and produced forty-five pages of contempt. Adams, Shipton wrote, "preached hate to a degree without rival" among New Englanders of his generation: "He taught his dog Queue to bite every Red Coat he saw, and took little children to the Commons to teach them to hate British soldiers."[10]

[9] Ralph Volney Harlow, *Samuel Adams: Promotor of the American Revolution* (New York, 1923), pp. 36–38, 64–65.

[10] Vernon Parrington, "Samuel Adams, the Mind of the American Democrat," in *The Colonial Mind, 1620–1800* (New York, 1927), pp. 233–47, esp. 233; Miller, *Sam Adams*, pp. 144, 152, 276, 342; Clifford Shipton, "Samuel Adams," in *Sibley's Harvard Graduates,* X, *1736–1740* (Boston, 1958), 420–65, esp. 463, 434. Shipton probably founded one of his accusations upon an incident involving John Quincy Adams. See John

The writings Adams left posterity have been all but irrelevant to this image of their author, for historians have been
characteristically suspicious of the papers Adams left for
their inspection. Shipton, for example, charged that Adams's
papers were censored by him and later by John Avery. John
Adams did leave a graphic picture of Samuel at Philadelphia
throwing bundles of correspondence into the fire or, in
summer, cutting the papers into shreds with a pair of scissors
and tossing the scraps to the wind. "Whatever becomes of
me," he explained, "my friends shall never suffer by my
negligence." But then the danger to his friends was real: the
nation was at war; their opponents might hang them as
traitors. The substantial collection of writings Samuel nonetheless left at his death was diminished, it seems, less
through conscious censorship than through a neglect that
left them open to the ravages of autograph hunters, children,
and "an ignorant servant, who used no inconsiderable portion to kindle fires."[11] What remains is dismissed as de-
ceitful in character because it was the work of a man whose
consistent technique, as Shipton claimed, was that of "the
lie reiterated." That charge echoes through modern biographies. Hosmer agreed with those Loyalists who found
"great duplicity" in Adams's conduct; Miller found his "sincerity open to question"; for Harlow, Adams's writings were
but the "psychopathic effusions" of a man who "evaded the

---

to Samuel Adams, Auteuil, France, April 27, 1785: "The child whom
you used to lead out into the Commons to see with detestation the British
troops, and with pleasure the Boston militia, will have the honor to deliver
you this letter. He has since seen the troops of most nations in Europe,
without any ambition, I hope, of becoming a military man. He thinks of
the bar and peace and civil life." Samuel considered the episode a lesson
in patriotism, not hate. He replied from Boston, April 13, 1786, that "the
child whom I led by the hand, with a particular design, I find is now
becoming a promising youth. . . . If I was instrumental at that time
of enkindling the sparks of patriotism in his tender heart, it will add to my
consolation in the latest hour." Letters quoted in Wells, *Samuel Adams,*
III, 220.

[11] Shipton, "Samuel Adams," p. 444; John Adams to William Tudor,
Quincy, June 5, 1817, in Adams, ed., *Works of John Adams,* X, 264; Wells,
Samuel Adams, I, x, xi. There remains, however, a hint of censorship in
Wells's remark that "there is . . . reason to believe that letters were ab-
stracted early in the present [nineteenth] century by persons interested in
their suppression."

truth, and mishandled the facts so glaringly that almost everything he wrote is a demand for refutation." There is in the historical record some proof of duplicity in Adams's politics—in the newspaper essay he signed "A Letter from the Country" to suggest his cause had support outside the metropolis, in the ruse he used to allow the publication of Hutchinson's letters, or in the deception he practiced so the Loyalist Daniel Leonard would be absent from legislative deliberations critical to the revolutionary cause. But biographers' accusations turn more often upon an unwillingness to question their own assumptions when confronted with documents that suggest a contrary view. Instead they reject the evidence. As Harlow put it, Adams "pretended to be a peace-loving colonist, desiring nothing so much as peace and quiet," only to "veil his real aggressions upon British authority."[12]

---

[12] Shipton, "Samuel Adams," p. 444; Hosmer, *Samuel Adams,* pp. 120–21; Miller, *Sam Adams,* pp. 228–29; Harlow, *Samuel Adams,* pp. 190, 357, 87–88. Handwritten manuscript of "A Letter from the Country," December 28, 1772, in the Samuel Adams papers, Manuscripts and Archives Division, New York Public Library, Astor, Lenox and Tilden Foundations (NYPL), New York City. (The essay does not appear in Adams's printed works, and may not have been published.) On the Hutchinson ruse, see above, n. 8; on Leonard, see Robert Treat Paine's "Account of Strategem," Paine Papers, Massachusetts Historical Society, Boston. I am grateful to Jack N. Rakove for the last reference.

The general charge of dishonesty is particularly complex. Today many of the issues that inspired fears in the eighteenth century seem benign, such that unless biographers consider the revolutionaries' distinctive political assumptions, Adams's treatment of events, his "persistence in attributing evil motives to those men he fought," seems not just mistaken but dishonest. See for example biographies by Harlow, pp. 357–58, and Shipton, p. 444. Shipton also claimed that "a comparison of the letters which Adams wrote to those of his friends who knew what was going on in Boston with those written to friends who were not in a position to know the truth will show that he was not simply the victim of blind prejudice," p. 426. He cited no specific letters, however, and this reader finds his accusations difficult to sustain. On independence, for example, Adams's position was consistent in any one time period regardless of his correspondent. The original Loyalist charge that Adams would stoop to anything to serve his cause stemmed, no doubt, from his political maneuvering. After the publication of his letters, Hutchinson, for example, questioned whether there was a man in all the King's dominions "of greater malignity of heart" than Adams, "or who less scruples any measures ever so criminal to accomplish his purposes." Letter to Thomas Pownall, July 1771, in Wells, *Samuel Adams,* I, 410. The Loyalists' charge that Adams was fallacious came also from their disagreement with his political judgments, as

The negative interpretation of Adams, which reached a certain culmination in Shipton's portrait, has, however, a meaning that goes beyond Adams alone; it reflects a broader ambivalence toward the earliest days of the Revolution. With the establishment of the republic came a rejection of extra-legal opposition to authority. As Adams himself fully understood, a continuation of resistance as practiced before 1776 would imperil the successful conclusion of America's experiment in popular self-government. Yet the Revolution remained the one common, identifying experience of Americans. If cleansed of its anarchistic implications, it could serve as a powerful symbol to counteract the forces of disintegration and so serve the establishment of an American nation. As a result the Revolution was subtly transformed into the war for independence (as it remains for many), a more suitable heroic rallying point than the fundamental reformation that revolution implies. Persons whose importance was confined to the period before 1776—who rallied colonists against established authority—were forgotten or, where their prominence precluded obfuscation, mythologized over time into symbols of all that had to be rejected in the revolutionary heritage. In their place as national heroes stood military men and the Founding Fathers of later years, who were then sanctified—as by Weems, whose superhuman Washington symbolized the Revolution for generations of American schoolchildren.

The Adams myth had its roots, then, in the earliest decades of the new nation. But it appropriately took modern form during the 1880s in the hands of James Hosmer, who, like other historians of his time, regretted the division of English people that independence imposed. The sympathies of such men went to those Loyalists who found more to fear in "the breaking down of the old system" than in submission to Parliament, "honest men" who, as Shipton said, were forced to flee from "the unreasoning rage of people among whom their families had lived as friends and public servants for generations." The rapprochement of America and England

do the similar charges of later writers. As a result the accusation of dishonesty is to a considerable extent incapable of direct refutation or verification. It reflects the observer's politics more than the subject's morality.

in the late nineteenth century came as increasing numbers of non-English immigrants flocked to the New World, as the political machines of first- and second-generation Americans transferred power from old elites to the supporters of more recent arrivals. Adams became a caricature of the urban boss, a man whose power extended beyond the reaches of a William Marcy Tweed or a George Washington Plunkitt, for he controlled both a city and a nation and he destroyed an empire. And in rejecting Adams, historians rejected still more: they renounced all strains in American life of what the Federalists had called "Jacobinism." Harlow asked the critical question: "How many of the vociferously 'loyal' Americans of today, those staunch enemies of twentieth century radicalism, would have looked with favor upon rebellion against established authority in 1775. The latter-day patriots profess great admiration for the 'fathers' of the Revolution, but the real test is to be found . . . in the attitude toward the spirit of revolution today."[13] For all these reasons, Samuel Adams was rejected with increasing vehemence.

In recent years the tide has begun to turn. An article by William Appleman Williams in 1960, a biography by Stewart Beach five years later, Richard D. Brown's 1970 study of the Boston committee of correspondence, a still more recent essay by Charles W. Akers—all dismiss what Akers called "the myth of Sam Adams as the Boston dictator who almost singlehandedly led his colony into rebellion." Boston politics, Brown says, was a "mixture of planning and spontaneity." The capital's relationship with outlying towns was too reciprocal, the restrictions on central leadership were too pervasive to justify any simple interpretation of politics founded upon Adams's control. Beach questioned whether Adams sought independence before the mid-1770s, rejected outright the common notion that Adams was "a rabble-rousing dema-

---

[13] Shipton, "Samuel Adams," p. 428; Harlow, *Samuel Adams*, pp. 265–66. On the simultaneous rejection of the Revolution and revival of Loyalist studies in the late nineteenth century, see Bailyn, *Ordeal of Thomas Hutchinson*, pp. 393–403. The contemporary political bias of this historical view is often clearer in popular histories. See, for example, Stewart H. Holbrook's *Lost Men of American History* (New York, 1946), pp. 11–32, esp. 22–23, where he dismisses local resistance leaders as "all left-wingers in their respective regions" who circulated "the Adams brand of poison."

gogue who stood on street corners in Boston directing the mob," and tried to depart from the entire framework of interpretation that was established in the nineteenth century. "It is not necessary," he said, "to approach Samuel Adams as a hero to find him an intensely human and fascinating individual." Biographies written despite the relevant documents risk unfounded conclusions; the results are different when, as Akers urged, historians "attribute to Samuel Adams only those actions, influences, intentions, and writings for which there is reasonably direct and certain evidence."[14] Yet the old view persists in Hiller Zobel's *The Boston Massacre* (1970), which rejected in the person of Samuel Adams all who were concerned with "percolating public dissatisfaction with the established order"; in the catalogue for a special exhibition in Adams's hometown on "Paul Revere's Boston," which identifies him as "a central figure in stirring up mob violence"; in popular consciousness.[15] Behind that persistence lies the normal time lag between the appearance of new views among scholars and their absorption into common knowledge, and a complex of political needs that effectively separates a more modern world from the age of Samuel Adams.

Why was Adams so important for contemporaries? In part through the accidents of time and place. He was older than other remembered partisans of independence, and so claimed a certain seniority in an era when age merited respect. He came, moreover, from Boston, which rapidly became the

[14] William Appleman Williams, "Samuel Adams: Calvinist, Mercantilist, Revolutionary," *Studies on the Left*, I (1960), 47–57; Beach, *Samuel Adams*, esp. pp. 9, 78, viii, x; Brown, *Revolutionary Politics in Massachusetts: The Boston Committee of Correspondence and the Towns, 1772–1774* (Cambridge, 1970), p. 124n and *passim*; Charles W. Akers, "Sam Adams—and Much More," *New England Quarterly*, XLVII (1974), 120–31, esp. 120, 130.

[15] Zobel, *The Boston Massacre* (Boston, 1970), p. 57, and *Paul Revere's Boston, 1735–1818* (Boston, 1975), p. 124, pl. 172. See also Garry Wills, *Inventing America: Jefferson's Declaration of Independence* (New York, 1978), esp. pp. 19–33. Wills depended heavily upon Zobel.

center of colonial resistance to Britain and the focus of British efforts to suppress the Americans. His exclusion from General Gage's Proclamation of Amnesty welded the name of Adams to that of his city and province, and so established and heightened his fame—perhaps even, Mercy Warren suggested, beyond what was justified by his abilities and contributions to the American cause.[16]

Boston was critical to Adams's reputation not just for what it became in the course of the Anglo-American conflict, but for what it had been for decades before: a large (by colonial standards) trading center governed by a town meeting, an urban community in which popular politics had long been the order of the day. The American Revolution involved of necessity a massive mobilization of the population, even where the political role of the people had been far more circumscribed than in Boston, such that all revolutionary leaders were or of necessity became popular politicians. And there Samuel Adams had much to teach, for he had made politics his life's work even before there was an accepted profession of politics. His enemies, like subsequent biographers, exaggerated his power: "Would you believe it," a British captain wrote his father from Boston in February 1775, "that this immense continent, from New England to Georgia, is moved and directed by one man!—a man of ordinary birth and desperate fortune, who, by his abilities and talent for factious intrigue, has made himself of some consequence. . . . This is the case of our great patriot and leader, Sam[uel] Adams."[17] He did serve as an experienced adviser— though not a dictator—in the politics of revolution. The network of correspondence committees Adams began at Boston in 1772 became a model of revolutionary organization throughout the continent. When Rhode Islanders were threatened by the *Gaspée* commission, they turned to him for advice on how to respond; and there is little doubt that while at the Continental Congress he advised Thomas

[16] Mercy Warren, *History of the Rise, Progress and Termination of the American Revolution* (Boston, 1805), I, 211–12.

[17] Captain W. Glanville Evelyn to his father, Boston, February 18, 1775, *Proceedings of the Massachusetts Historical Society*, XVII (Boston, 1880), 289.

Young and his fellow Philadelphia radicals in their efforts to revolutionize Pennsylvania.

His popular politics were founded on consistent principles. Adams believed in leadership but was also strongly impressed by the constraints within which leaders must act. "A Politician," he wrote in 1778, "must take men as he finds them" and try to make their "Humours and Prejudices, their Passions and Feelings, as well as their Reason and Understandings subservient to his Views of publick Liberty and Happiness." Adams held that men were ruled more by their feelings than by reason, that the people could in the short run be deluded or mistaken, that when their passions were aroused, the masses were capable of great "tumults," comparable to the ragings of the sea, and they were then as open to reason as "the foaming billows . . . to a lecture of morality and . . . quiet." Still, he saw profound limitations upon the masses' malleability and irrationality. He denied that the people were an "unthinking herd." Calm would succeed disorder; and prudent patriots could help recall the people from prejudice and passion to "the Exercise of Reason." Adams emphasized the people's ability to make valid political judgments, particularly when they acted as a body and had sufficient time for reflection. "The inhabitants of this continent are not to be dup'd," he wrote. "They can judge, as well as their betters, when there is a danger of *slavery*."[18]

The "true patriot," then, did not—indeed, could not—create disaffection. The task of a popular leader, as Adams explained it, was to explore the causes of popular discontent and then, if he found his country's *"fears and jealousies"* were well grounded, to encourage them "by all proper means in his power." He would "keep the attention of his fellow citizens awake to their grievances; and not suffer them to be at rest, till the causes of their just complaints are removed." The Boston committee of correspondence, which Adams

---

[18] Adams to Samuel Cooper, Philadelphia, December 25, 1778, and April 30, 1776; to Elbridge Gerry, Boston, March 25, 1774; as "Candidus," in *Boston Gazette,* April 12, 1773; Boston committee of correspondence to Marblehead committee, Boston, April 12, 1774; and as "Vindex," in *Boston Gazette,* December 21, 1771, in Harry Alonzo Cushing, ed., *The Writings of Samuel Adams* (Boston, 1904–08), IV, 107; III, 284, 83, 29, 96; II, 148–50.

founded, embodied this attitude. The stated purpose of the committee was to survey public opinion upon British actions, of which it took pains to inform its rural correspondents. Since the towns' responses strongly suggested they shared Boston's viewpoint, the committee simply reinforced local patriotism by a sophisticated system of flattery: quotations from a town's previous letter were, for example, often incorporated in Boston's reply along with fulsome statements of approval.[19]

The function of the Boston committee of correspondence and of the radical group in the Continental Congress was much like that of the old Boston caucus. From the 1720s the caucus had concerted support among merchants, tradesmen, and other groups for men and measures that would be decided in Town Meeting, using its power over tax collecting to relieve hard-pressed friends and perhaps also to court the hesitant. (Samuel Adams's accounts for his terms as tax collector, 1763–65, were far in arrears; but his neglect to collect the town's revenues was part of a tradition that went back at least to 1736.) By such methods the caucus achieved in Boston a cohesion and political continuity that some smaller New England towns secured without such systematic effort. At Philadelphia Adams was again involved in testing the ground before issues were brought to a test—in consolidating allies and neutralizing enemies so favored positions could triumph without acerbic public division. Thus his nomination of the Rev. Jacob Duché, an Episcopalian, to read an opening prayer at the First Continental Congress: he was no bigot, Adams declared, and he "could hear a prayer from a gentleman of piety and virtue, who was at the same time a friend to his country." By that gesture Adams undercut suspicions of New England bigotry, and disproved assertions that Congress could not worship together because of the diversity of its members' creeds. Duché responded, moreover, with a moving extemporaneous prayer "for America, for the Congress, for the Province of Massachusetts Bay, and especially the town of Boston." The prayer

---

[19] Adams as "Vindex," in *Boston Gazette,* December 21, 1771, ibid., II, 148–50; Brown, *Revolutionary Politics,* pp. 126–31, 244–45.

"had an excellent effect," John Adams noted, "upon everybody here." John Adams's nomination of George Washington as commanding general of the American army, which Samuel seconded, was similarly politic. Only once did Samuel Adams's judgment fail badly, in 1774 when he and the committee of correspondence circulated among Massachusetts towns a "Solemn League and Covenant" calling for economic sanctions against Britain far more rigorous than those the Town Meeting had endorsed, and so provoked a divisive debate that threatened for a time the very continuation of the committee.[20]

That episode is striking because it provides so dramatic an exception to the caution Adams adopted where haste threatened American unity, which was, he frequently stressed, critical to success. "Patience," he once reminded the fiery Thomas Young, ". . . is characteristic of the Patriot." His final published words, from an 1802 letter to Thomas Paine, were "Felix qui cautus," happy the man who is cautious. Patience demanded of Adams conscious efforts at self-control. "While I am in this world," he once wrote John Adams, "I am resolvd that no Vexation shall put me out of Temper if I can possibly command myself. Even old Age . . . shall not prevail to make me peevish." An older man than he, Adams noted in his late fifties, "can in the apparent Coolness of Mind, stabb a dreaded Rival to the Vitals. His Words are like Honey, but there is a large Mixture of Poison." He knew well the distinction between patience and submission, and inveighed against that false prudence "which leads men to acquiesce in measures of the most destructive tendency for the sake of present ease." But there were times when responsible public leaders had to wait. "We cannot make Events," he counseled Samuel Cooper in 1776. "Our Business is wisely to improve them. . . . It requires time to bring honest Men

---

[20] On the caucus, see especially E. B. Warden, "The Caucus and Democracy in Colonial Boston," *New England Quarterly,* XLIII (1970), 19–45; also Alan and Katherine Day, "Another Look at the Boston 'Caucus,'" *Journal of American Studies,* V (1971), 19–45. Wells, *Samuel Adams,* I, 85–86; II, 223 (on Duché), 308–09; Brown, *Revolutionary Politics in Massachusetts,* pp. 190–99.

to think and determine alike even in important Matters."
Thus in the revolutionary struggle America's enemies proved
far more effective than her friends in effecting American
unity. The Boston Port Act, Adams wrote, like the can-
nonading of Norfolk, Virginia, "wrought a Union of the
Colonies which could not be brot about by the Industry of
years in reasoning on the necessity of it for the Common
Safety."[21]

Nowhere was his patience and the restraining influence of
his political sense so clear as on the question of independence.
Adams did not favor that resort when the Anglo-American
conflict began, but moved toward it slowly, in defined stages,
under the pressure of events, sensitive always to their political implications for both England and America. Nothing in
Adams's writings before, during, or immediately after the
Stamp Act crisis (1765–66) suggests a desire for independence. His earliest known political writings—from the 1740s
—include strong praise of the British constitution. He admitted, however, a significant prejudice in favor of Massachusetts government, which was modeled on that of England,
but with improvements. The colonists' demand that they be
taxed only by their own representatives, even their resistance
to the Stamp Act, seemed to him in perfect accord with British tradition. There was no reason to doubt that colonists
would continue "faithfull and loyal Subjects," he wrote in
1765—were they allowed the same governmental powers to
which they had long been accustomed, powers he understood to be those not of a sovereign state but a "subordinate
civil Governmt." Adams's disavowal of independence
reached the height of explicitness in a letter he drafted for
the Massachusetts assembly to Lord Rockingham, dated
January 22, 1768: the House and its constituents were "so
sensible . . . of their happiness and safety, in their union
with, and dependence upon, the mother country, that they

---

[21] Adams to Young, Philadelphia, October [17,] 1774; to Paine, Boston,
November 30, 1802; to John Adams, March 9, [1779]; as "Candidus,"
December 9, 1771; and to Samuel Cooper, Philadelphia, April 30, 1776, in
Cushing, ed., *Writings of Samuel Adams*, III, 163; IV, 413, 131–32; II,
287 (and, also on false prudence, 334); III, 284 (and also 253–54).

would by no means be inclined to accept of an independency, if offered to them."[22]

Thereafter the situation rapidly became more serious. The arrival of British troops at Boston in the fall of 1768 was of particular importance; Adams was always a bitter foe of standing armies, whose use against civilians in time of peace he, like other Englishmen, considered a major sign of impending tyranny. Other measures also hastened his reassessment of the colonies' position. In promising to pay Crown appointees with customs revenues, the Townshend Act (1767) threatened both the colonial assemblies' exclusive right to tax their constituents and their traditional role as paymaster, by which the legislatures had exercised a crucial check on executive power. It was rumored, then confirmed, that the Crown would pay the Massachusetts governor and judges. Meanwhile the removal of the General Court from Boston to Cambridge by the acting governor, Thomas Hutchinson, and his surrender of the harbor garrison at Castle William to the Royal Army suggested that the colony's executive officer was no longer so independent an agent as his predecessors had been, but now acted on orders from London, even when they conflicted with the Massachusetts Charter.[23] The danger of colonial government by "ministerial mandates" was equal to that of parliamentary taxes or standing armies, Samuel Adams warned; the dissolution of popular checks on the governor made him a tyrant, and the addition of judges to the Crown payroll completed the transformation of the free government of Massachusetts into a despotism. Nor was the problem confined to the Bay Colony: the *Gaspée* commission's infringement of jury rights in Rhode Island (1772) showed that the menace of executive power surmounted provincial boundaries, while events abroad, particularly in Ireland and England—which Adams followed closely—seemed to prove that the threat of

---

[22] Adams essay from the *Independent Advertiser* in Wells, *Samuel Adams,* I, 21–22; Adams to DeBerdt, Boston, December 16, 1766; to G——W——, Boston, November 13, 1765; and assembly letter in Cushing, ed., *Writings of Samuel Adams,* I, 113, 39, 170.

[23] For an account of these events see Bailyn, *Ordeal of Thomas Hutchinson,* pp. 169–75.

despotism permeated the empire. The effort to undermine democratic checks on executive power was not, Adams thought, new. It went back perhaps to the British administration of Sir Robert Walpole. But the spate of recent advances made the danger urgent. The entire British world seemed on a precipice; tyranny was at the door.[24]

Under the force of these unfolding events, Adams moved toward predicting independence, warning that it was an increasingly possible outcome of the Anglo-American conflict. In an article signed "Alfred," published in the *Boston Gazette* on October 2, 1769, for example, he expressed fears that the "jealousy between the mother country and the colonies" first raised in the Stamp Act crisis might "finally end in the ruin of the most glorious Empire the sun ever shone upon." But hopes for a changed British policy became ever dimmer. By October 1771 Adams wrote his trusted friend Arthur Lee, then in London, "I have no great Expectations from thence, and have long been of Opinion that America herself under God must finally work out her own Salvation." Independence might, however, be far off. To the Rhode Island radical Henry Marchant, Adams wrote of it in 1772 only as a probability for "some hereafter." He saw no reason either side should hasten the crisis. "I am a friend to both," he wrote, "but I confess my friendship to [the colonies] is the most ardent."[25]

Prediction, therefore, fell short of advocacy. Always Adams's forecasts of independence were contingent. As he said in a letter to Arthur Lee of April 1774, separation would come only "if the British administration and government do not return to the principles of moderation and equity." During the early 1770s this seemed possible as the colonists' confidence in the mother country was not yet "in too great a Degree lost." Adams's disillusionment did not yet extend be-

[24] Adams as "A Chatterer," in *Boston Gazette,* December 3, 1770; Adams to Darius Sessions, Boston, December 28, 1772; to Arthur Lee, Boston, September 27, 1771; and as "Candidus," in *Boston Gazette,* October 14, 1771, in Cushing, ed., *Writings of Samuel Adams,* II, 70–71, 389–92, 231–32, 252.

[25] Adams as "Alfred," in *Boston Gazette,* October 2, 1769; to Lee, October 31, 1771; and to Henry Marchant, January 7, 1772, in Cushing, ed., *Writings of Samuel Adams,* I, 386–87; II, 267, 309.

yond the Parliament and ministry to the King or nation at large. And so his position was reformist, for "a Change of Ministers and Measures," not for so revolutionary a transformation as independence implied.[26] He worked actively, moreover, for reform. Even his predictions were phrased as warnings to Britain, designed to awaken the mother country to the serious consequences her actions portended, and so to inspire political change. The publication in 1773 of private letters by Hutchinson and other royal officials, which so disturbed Hosmer, was itself an effort to facilitate reconciliation. Adams, like others of his colleagues, believed the current campaign against American freedom had been inspired by "a few men born and educated amongst us, and governd by Avarice and a Lust of power" and later "adopted" by Britain. If these men—now so fully exposed and condemned by their own words—could be removed from office on the demand of outraged Massachusetts freemen, "effectual measures might then be taken to restore 'placidam sub Libertate Quietam,'" a peace consonant with liberty. It might be necessary, however, that some in England also be "impeachd and brot to condign punishment."[27]

Adams's interest in cooperation between English and American opponents of Crown policy also argues strongly—more so perhaps than his explicit disavowals of independence—that he wanted reform within the context of empire in the early 1770s. He personally wrote to the English radical John Wilkes in December 1770 and subsequently carried on an active correspondence with the American Wilkesite Arthur Lee. "The Grievances of Britain and the Colonies . . . are of the same pernicious Growth," he wrote Lee in September 1771, and so the cooperation of patriots in both countries was "by all means to be cultivated." His earliest proposal for a correspondence union was designed to facilitate just such

---

[26] Adams to Lee, Boston, April 4, 1774; and to Marchant, January 7, 1772, in ibid., III, 100; II, 309. For other contingent predictions of independence, see ibid., III, 101, 66.

[27] Adams to Lee, June 21, 1773, in ibid., III, 44, and see also 42. The purpose behind the letters' publication, then, was essentially the same as that of Benjamin Franklin in sending the letters to Massachusetts. Only subsequently did Franklin and Adams lose faith in the empire. See Bailyn, *Ordeal of Thomas Hutchinson*, pp. 233, 38.

a coordination of patriotic activities throughout the empire. Three years later he continued to emphasize the importance of coordinating American and British efforts against the growth of Crown power. In 1774 he also discussed with Lee the terms of a possible American bill of rights, which might have made possible the Americans' continued participation in the British governmental system.[28] Within two years, however, the lack of such a document "fixing" Americans' rights under the British constitution, and the apparent impossibility of achieving one, had become a major pillar of his case for colonial separation from Britain.

When, then, did Samuel Adams become an advocate of independence? In November 1775, well after the war had begun, he finally wrote James Bowdoin that he could no longer "conceive that there is any room to hope from the virtuous efforts of the people of Britain" against a "Tyrant . . . flushed with expectations from his fleets and armies" and possessed of an *"unalterable* determination, to *compel* the colonists to *absolute* obedience." By January 1776 he was acutely distressed by evidence that Portsmouth, New Hampshire, was opposed to separation, and wrote John Adams of his efforts in Congress to prevent further disavowals of independence. The next month he published a newspaper essay forthrightly arguing for separation: the lack of any "Britannico-American Magna Charta" stating precisely the terms of America's connection with Britain meant that the colonies faced "an indefinite dependence upon an undetermined power," currently exercised by "a combination of usurping innovators" who had "established an absolute tyranny in Great Britain and Ireland, and openly declared themselves competent to bind the Colonies in all cases whatsoever." America was in fact independent; the administration had "dissevered the dangerous tie."[29]

This chronology is not extraordinary. Thomas Jefferson, Elbridge Gerry, and others of their generation went through

---

[28] Adams to Lee, September 27, 1771, and April 4, 1774, in Cushing, ed., *Writings of Samuel Adams,* II, 234; III, 101.

[29] Adams to James Bowdoin, Philadelphia, November 16, 1775; to John Adams, Philadelphia, January 15, 1776; and article signed "Candidus," in *Boston Gazette,* February 3, 1776, in ibid., III, 241, 258–60, 261–66.

much the same progression, and their disillusionment with Britain was inspired by many of the same events. Indeed, Adams was less anxious for a declaration of independence than several of his fellows at home in Massachusetts. "Let us not be impatient," he counseled Joseph Hawley. "It requires Time to convince the doubting and inspire the timid."[30] And on July 9, 1776, he wrote Hawley that had independence been declared nine months earlier "we might have been justified in the Sight of God and Man"—then altered the sentence so it read three months instead of nine! Thereafter in letters to his most trusted friends, Adams continued to rethink the question of when independence should have been declared, even though the issue was by then academic. He would have been more satisfied, he suggested in December 1776, had the declaration immediately followed Lexington and Concord. But on the whole, he was inclined to think that the course actually taken was best. He had once believed an earlier declaration would have invigorated the American Northern Army and so brought Canada into the Union, "but probably I was mistaken. The Colonies were not then all ripe for so momentous a Change."[31]

Just as Adams's concern for unity affected his advocacy of independence, so, too, it shaped his attitudes toward popular violence. He was no more a man who scored "triumphs" like the Boston Massacre and Tea Party, as the "Adams myth" suggests, than he was the first for independence. He never justified force as a first response to oppression. His

[30] Adams to Joseph Hawley, April 15, 1776, in ibid., III, 281. See also Adams to Benjamin Kent, Philadelphia, July 27, 1776, in ibid., III, 305: "Perhaps if our Friends had considered how much was to be previously done they wd not have been, as you tell me some of them were, 'impatient under our Delay'" in declaring independence. On the colonial leaders' conversion to independence, see Pauline Maier, *From Resistance to Revolution: Colonial Radicals and the Development of American Opposition to Britain, 1765-1776* (New York, 1972), pp. 228-70.

[31] Adams to Hawley, Philadelphia, July 9, 1776; to Warren, Baltimore, December 21, 1776; to Kent, Philadelphia, July 27, 1776; and see also letters from Philadelphia to R. H. Lee, July 15, 1776; to Warren, July 16, 1776; to John Pitts, July 17, 1776; and from Baltimore to Arthur Lee, January 2, 1777, in Cushing, ed., *Writings of Samuel Adams,* III, 295, 338, 304-05; also 297-98, 299, 300-01, 339-40. The last statement is consonant with a tendency of Adams to consider his own position mistaken if it was rejected by a democratic legislature.

famous Master of Arts declaration of 1743 affirmed only that it was "lawful to resist the Supreme Magistrate, if the Commonwealth cannot otherwise be preserved"—not so unacceptable a proposition even in more submissive times. Although Samuel Adams was "staunch and stiff and strict and rigid and inflexible in the cause," he was always for "softness and delicacy, and prudence," John Adams testified, "where they will do." Where they would not, he justified forcible resistance, but only if it fitted defined criteria of acceptability. He was as ready to condemn "a lawless attack upon property in a case where if there had been right there was remedy" as he was to defend "the people's rising in the necessary defence of their liberties, and deliberately, . . . rationally destroying property, after trying every method to preserve it, and when the men in power had rendered the destruction of that property the only means of securing the property of *all*." As such he approved the Stamp Act uprising of August 14, 1765, since the cause was important, resistance had widespread support—the "whole People" thought their essential rights invaded by Parliament—and all legal means of redress had been tried to no effect. But he condemned the attack on the homes of Thomas Hutchinson and others on August 26, 1765, as a transaction of "a truly *mobbish* Nature." There is no evidence that he prompted the Boston Massacre riot, although he served thereafter as spokesman for the town in demanding that troops be removed from Boston. Adams is said to have signaled the Boston Tea Party, and, although his precise role on December 6, 1773, is disputable, the words attributed to him in the final "Tea Meeting" are in perfect accord with his philosophy: "This meeting can do nothing further to save this country." In effect, all peaceful means of preventing payment of the tea duty, and accepting all it implied, had been exhausted. Only then was the destruction of property justified.[32]

[32] Wells, *Samuel Adams,* I, 10; John Adams's diary, December 23, 1765, in Adams, ed., *Works of John Adams,* II, 163; Samuel Adams to Elbridge Gerry, March 24, 1774; and to John Smith, "20th 1765," in Cushing, ed., *Writings of Samuel Adams,* III, 83–84; I, 59–60. For a traditional account of Adams's role in precipitating the Tea Party, see, for example, Miller,

But violence was not his cause. Samuel Adams was above all a master politician, an organizer and coordinator who believed in constitutional government. Already in 1748 he affirmed that "the true object of loyalty is a good legal constitution," an opinion he sustained through old age. He advised moderation and prudence because these were instruments of political effectiveness. Redress, he understood, depended upon American strength, which depended upon internal unity, which was itself best achieved in what the people "easily see to be a constitutional opposition to tyranny." Violence, by contrast, was divisive, and so Adams stressed not only the limits of its theoretical justifiability but also its political disutility. His advice to Rhode Islanders in 1773, that they prevent the *Gaspée* commission from becoming the occasion of bloodshed, continued the following year in letters from Philadelphia to his besieged Boston colleagues. "Violence and Submission would at this time be equally fatal," he wrote; and again, "Nothing can ruin us but our Violence." He urged James Warren "to implore every Friend in Boston by every thing dear and sacred to Men of Sense and Virtue to avoid Blood and Tumult" so as to *"give the other Provinces opportunity to think and resolve."* When independence was finally declared, he was delighted that so important a revolution had been achieved "without great internal Tumults and violent Convulsions."[33]

His medium was not the mob but the press, the public celebration—like the Sons of Liberty dinner at Dorchester

Sam Adams, p. 294. It conflicts with a narrative in the Sewell Papers, Public Archives of Canada, Ottawa—"Proceedings of Ye Body Respecting the Tea"—which suggests that violence was detonated by an announcement that Governor Hutchinson had refused to issue a pass for the tea ships to leave Boston Harbor, and that Adams and his colleagues "called out to the People to stay" in the meeting despite the call of "hideous Yelling in the Street" because "they said they had not quite done." The document, edited by L. F. S. Upton, is in the *William and Mary Quarterly,* 3d Ser., XXII (1965), 297–98.

[33] Adams in the *Independent Advertiser,* quoted in Wells, *Samuel Adams,* I, 17; to Joseph Warren, Philadelphia, September 1774; to Darius Sessions, Boston, January 2, 1773; to Charles Thomson, Boston, May 30, 1774; and, on independence, to Benjamin Kent, Philadelphia, July 27, 1776, in Cushing, ed., *Writings of Samuel Adams,* III, 157; II, 398–400; III, 124, 304; Adams to James Warren, Philadelphia, misdated as May 21, 1774, in *The Warren-Adams Letters* (Boston, 1917–25), I, 26.

in August 1769, where some 350 patriots ate, saw a mimic show, and sang the "Liberty Song"—and, above all, the committee or association. This was true in 1772, when Adams believed tyranny was at hand in Massachusetts. "Let us . . . act like wise Men," he counseled, and "calmly look around us and consider what is best to be done. Let us converse together. . . . Let it be the topic of conversation in every social Club. Let every Town assemble. Let Associations and Combinations be everywhere set up to consult and recover our just Rights." It remained true in 1776, when Adams complained that his compatriots were not doing enough to encourage enlistments in the American army. "Your Presses have been too long silent," he scolded from Congress. "What are your Committees of Correspondence about? I hear nothing of circular Letters—of joynt Committees, &c. Such Methods have in times past raised [the] Spirits of the people —drawn off their Attention from *picking up Pins,* and directed their Views to great objects." Even his Loyalist detractors testified to Adams's skill as a writer, whether of legislative documents or for the press, and as an organizer. Joseph Galloway stressed his incredible energy as the leader of political factions both in Massachusetts and in Philadelphia; Peter Oliver mentioned that Adams had organized a singing society for Boston mechanics and somehow "embraced such Opportunities," as Oliver saw it, "to the inculcating Sedition."[34]

All of this was radical enough for an age that could not

---

[34] Adams as "Valerius Poplicola," in *Boston Gazette,* October 5, 1772; and to James Warren, Philadelphia, May 12, 1776, in Cushing, ed., *Writings of Samuel Adams,* II, 337, III, 289–90; Hutchinson, *History of Massachusetts Bay,* III, 212; Galloway, *Historical and Political Reflections,* pp. 67–68; Adair and Schutz, eds., *Peter Oliver's Origin & Progress of the American Rebellion,* p. 41. See also John Adams's diary for August 14, 1769, in Adams, ed., *Works of John Adams,* II, 218, on the Sons' dinner: "This is cultivating the sensations of freedom. There was a large collection of good company. Otis and Adams are politic in promoting these festivals; for they tinge the minds of the people; they impregnate them with the sentiments of liberty; they render the people fond of their leaders in the cause, and averse and bitter against all opposers." See also entry for September 3, 1769, in ibid., p. 219: "supped with Mr. Otis, in company with Mr. Adams, Mr. William Davis, and Mr. John Gill. The Evening spent in preparing the next day's newspaper—a curious employment, cooking up paragraphs, articles, occurrences, & c., working the political engine!"

yet easily accept nongovernmental political groups as legitimate. Conventions and committees, like the factions that had frequently emerged in prerevolutionary colonial politics, were often condemned as seditious in their efforts to exercise or gain power normally held by regular institutions, indistinguishable from common "mobs." However advanced he might be in the practice of popular politics, Samuel Adams never broke with these consensual assumptions of a traditional world, and so never made his peace with parties or public political conflict. "Neither religion nor liberty can long subsist in the tumult of altercation, and amidst the noise and violence of faction," he wrote Thomas Paine in 1802. Candidates for public office were not to solicit support, which would indicate that they were moved by ambition and avarice, "Passions which have in all Ages been the Bane of Human Society." Citizens were to cast their ballots freely, motivated by a commitment to the constitution, not a *"Devotion to Persons"* which to Adams suggested a "Spirit of Faction" incompatible with that of Liberty. The Boston caucus, the committee of correspondence, these were to concert support for measures right in an absolute sense, as Adams saw it, for the common good as God and all men not distracted by selfishness would recognize it. Unity here was always his cause, his mission. Adams never regretted participating in the popular organizations of the resistance movement, for they had served "an excellent Purpose" in facilitating public watchfulness over those in authority under the old regime. But with the establishment of regular, constitutional, republican government, in which all public officials depended upon free annual elections, committees and conventions became "not only useless but dangerous." Decency and respect were due constitutional authority; bodies of men who convened to deliberate and adopt measures cognizable by legislatures might bring legislatures into contempt and "lessen the Weight of Government lawfully exercised."[35]

---

[35] Adams to Paine, November 30, 1802; in unsigned article in *Boston Gazette,* April 2, 1781; to John Adams, April 16, 1784; and to Noah Webster, April 30, 1784, in Cushing, ed., *Writings of Samuel Adams,* IV, 413, 251–53, 296, 305–06.

And so Adams became a firm opponent of popular uprisings much like those he had condoned in the pre-republican era. He served in 1782 on a legislative committee to visit Hampshire County and "inquire into the grounds of disaffection" there, to quiet any "misinformations" and "groundless jealousies" that lay behind local insurrections. Four years later he acquiesced fully in measures to suppress Shays's Rebellion, which he considered a Tory effort to undermine the Revolution. He may even have argued, as one memorialist claimed, that "in monarchies the crime of treason and rebellion may admit of being pardoned or lightly punished; but the man who dares to rebel against the laws of a republic ought to suffer death." He was no less definite in condemning Pennsylvania's "Whiskey Rebels," who rose against the federal excise tax in 1794. "No people can be more free [than] under a Constitution established by their own voluntary compact, and exercised by men appointed by their own frequent suffrages," Governor Adams told the Massachusetts legislature. "What excuse then can there be for forcible opposition to the laws? If any law shall prove oppressive in its operation, the future deliberations of a freely elected Representative, will afford a constitutional remedy."[36]

To James Warren, an old revolutionary who opposed the suppression of Shays's Rebellion, Samuel Adams seemed to have forsaken his old principles, "to have become the most arbitrary and despotic Man in the Commonwealth."[37] There were, however, deep continuities in Adams's attitudes. Always he fought as the defender of the free constitutional government of Massachusetts, whether against Hutchinson, Britain, or western insurgents. Before 1776 he justified the resort to popular meetings and direct force only on rare occasions when all alternatives failed. With the foundation of the republic such occasions evaporated altogether. Henceforth even the most severe threats of power to freedom and constitutional rule, such as had prompted the English Revolution of 1688 and the American Revolution of 1776, could

[36] Wells, *Samuel Adams,* III, 162, 246; Adams to legislature, January 16, 1795, in Cushing, ed., *Writings of Samuel Adams,* IV, 373.

[37] James Warren to John Adams, Milton, May 18, 1787, in *Warren-Adams Letters,* II, 293.

be brought down through established, lawful procedures, as would be done in the "revolution of 1800" and that of 1974. Only in countries like France, where the republic had yet to be established, could the older type of revolution, with its popular associations and mass uprisings, be justly continued.

⤙∞⤚

There is another reason for Samuel Adams's importance among his contemporaries, one that goes beyond his station as senior statesman of his generation, as a Bostonian, and as a master of popular politics. More than any other American of his time he had absorbed into his being ascetic values that ran through the revolutionary movement North and South, and which were deeply founded in the Anglo-American Whig tradition. At first Adams was destined for the clergy; politics instead became his ministry. He was one of the first Americans willing to identify himself as a politician,[38] but only because he understood that role as akin to a religious vocation: there was great moral content in the cause of "Liberty and Truth," as he once called it. Virtue was the most emphatic theme of his writings and of his life. It implied austerity, a "Sobriety of Manners. . . . Temperance, Frugality, Fortitude," but above all a willingness to sacrifice private advantage for the cause of the community, to subject the self to a greater cause. Only a "virtuous people" could "deserve and enjoy" freedom. Should they become "universally vicious and debauched" they would, whatever the form of their institutions, become "the most abject slaves." Wherever freedom was lost and tyranny established, he wrote in 1772, "Immorality of every Kind comes in like a Torrent. It is in the Interest of Tyrants to reduce the People to Ignorance and Vice. For they cannot live in any Country where Virtue and Knowledge prevail."[39]

[38] As, for example, in a letter to Samuel Cooper, Philadelphia, December 25, 1778, in Cushing, ed., *Writings of Samuel Adams,* IV, 107.

[39] Adams to Samuel P. Savage, Philadelphia, October 6, 1778, ibid., IV, 67–68; essay in *Independent Advertiser,* 1749, in Wells, *Samuel Adams,* I, 23; as "Valerius Poplicola" in *Boston Gazette,* October 5, 1772, in Cushing, ed., *Writings of Samuel Adams,* II, 336–37.

A man who held such a creed so emphatically was less suited for the role of founding father than for that of a moral reformer. In late 1775, as Adams came to think George III's "Councils and Administration" would "produce the grandest Revolutions the World has ever seen," he suggested that he be recalled from Philadelphia, for his abilities were not up to the challenge of founding a new American empire. In that time of crisis he saw above all a "golden opportunity of recovering the Virtue and reforming the Manners of our Country." Americans might look to armies for their defence, he noted, "but Virtue is our best Security." And so he railed at the "Luxury and Extravagance" of Boston in 1778, fearing it would be "totally destructive of those Virtues which are necessary for the Preservation of the Liberty and Happiness of the People." He called for reformation and labored to keep the theater, that caldron of dissipation, out of Boston. The patriot was of course a virtuous man: he worked for the cause selflessly. "It would be the glory of this Age, to find Men having no ruling Passion but the Love of their Country, and ready to render her the most arduous and important Services with the Hope of no other Reward in this Life than the Esteem of their virtuous Fellow Citizens," he wrote in 1778. "But this, some tell me, is expecting more than it is in the Power of human Nature to give."[40]

Yet he himself lived this unlikely creed, privately as well as publicly. He eschewed wealth. John Eliot, that early compiler of New England biographies, described him as "a poor man, who despised riches, and possessed as proud a spirit as those who roll in affluence or command armies." So unconcerned with possessions and appearances was this short, stocky patriot that his neighbors felt compelled to reoutfit him before sending him off to Philadelphia, lest his shabby clothes prove an embarrassment to Massachusetts at the

[40] Adams to James Warren, Philadelphia, November 4, 1775; to Savage, Philadelphia, October 6, 1778; and to James Warren, Philadelphia, July 1778, in Cushing, ed., *Writings of Samuel Adams,* III, 234–35; IV, 67–68, 46. On the theater controversy, see Wells, *Samuel Adams,* III, 290–91; and S. E. Morison, "Two 'Signers' on Salaries and the Stage, 1789," *Proceedings of the Massachusetts Historical Society,* LXII (Boston, 1930), 55–63.

Continental Congress. To him poverty was a source of pride, an outward sign of inner commitment. He once recommended Hugh Hughes, an old New York Son of Liberty, as a man whose "Virtue . . . rendered him obnoxious to all the Tories of that City. . . . He is," Adams added, "perhaps as poor as I am but he 'goes about being good.' " Five years later he confessed to his wife, "I glory in being what the world calls a poor Man." At the age of seventy-four, when he finally retired from public office, Adams could justly observe that he had not been enriched in public service. According to the Rev. Thomas Thacher, Adams long derived the greater part of his income from the small stipend paid him as clerk of the General Court; and while he was at Congress, his wife helped support the family by "manual labor." He might have ended his days a ward of charity had it not been for a set of claims upon the United States earned by his son, who had served as a surgeon in the revolutionary war, and who left those claims to his father on his own death in 1788. The younger Adams had made his way into the military on his own: in a rare surviving reference to his son, Samuel insisted that the young man could "expect to derive no Advantage in point of Promotion from his Connection with me," for he had a longstanding policy against using his political influence to benefit relatives.[41]

He was as oblivious of family respectability as he was of material wealth. In a period when Harvard students were numbered according to social position, Samuel Adams stood sixth out of twenty-three in the class of 1740. Had the ordinary rules of ranking been followed, he would have been second. But this was of little concern to him. "Every kind of genealogy he affected to despise," Eliot noted, "as a thing which gives birth to family pride." Nor did he seek personal glory, either in his own time or in history. Here he con-

[41] Eliot, *Biographical Dictionary,* p. 16; Wells, *Samuel Adams,* II, 207–09, and III, 332–33; Adams to James Warren, Philadelphia, July 12, 1775, in *Warren-Adams Letters,* I, 82; Adams to Elizabeth Adams, Philadelphia, November 24, 1780, and March 19, 1775, in Cushing, ed., *Writings of Samuel Adams,* IV, 226; III, 363–64; Thomas Thacher, *A Tribute of Respect, to the Memory of Samuel Adams . . .* (Dedham, Mass., 1804), esp. pp. 19–22.

trasted dramatically with John Adams, who early in the Anglo-American conflict reflected upon the opportunity his times afforded a young man aspiring for fame like that of the Hampdens and Sidneys of ages past, and who scrupulously preserved his papers, dogging Samuel to do the same. But Samuel remained unimpressed by his cousin's pleas. "I do not keep copies of all my letters," he once wrote, "—they are trifles."[42] Nor was he ambitious for prominent office. Only in his later years did he take on executive positions, contenting himself through the greater part of his life with posts in representative bodies or committees, with those behind-the-scenes tasks that brought political effectiveness, and suspicion, but not prominence or distinction. Not even power rewarded his sacrifices. Adams never single-handedly set the policies of the patriots. Instead he was, as Charles Francis Adams noted over a century ago, "exclusively entitled to the merit of connecting them into one system, and infusing into the scattered efforts of many, all the life and energy which belongs to a single will." Inner rectitude was what he sought. "If my mind has ever been tinctured with Envy," he wrote his wife in 1780, "the Rich and the Great have not been its objects. If I have been vain, Popularity . . . is not the Phantome I have pursued. He who gains the Approbation of the Virtuous Citizens . . . may feel himself happy; but he is in Reality much more so, *who knows he deserves it.* Such a Man, if he cannot retreat with Splendor, he may with dignity."[43]

Such statements suggest that Adams, like Benjamin Frank-

---

[42] Shipton, "Samuel Adams," p. 420; Eliot, *Biographical Dictionary,* pp. 5–7; John Adams, "A Dissertation on the Canon and Feudal Law" (1765), in Adams, ed., *Works of John Adams,* III, 463; John to Samuel Adams, Paris, April 5, 1783, John Adams Papers, Manuscripts and Archives Division, New York Public Library, Astor, Lenox and Tilden Foundations (NYPL), New York City; Adams to Savage, Philadelphia, November 1, 1778, in Cushing, ed., *Writings of Samuel Adams,* IV, 87.

[43] Charles Francis Adams, "Life of John Adams," in Adams, ed., *Works of John Adams,* I, 124; Adams to Elizabeth Adams, Philadelphia, November 24, 1780, in Cushing, ed., *Writings of Samuel Adams,* IV, 226. Hutchinson noted how much more ambitious John Adams was than Samuel. See his *History of Massachusetts Bay,* III, 214. On Adams's contribution—"providing structure" to "an essentially unstructured situation"—see also Brown, *Revolutionary Politics,* 54n.

lin, may have mastered whole catalogues of virtues only to stumble on the sin of pride. Yet humility suffused his life, and contributed to his effectiveness as a leader. Adams had the rare ability to recognize, with others, that he was "not a man of ready powers," that his strengths were limited. And so he recruited others for roles he could not fulfill. Nor did he harbor the illusion that his contributions and sacrifices were such that the public was in any way particularly obliged to him. "No Man," he wrote, "has a Claim on his Country, upon the Score of his having renderd publick Service," since it was simply "the Duty of every one to use his utmost Exertions in promoting the Cause of Liberty and Virtue." Indeed "a Citizen owes everything to the Commonwealth." As a result he could greet a turn in his political fortune without the bitterness with which John Adams left office in 1801. In similar circumstances twenty years earlier, Samuel reminded his indignant friends "that in a free Republick, the People have an uncontrolable right of chusing whom they please" for public offices. And when time enfeebles a public servant's powers, his country "to preserve its own Vigour will wisely call upon others." If the retired servant then "decently retreats" to make room for his replacement, "he will show that he has not yet totally lost his Understanding." Again on his final retirement from politics sixteen years later, Adams reaffirmed a longstanding conviction that others more able could easily replace him.[44] This refusal to elevate the self shaped Adams's personality. He watched himself as closely as he counseled the people to scrutinize their rulers and learned to control a natural passion and temper much as he led his countrymen to eschew violence in the name of a larger good. "If Otis was Martin Luther . . . [who was] rough, hasty and loved good cheer," John Adams remarked, Samuel Adams was John Calvin,

[44] Bentley, diary, October 3, 1803, in *Diary of William Bentley,* III, 49; John Adams to William Tudor, Quincy, February 9, 1819, in Adams, ed., *Works of John Adams,* X, 364–65; Adams to Elizabeth Adams, Philadelphia, November 24, 1780; to Caleb Davis, Philadelphia, April 3, 1781; and to the legislature, January 27, 1797, in Cushing, ed., *Writings of Samuel Adams,* IV, 226, 254–55, 404.

"cool, abstemious, polished, refined, though more inflexible, uniform, consistent."[45]

This subordination of self to cause—Adams's "virtue"—penetrated even his writings. Like others of his generation, he seemed to hide behind a rhetorical facade, for by the ethic of the Revolution and its Whig tradition, political literature was to be as selfless as politics itself, designed to promote its cause, not its author. Even Adams's private letters are remarkably impersonal. He wrote to his daughter much as the Boston committee of correspondence wrote to outlying towns. On September 8, 1778, for example, he quoted back passages from the girl's own previous letter, which informed him of his wife's illness, drawing inferences, approving proper sentiments: "I am satisfied 'you do all in your power for so excellent a mother.' You are under great obligations to her, and I am sure you are of a grateful disposition. I hope her life will be spared, and that you will have the opportunity of presenting to her my warmest respects." Always the cause, or lesson, is primary, whether filial duty or, as in a letter of 1780, religion. At most he adds personal assurances "that I have all the feelings of a father" —then signs, "S. Adams."[46] Such letters assault the expectations of modern readers, whose critical standards contradict those of two centuries earlier, and who expect writers to produce advertisements for themselves. This conflict of cultures fostered biographers' suspicions of Adams and of his writings, which are not artifacts of deceit but testimonials to the fullness of his achievement—to the reason he became for contemporaries the embodiment of the virtuous patriot, and so of the meaning of the Revolution of 1776. Those qualities of "untainted probity, simplicity, modesty, and . . . firmness" that Brissot de Warville recognized in Adams were "Republican virtues," brought into the eighteenth century from the ancient world, via Machiavelli and the Renaissance. It was above all Adams's consistency here that marked him out from others. In him one could find—as the marquis

---

[45] John Adams to J. Morse, Quincy, December 5, 1815, in Adams, ed., *Works of John Adams*, X, 190.

[46] Letters to his daughter, Hannah, in Wells, *Samuel Adams*, III, 53–54.

de Chastellux observed after an interview—"the satisfaction one rarely has in society, or even at the theatre, of finding the person of the actor corresponding to the role he plays." His "simple and frugal exterior," his conversation, his writings, his personal identity were all of a piece.[47]

Having denied himself special significance, he naturally respected others who had still fewer traditional claims to respectability. "No man ever despised more those fools of fortune, whom the multitude admire" than did Adams; "and yet," Eliot noted, "he thought the opinion of the common people in most cases to be very correct." He was "well acquainted with every shipwright, and substantial mechanick, and they were his firm friends through all the scenes of the revolution, believing that to him more than any other man in the community we owed our independence." His writings often took on the guise of speaking for the people. Indeed, so great was Adams's confidence in the people and his personal modesty that he "sometimes doubted his own judgment when it differed from the democratic instincts," as when the resolutions of leading Boston mechanics, meeting at the Green Dragon Tavern, led him to overcome his original misgivings and favor the federal constitution of 1787.[48]

Adams's attitude toward women and marriage suggests that his equalitarianism was instinctual. He posed no objections to the model of familial relationships taught by tradition and the Bible, but he found it difficult to live by. "It is acknowledged," he wrote his future son-in-law, Thomas Wells, in 1780, "that the Superiority is and ought to be in the Man." But since "the Mannagement of a Family in many Instances necessarily devolves on the Woman, it is difficult always to determine the Line between the Authority of one and the Subordination of the other." Nor could he maintain standard notions of the separate and proper concerns of the

[47] De Chastellux, *Travels in North America*, I, 142. Note that in comparing Samuel Adams with Calvin, John Adams also stressed his consistency. Citation above, note 45.

[48] Eliot, *Biographical Dictionary*, pp. 5–7. Account of efforts to secure ratification of the federal constitution in Massachusetts by Col. Joseph May in Wells, *Samuel Adams*, III, esp. 260, but see also 261ff., where Wells suggests this episode was exaggerated in local tradition.

sexes, however embarrassed he might feel by his breaches of propriety. "I forget that I am writing a female upon the Subject of War," he apologized in a letter to his wife from Philadelphia. And again, "I can scarsely find time to write you even a Love Letter. I will however for once give you a political Anecdote." He sent her so much political news, he once explained, because his letters were meant also for his male colleagues in Boston. But after a time he recognized that no excuses were necessary; his wife's "whole Soul" was "engagd in the great Cause." Here were the foundations for a new mutuality in marriage, upon which he offered Wells his developed opinions. "The Marriage State was designd to complete the Sum of human Happiness in this Life," he noted. Where it proved otherwise, the fault was often in "the Parties themselves, who either rush into it without due Consideration, or fail in point of Discretion in their Conduct towards each other afterwards." A good marriage required judgment on both sides, honor and justice, and above all concessions on minor points in the interest of a larger harmony. "Of what Consequence is it," he asked Wells, "whether a Turkey is brought on the Table boild or roasted? And yet, how often are the Passions sufferd to interfere in such mighty Disputes, till the Tempers of both become so sowerd, that they can scarcely look upon each other with any tolerable Degree of good Humor."[49]

All of this is strongly reminiscent of Adams's revolutionary politics—his consistent patience, counseling the importance of avoiding haste in espousing war and independence; his mindfulness of the need for concession and consultation in achieving and maintaining unity within the revolutionary movement; his unwillingness to stand on pretense; his readiness to respect and even to prefer the judgment of the humble to that of the esteemed. Adams himself seems to have recognized the confluence of his private and public politics, for soon after writing Wells he commented to John Scollay that there was great uniformity in the practices that promote

---

[49] Adams to Thomas Wells, Philadelphia, November 22, 1780; and to Elizabeth Adams, Philadelphia, esp. August 8, 1777, and February 26, 1776, in Cushing, ed., *Writings of Samuel Adams,* IV, 224; III, 404, 267.

stability for families, cities, and states. The strength of a marriage came from both partners, of a democracy from its people as well as its magistrates. The foundation of success for both lay in mutual respect. It seemed appropriate to him that, with the Revolution, Boston should consider improvements in the education of female children. And for the family as, it would seem, for the state, it was best that men "not . . . govern too much."[50]

There were limits to the extremes these democratic tendencies sustained. Adams was in no sense a proto-socialist or a leveler. "Utopian schemes of levelling, and a community of goods" were to him "as visionary and impracticable" as attempts to "vest all property in the Crown" had been "arbitrary, despotic, and . . . unconstitutional." Laws that threatened the security of property were for him "subversive of the end for which men prefer society to the state of nature" and so "subversive of society itself."[51] Inspired by the French Revolution, he emphasized equality along with liberty in the 1790s; but so early as 1771 he favored "that constitution of civil government which admits equality in the most extensive degree"—so long as it remained "consistent with the true design of government," which demanded that some rank and subordination be continued. Leadership was, however, to be drawn from men of all ranks and conditions. "The cottager may beget a wise son; the noble, a fool. The one," he wrote, "is capable of great improvement; the other, not." Samuel Adams's politics, according to William Bentley, came from "two maxims, rulers should have little, the people much. The rank of rulers is from the good they do, and the difference among the people only from personal virtue. No entailments, no privileges. An open world for genius and industry." Even wealth, which some revolutionaries accepted as a rough index of ability, and which had long

---

[50] Adams to John Scollay, Philadelphia, December 30, 1780; to John Adams, Boston, December 19, 1781; and to Thomas Wells, Philadelphia, November 22, 1780, in ibid., IV, 236–37, 270, 224.

[51] Adams for the Massachusetts House of Representatives to Dennys DeBerdt, January 12, 1768; and as "Candidus" in *Boston Gazette,* January 20, 1772, ibid., I, 137; II, 316–17.

served to identify the colonies' natural leaders for a deferential electorate, was for Adams a dishonorable and dangerous criterion for public office. It would be better, he once argued, to prefer men in want over those with riches, for while the former could be done "from the feelings of humanity, . . . the other argues a base, degenerate, servile temper of mind." Ability and virtue were alone appropriate qualifications. But once the people put men in office, their authority was to be honored without fail—as Adams made clear in his ringing condemnations of the Shaysites and the Whiskey Rebels. Indeed, once the republic had been founded it was the office far more than the officeholder that demanded a rigid and formal respect, even from incumbents, for positions of authority had been created by and for the sovereign people.[52]

Adams's personality, his politics, his revolutionary career —all these were to him tightly linked with his New England background. No man was more aware than he of the legacy of his Puritan forebears, more proud of their achievements, more determined to perpetuate them into the future. Ancestors and posterity rank only with virtue as leading concepts in his writings; all were interrelated and laden with emotional as well as intellectual significance. New England's founders, he believed, had retreated to "this distant Part of the Earth" at a time when "Tyranny had laid its oppressive Hand on Church and State in their Native Country." They sought to establish a government "upon the true principles of Liberty," and defended their achievement against the Randolphs, the Androses—against all who would interfere with their freedom and that of their heirs. And so the peculiar glory of that Massachusetts constitution which Adams preferred to the much-admired government of England be-

[52] Equality: Adams to legislature, January 17, 1794; and as "Vindex," *Boston Gazette,* January 21, 1771, ibid., IV, 357–59; II, 151–52. Samuel to John Adams, Boston, November 20, 1790, in Adams, ed., *Works of John Adams,* VI, 425; entry for October 3, 1803, in *Diary of William Bentley,* III, 49; Adams to Elbridge Gerry, Philadelphia, January 2, 1776, in Cushing, ed., *Writings of Samuel Adams,* III, 247. For an extreme example of the rigidity with which Adams came to believe elective office should be respected, see James T. Austin, *Life of Elbridge Gerry* (Boston, 1828–29), I, 474.

cause the Bay Colony's "invaluable charter secures to us all the English liberties, besides which we have some additional privileges which the common people there have not."[53]

The founders' legacy lay, however, not just in their institutions, but in their virtue, in the morals they taught their children. "Our Bradfords, Winslows and Winthrops would have revolted at the Idea of . . . Dissipation and Folly," Adams wrote, "knowing them to be inconsistent with their great Design, in transplanting themselves into what they called this 'Outside the World.' " They left luxury and affluence behind, contented themselves with humble fare, and provided a compelling example for their descendants. There was, then, an obligation upon the living to make "every laudable Effort" to continue the ways of the fathers, to secure for posterity "the free and full Enjoyment of those precious Rights and privileges for which our renowned forefathers expended so much Treasure and Blood."[54]

No motif gave such force to the letters Adams wrote before independence for the town of Boston than his urging of New England's historic mission. To Plymouth, to Rowley, to Duxbury he encouraged perseverance in "the truly noble Spirit of our renowned Ancestors." He continued this theme in the 1780s, recalling errant kinsmen to the example of their heroic forefathers; and even in his final years, as Eliot noted, he held up New England's Puritans as a model for the world. Local tradition was for Adams in effect a property that gave him identity, much as other men identify

[53] Adams, with John Ruddock and John Hancock, to the town of Plymouth, March 24, 1776; and to Arthur Lee, Boston, September 27, 1771, in Cushing, ed., *Writings of Samuel Adams,* I, 72–73; II, 236. Adams quoted in Wells, *Samuel Adams,* I, 22. In the final passage, Adams referred, perhaps, to the fact that New England towns were governed by town meetings, in which the people had a far greater role than in the municipal corporations of England or of New York and Philadelphia. He no doubt thought as well of the Massachusetts upper house, whose members were under the Charter of 1691 elected by the province's lower house. In England, of course, men inherited seats in the House of Lords, whereas in other colonies members of the upper houses were most often appointed by the Crown or the proprietor.

[54] Adams to John Scollay, Philadelphia, December 30, 1780; and, for the Boston committee of correspondence, to Thomas Mighill, Boston, April 7, 1773, in Cushing, ed., *Writings of Samuel Adams,* IV, 238; III, 18.

themselves through office or wealth. And it gave him direction. He understood himself as an intermediary, passing
the achievements of the past on to the future. Not for him
the breaking of new paths, the discovering of new worlds;
he traveled a well-marked highway, which gave him rectitude and confidence, the "sternness of stuff" that John
Adams recognized as so critical in sustaining a revolutionary
past the obstacles that impede his course. "I am not more
convincd of any thing," Adams wrote his wife in 1777,
"than that it is my Duty, to oppose to the utmost of my
Ability the Designs of those who would enslave my Country; and with Gods Assistance I am resolvd to oppose them
till their Designs are defeated or I am called to quit the Stage
of life."[55]

This self-conception explains the critical role his conflict
with Thomas Hutchinson played in Adams's development
as a revolutionary. Those two men had much in common.
Both were Harvard men from old Massachusetts families
who had spent their lives in public service. Hutchinson, like
Adams, inclined toward a simplicity of taste which led his
biographer to call him a "neo-Puritan ascetic." But Hutchinson was as keenly sensitive to gradations in rank as Adams
was oblivious of them; he was acquisitive and ambitious,
having left a successful career in trade to become chief justice, lieutenant governor, and finally governor of the Bay
Colony. By his influence Hutchinson helped place close relatives in nearly all the colony's prominent offices. Worse yet,
he failed to share Adams's reverence for the Massachusetts
past; the founders had, after all, persecuted his ancestor
Anne Hutchinson just as their descendants would turn on
him. In his history of Massachusetts Bay, Hutchinson even
had the effrontery, as Adams read it, to suggest that the
colony's fathers had misunderstood their relationship to
England. Indeed, in hard times before the Revolution when
Hutchinson considered returning to the land of his fathers,
it was not of Massachusetts that he thought, but of an ancestral town in England. And so when, as governor, he

[55] See, for example, Boston committee of correspondence letters in ibid.,
I, 71 (quotation), II, 395; III, 17–18, 32–33. Also Adams to Elizabeth
Adams, Baltimore, January 29, 1777, III, 349.

proved ready to compromise the Bay Colony's charter on royal orders, he easily became for Adams a traitor of traitors, a son of New England ("bone of our Bone, and flesh of our flesh") who turned on his native land, a man who would "aid the Designs of despotick power," even to recommend an abridgment of American liberty, all to satisfy his lust for rank and power. Because he was so successful in gaining power, Hutchinson threatened that continuity of past and future that was so critical to Adams.[56]

From these local origins, Adams's radicalism spread until he opposed not only England, whose politics shaped and sustained a Hutchinson while they assailed a Wilkes, but also the old order throughout Europe. For in his effort to preserve his vision of a pure and virtuous past, Adams, like other revolutionaries, became of necessity an innovator. At the outset of his political career, he had betrayed no uneasiness with the inherited powers of Britain's "mixed constitution," but he came to understand that with the development of American independence monarchy had been "exploded" and the "Aristocratick Spirit" that seemed so deep-rooted in certain colonies began to give way "to that of Democracy." His conversion was total: "I firmly believe," he wrote Richard Henry Lee in April 1785, "that the benevolent Creator designed the republican Form of Government for Man." All other known institutions were, he suggested, "unnatural" by comparison and tended "to distress human Societies." He fully understood what a threat the new American republic posed for the traditional governments of Europe, and so expected an era of turmoil and repression before the triumph of republicanism would bring a new peace. "Will the Lion ever associate with the Lamb or the Leopard with the Kid," he asked Lee, "till our favorite principles shall be universally established?"[57]

[56] On Hutchinson, see Bailyn, *Ordeal of Thomas Hutchinson,* esp. pp. 20, 25–26, 30–31, 139, and *passim.* Adams, as "Valerius Poplicola," October 28, 1771 (on Hutchinson's history); to Stephen Sayre, Boston, November 23, 1770; to John Scollay, Philadelphia, December 30, 1780; and to Mrs. Adams, Philadelphia, March 23, 1779, in Cushing, ed., *Writings of Samuel Adams,* II, 256–64, 67–68 (quotation); IV, 237–38, 138.

[57] On the conservative beginnings of revolutionary change, see Hannah Arendt, *On Revolution* (New York, 1965), pp. 34–40, 153. Adams to

Yet even revolutionary republicanism constituted only a revival of his ancestors' ways. The Continental Congressmen who met under unpretentious circumstances in York, Pennsylvania, reminded Adams of those early New Englanders who were satisfied with bread and cheese, or "Clams and Muscles." It was, he claimed, the "Principles and Manners of New England" which "producd that Spirit which finally has established the Independence of America." And "the genuine Principles of New England," he suggested, were quite simply "Republican Principles." Thus Adams, in what had been for his ancestors a New World Israel, took on the role of his Old Testament namesake, Samuel the prophet, insignificant except as God's instrument, who chastised Saul for his perfidy, knew that kingship was a rejection of the Lord's rule and wicked in His eyes, and remained determined that for all their falling from grace, his people's wanderings through the wilderness would become not a fool's errand but the foundation of a new state conformable to God's will.[58]

⌐∞⌐

The traits that made up Samuel Adams were faults to some men, and many of them would be accounted faults by most men in most times. The departures from strict candor that can be documented and are justly charged to him are not at issue here. They distinguish Adams from Washington of the cherry tree; but Weems's Washington was a myth. Adams's subordination of self to cause did, however, have real human

---

Benjamin Kent, Philadelphia, July 27, 1776; and to Richard Henry Lee, Boston, April 14, 1785, in Cushing, ed., *Writings of Samuel Adams,* III, 305; IV, 314–15.

[58] Adams to James Warren, "York Town," May 25, 1778, in *Warren-Adams Letters,* II, 13; to William Checkley, Boston, June 1, 1774; to James Warren, Philadelphia, February 12, 1779; and to Samuel Cooper, Philadelphia, April 23, 1781, in Cushing, ed., *Writings of Samuel Adams,* III, 128; IV, 124, 259–60. The story of Adams's namesake is told in the Old Testament's Book of Samuel. Adams referred to the prophet Samuel at least once—see his article as "Candidus," *Boston Gazette,* November 11, 1771, ibid., II, 271–72.

costs. Having so denied himself personal consideration, he found it difficult to respond to the sufferings and sacrifices of others. The publication of Hutchinson's letters ruined the career of a man who had been faithful to the province of his birth according to his understanding of its welfare and led to a painful exile, in which Hutchinson learned how little an Englishmen he was, how much an American. But long after he had been forced from the Bay Colony, Hutchinson remained for Adams a paragon of corruption, of all the republic would have to repress if it was to survive. The failures of his empathy were not, however, limited to opponents. The historian James Hosmer noted long ago that Adams's peculiar inability to grieve after the death at Bunker Hill of his close colleague Joseph Warren was part of a characteristic "reticence as to his own emotions." The death of "our truly amiable and worthy Friend Dr. Warren is greatly afflicting," he wrote his wife. "The Language of Friendship is, how shall we resign him! But it is our Duty to submit to the Dispensations of Heaven." Warren "fell in the glorious Struggle for the publick Liberty." Similarly, Adams seemed startlingly unmoved in 1777 when the Continental Congress condemned one of his old protégés, Dr. Thomas Young, a man who had recently died in the service of his country. The resolutions that included Young's censure were "a matter . . . not worth your while to have explaind to you," Adams wrote Richard Henry Lee at the time, one of "a Thousand and [one] little Matters" that "too often throw out greater ones," like the Confederation both he and Lee ardently sought.[59]

Yet it is unlikely that Adams seemed so removed to his revolutionary colleagues as William Bentley later claimed. His confidences were limited to a handful of men,[60] but with these he found it painful to keep secrets, and longed

---

[59] Hosmer, *Samuel Adams,* pp. 337–38; Adams to Elizabeth Adams, Philadelphia, June 28, 1775; and to Richard Henry Lee, Philadelphia, June 26, 1777, in Cushing, ed., *Writings of Samuel Adams,* III, 220, 378. Adams did, however, move in Congress that the United States adopt Warren's eldest son and educate him at public expense. See Adams to James Warren, Baltimore, February 1, 1777, ibid., p. 353.

[60] Cf. Adams to Darius Sessions, Boston, December 28, 1772; and to John Adams, February or March 1773, in ibid., II, 389, 430.

for those private conversations where like-minded men could "disclose each others Hearts." Among these friends Adams won respect and, his correspondence occasionally reveals, affection even for his idiosyncrasies. In December 1777 he visited Plymouth to help celebrate the anniversary of the Pilgrims' landing, the sort of event he particularly enjoyed, and sent James Lovell an account that stressed above all the merits of the day's sermon. "An epicure would have said something about the clams," Lovell replied, "but you turn me to the prophet Isaiah."[61]

By the early nineteenth century, however, Samuel Adams had become a remote figure, "one of Plutarch's men. Modern times have produced no character like his that I can call to mind," one clergyman commented. If he marked a New World reincarnation of the Old Testament Samuel, he was for Edward Everett "the last of the Puritans," a man who, as the historian William Lecky noted, "exhibited in perfection the fierce and sombre type of the seventeenth-century Covenanter. Poor, simple, ostentatiously austere and indomitably courageous, the blended influence of Calvinistic theology and of republican principles had permeated and indurated his whole character, and he carried into politics all the fervour of an apostle and all the narrowness of a sectarian." This was not a man for all seasons, but one who was "born for the revolutionary epoch," who "belonged to the revolution." Had he lived in any age when abuses of power invited resistance, he would have been a reformer, William Tudor claimed: "he would have suffered excommunication rather than have bowed to papal infallibility"; he would have "gone to the stake, rather than submit to the prelatic ordinances of Laud; he would have mounted the scaffold, sooner than pay a shilling of illegal ship-money." In his severe Spartanism, Adams was in fact a classic revolutionary, comparable to later French Jacobins of the "Republic of Virtue," to Bolsheviks in the early days of the Russian Revolution, the Chinese in Yenan, even the Vietcong in the Mekong Delta. The myth of Samuel Adams may then be

---

[61] Adams to James Warren, Philadelphia, November 4, 1775; and to Samuel Cooper, Philadelphia, April 23, 1781, ibid., III, 234; IV, 259 (quotation). Lovell to Adams, January 20, 1778, Samuel Adams Papers, NYPL.

wrong not just in misconceiving his personal identity, but also in its more fundamental assumptions about the character of a revolutionary. Successful revolutionary leaders are not violent and irresponsible anarchists but politic persons of intense discipline for whom the public cause purges mundane considerations of self.[62]

Men such as these are destined to be misunderstood by later generations, for they play transitional roles in their revolutions. "They . . . helped carry men through a time of change" but "had no place in a time of stability." With the consolidation of the new order their asceticism becomes uncomfortable, outmoded. By the time of Samuel Adams's death, his contempt for opulence was so out of date that his eulogist Thacher feared it might be taken as evidence of indolence or "the want of wisdom to estimate riches by their just value," and felt obliged to tell his listeners that "in the most splendid eras of antiquity, nay in some former period of our own history, such temperance . . . would have been highly applauded."[63]

Revolution, moreover, accelerates the pace of change that divides past and present, and often takes a course far different than that anticipated by its earliest supporters. As a result the old men of a revolution are more likely than most aged humans to die aliens in time, the citizens of an earlier era. The republican emphasis upon earned over inherited status and the unleashing of new economic opportunities during and after the revolutionary war opened the way in America for a new individual ambition and aggressive materialism that contrasted sharply with the older vision of a republic of virtue. When James Warren made a sentimental pilgrimage to Concord in 1792 he found "few of the old hands, and little of that noble spirit, and as little of those comprehensive views and sentiments which dignified the early days of the revolution. Thus," he concluded, "I have

---

[62] Clergyman quoted in Wells, *Samuel Adams,* II, 185. Everett, "The Battle of Lexington," April 19, 1835, in his *Orations and Speeches* (Boston, 1850–68), I, 545; Lecky, *The American Revolution, 1763–1783* (New York, 1922), p. 120; Tudor, *Life of Otis,* pp. 275, 276. See also Michael Walzer, *The Revolution of the Saints: A Study in the Origins of Modern Politics* (Cambridge, 1965), esp. pp. 310–20.

[63] Walzer, *Revolution of the Saints,* p. 320; Thacher, *A Tribute,* p. 22.

lived long enough to feel pains too great for me to describe."
Nor did a newly sovereign people show the respect for their
betters, or continue the traditional practice of rewarding
and retaining in office persons of quality as some from the
generation of 1776 had expected. The decline from influence
of "oldstanders and independent men of long well-tried
patriotism, sound understanding, and good property" was
for South Carolina's Christopher Gadsden evidence that the
new world for which he had helped prepare the way was a
"mere bedlam." "Look around our whirling globe, my
friend, where you will," he wrote John Adams in 1801,
"east, west, north, or south, where is the spot in which are
not many of these mad lunatics? . . . More and more
happy, I bless God, do I every day feel . . . to find that my
passage over this life's Atlantic is almost gained. . . ."[64]

Samuel Adams never succumbed to such disillusionment.
He came to doubt whether Boston, much less America,
would ever become a Christian Sparta, as he had once hoped,
but never lost his deeper faith in the people, never despaired
of the Revolution. His hope for a "golden age" centered increasingly on widespread public education to shape the
minds and morals of children that they might carry on the
work of their fathers. Here again, his model for the future
lay in the past, in early New England where, he thought, the
founders had taken care amid the hardships of settlement to
provide a system of education "by which . . . wisdom,
knowledge, and virtue have been generally diffused among
the body of the people."[65]

Adams supported the French Revolution, and saw in the
election of 1800, which so disturbed Gadsden, the conclusion
to a brief nightmare of armies and repression. "The storm is

[64] James Warren to Elbridge Gerry, Plymouth, December 18, 1792, in
C. Harvey Gardiner, ed., *A Study of Dissent: The Warren-Gerry Correspondence* (Carbondale, Ill., 1968), p. 251; Gadsden in Richard Walsh,
ed., *The Writings of Christopher Gadsden, 1764–1805* (Columbia, 1966),
pp. 306–07.

[65] Adams to John Scollay, Philadelphia, December 30, 1780; to James
Warren, Philadelphia, November 4, 1775, and February 12, 1779; and to
the Massachusetts legislature, June 3, 1795, in Cushing, ed., *Writings of
Samuel Adams,* IV, 238; III, 235–36; IV, 124–25, 377–79; Samuel to John
Adams, Boston, October 4, 1790, and November 20, 1790, in Adams, ed.,
Works of John Adams, VI, 414, 422–25 (quotation at 422).

now over," he wrote Thomas Jefferson, "and we are in port," with peace and harmony ahead. The eyes of the people had "too generally been fast closed from the view of their own happiness, . . . but Providence, who rules the World, seems now to be rapidly changing the sentiments of Mankind in Europe and America." Was there not reason to believe "that the principles of Democratic Republicanism" were already "better understood than they were before; and that by the continued efforts of Men of Science and Virtue, they will extend more and more till the turbulent and destructive Spirit of War Shall cease? The proud oppressors over the Earth shall be totally broken down," he predicted, "and those classes of Men who have hitherto been the victims of their rage and cruelty shall perpetually enjoy perfect Peace and Safety till time shall be no more."[66]

And so Samuel Adams—the American revolutionaries' American revolutionary, a committed democratic-republican, a classic revolutionary—rode out a storm of change, confident that the ways of his forefathers were winning their rightful place in the history of mankind, and died looking forward to a great liberation not from this earth but upon it.

[66] Adams to Jefferson, April 24 and November 18, 1801, in Cushing, ed., *Writings of Samuel Adams,* IV, 408–11.

CHAPTER TWO

·······◆◆◆◆◆·······

ISAAC SEARS

AND THE BUSINESS

OF REVOLUTION

*"Work & Be Rich"**

NOT ALL REVOLUTIONARIES of New England origin were modeled after Samuel Adams. Isaac Sears was a fifth-generation New Englander whose first American paternal ancestor, Richard Sares, appeared on a Plymouth tax list for 1633. His bonds with New England's faith were as strong as those with her soil: one forebear had been a deacon, another a minister in the Congregational Church. When Isaac was a young child his parents left the family seat on Cape Cod, but carefully transferred their membership from the congregation at Harwich, Massachusetts, where Isaac had been baptized in July 1730, to that of their new home in Norwalk, Connecticut. The weight of the past—so directive in Adams's life—seems, however, to have rested lightly on Sears's shoulders. He became an Anglican, marrying Sarah Drake at Trinity Church in New York. His own children were raised on Manhattan. There, in the city's busy trading streets and among the seamen who frequented the Water Street tavern of his father-in-law, Jasper Drake, he was more at home than

---

* Watermark in American-made paper used by the Albany committee of correspondence. James Sullivan, ed., *Minutes of the Albany Committee of Correspondence, 1775–1778* (Albany, 1923), x.

in the New England towns of his forefathers. He spent several years in New Haven and Boston during the revolutionary war, but packed up his furniture and returned to Manhattan at the earliest possible moment once the British occupation was ended.[1] The New Englander had become a New Yorker. And as a New Yorker Sears made a name within the resistance movement comparable to that of Boston's Adams, though as different in character as were the societies and politics of the cities where the two men lived and worked.

⨾⨾

The home Sears chose was by twentieth-century standards a small and even intimate town, but a changing one. Its population grew rapidly between 1760 and 1775, reaching in the year of Lexington and Concord perhaps 25,000 people, all confined within an area roughly a mile in length and a mile and a half in breadth on the lower tip of Manhattan, or "New York Island" as it was sometimes called.[2] At the upper reaches of Broadway, then as now a major thoroughfare, were the "Fields" or Commons on the site of the present City Hall. There too were the town's prison and poorhouse, and the barracks for British soldiers who played a prominent role in its prerevolutionary disorder. But these served as a frontier. Beyond them lay only the gardens and country houses of a suburban countryside.

[1] Biographical information is available in Samuel P. May, *The Descendants of Richard Sares (Sears) of Yarmouth, Massachusetts, 1638–1888* (Albany, 1890), esp. pp. 113–18; Robert Jay Christen, "King Sears: Politician and Patriot in a Decade of Revolution," unpublished Ph.D. dissertation, Columbia University, 1968; and Christen, "Isaac Sears: Radical in Rebellion," unpublished M.A. thesis, Columbia University, 1953. Sears and Pascal Smith to General Henry Knox, Knox collection, Massachusetts Historical Society (MHS), Boston.

[2] Carl Bridenbaugh, *Cities in Revolt: Urban Life in America, 1743–1776* (New York, 1955), p. 216. Bridenbaugh's population figures may be too high. Gary Nash, "Urban Wealth and Poverty in Pre-Revolutionary America," *Journal of Interdisciplinary History*, VI (1976), 557, gives the city's 1775 population as 22,600. Esther Singleton, *Social New York Under the Georges, 1714–1776* (New York, 1902), esp. pp. 5, 7.

Within the settled areas, neighborhoods could already be distinguished by their residents' social and economic standing. Lower Broadway, near Fort George and the Bowling Green, was a fashionable address, attractive to New York's powerful aristocrats, for whom there were no equivalents in Boston, men who combined mercantile fortunes with extensive inherited landholdings in the Hudson Valley. Working people clustered in the opposite, northeastern corner of the city in a thinly populated area beyond the "Fresh Water," and on the eastern side of the island more generally, above all in the Out Ward and in Sears's own Montgomerie Ward. This tendency toward residential separation had, however, not gone so far as to disrupt the intimacy of what was far more a small town than a modern city. Along its principal streets were juxtaposed almost at random "fashionable private residences, merchants' stores, lawyers' offices, mechanics' workshops." Visitors were struck not by tall buildings but by the rows of trees New Yorkers had planted along their streets—beech and locust for shade and flowers, with an occasional elm or lime (that is, linden)—or by the balconies perched atop the "strong and neat" brick houses of their more prosperous members "where company sit in the summer evenings, to enjoy the prospect of the shores and harbor," or by the clatter of frogs on a summer night. The visual perspective of the old city was then, as it remained on into this century, more horizontal than vertical—out toward the East River where its harbor lay, on one side, and on the other toward what one mapmaker labeled the North or "Hudson's" River.[3]

New York was a city of peoples. Unlike Boston, it possessed no common unifying culture. It was an English port whose Dutch origins were apparent in its old gabled houses. And New York was more than Dutch and English: from its earliest decades French, Sephardic Jews, and Africans had also walked its streets. Germans and Irish Protestants (Scots-Irish, as they were later called) came in the mid-eighteenth century, finding in New York a welcome they would not

---

[3] *New York City During the American Revolution* (New York, 1861), "Introduction," esp. p. 14; Singleton, *Social New York,* pp. 5–7.

"Plan of the City of New York," by Bernard Ratzer, 1767.

To the Public.

THE long expected TEA SHIP arrived laſt night at Sandy-Hook, but the pilot would not bring up the Captain till the ſenſe of the city was known. The committee were immediately informed of her arrival, and that the Captain ſolicits for liberty to come up to provide neceſſaries for his return. The ſhip to remain at Sandy-Hook. The committee conceiving it to be the ſenſe of the city that he ſhould have ſuch liberty, ſignified it to the Gentleman who is to ſupply him with proviſions, and other neceſſaries. Advice of this was immediately diſpatched to the Captain; and whenever he comes up, care will be taken that he does not enter at the cuſtom-houſe, and that no time be loſt in diſpatching him.

New-York, April 19, 1774.

"To the Public. The long expected TEA SHIP arrived last night at Sandy-Hook," broadside, 1774.

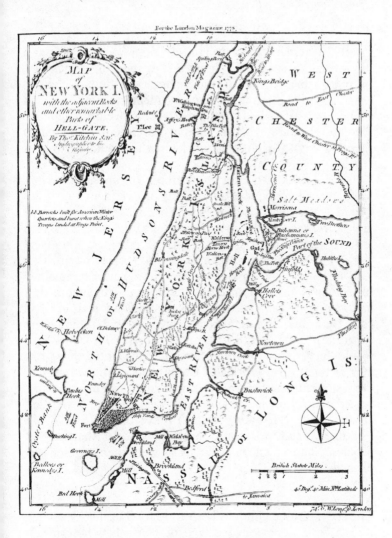

"MAP of NEW YORK, I," showing "New York Island" with only the lower tip settled, 1778.

have received in Boston. As a result the city was more cosmopolitan, marked by its greater endurance of different peoples and faiths, a municipality which, for lack of a shared tradition binding its peoples, was less restricted by the past. Sears preferred that openness and mobility. In 1775, as a member of New York's Provincial Congress, he approved a stirring endorsement of "the free enjoyment of conscience" as "of all others, the most valuable branch of human liberty." Later, while in Boston, he signed a memorial that included an unusual defense of "the Liberty of moveing, from one Place to another" as "one of the dearest Gifts of God to Men," a natural right that no legislature could destroy or restrain.[4]

It was, however, not for freedom but for opportunity that Sears moved to New York, taking up residence on busy Queen (later Pearl) Street. New York was a trading town, and Sears was a trader, a pioneer in what became after 1800 a great migration of southern New Englanders into New York. The assimilation of Yankees and Yorkers was neither easy nor complete. In Sears's day New Yorkers remained suspicious of their Connecticut neighbors, with whom they had a long history of conflict. New England men are bad pay, Gerardus Beekman commented in 1754; they were "d[amne]d ungreatfull cheating fellows." He vowed he would "never trust any more men of that Cuntry. The great Part of them turns Out bad." Complaints continued on into the nineteenth century, as transplanted New Englanders assumed control of the port between 1820 and the Civil War, all the while celebrating their Yankee origins and habits ("industry, enterprise and shrewdness"). In that city of peoples, Connecticut men like Sears were themselves a people apart.[5]

The sixth of nine children born to Mary Thacher Sears and Joshua Sears, a respected citizen of Norwalk whose means

[4] *Journals of the Provincial Congress . . . of the State of New York,* I (Albany, 1842), 53–54; *Boston Town Records, 1778–1783,* in *A Report of the Record Commissioners of the City of Boston,* XXVI (Boston, 1895), 282.

[5] Robert G. Albion, *The Rise of New York Port* (New York, 1970; orig. 1939), pp. 241–52; Beekman to Samuel Fowler, April 2, 1754, in Philip L. White, ed., *The Beekman Mercantile Papers, 1746–1799* (New York, 1956), I, 210; Philip L. White, *The Beekmans of New York in Politics and Commerce, 1647–1877* (New York, 1956), pp. 223–24. For the larger story of New York-Connecticut conflict, see Dixon Ryan Fox, *Yankees and Yorkers* (New York, 1940).

were neither insubstantial nor lordly, Isaac as a young boy "hawked" shellfish through the country, according to the Loyalist historian Thomas Jones, for whom humble origins were a proof of unworthiness. At age sixteen Sears was apprenticed to the captain of a New England coastal vessel. The boy proved able. He soon became an officer, and by his early twenties commanded small sloops that plied the North American coast between Halifax and New York and that made winter voyages to the West Indies. Like all colonial captains he enjoyed considerable freedom in negotiating the commercial affairs of his employers, who were frequently New Yorkers, in ports of call abroad.[6]

A fuller field for his gifts came with the Seven Years' War. Sears became a captain of privateers—private vessels especially commissioned in time of war to attack and seize enemy shipping. The profits of privateering could be high. Officers and crew often received half of the condemned "prize," which they divided among themselves according to rank as specified in the ship's articles of agreement. Special provisions allowed for compensation to the injured, or for incentives to the courageous: the articles of agreement for the privateer *Mars,* concluded at New York on June 23, 1762, allocated an additional half share of the returns for "the first Man who enters on boarding a Prize in an engagement, and strikes her Colours." Risks were also great, even apart from the violence that was a privateersman's lot. The small, lightly armed privateers were built more to run than fight. Heavily rigged to catch the wind on masts "like church steeples," the fast and maneuverable American vessels won the admiration of British naval designers, but ran a distinct risk of capsizing. They had once served well the needs of colonial smugglers. The work of privateers resembled, however, that of pirates more than smugglers. Like the colonial crowds in which seamen often participated, and which could act at one moment as a militia or posse and in another as rioters, privateers existed on the margins of legality and respectability. Between them and piracy lay their commis-

[6] Thomas Jones, *History of New York During the Revolutionary War* (New York, 1879), II, 340; Christen, "King Sears," pp. 10–12.

sions or letters of marque, but where the authority of those commissions was questioned, or where the privateersmen acted outside the limits of their commissions, they easily slipped into the pirates' ranks. Even courts sometimes found it difficult to draw the narrow line between piracy and privateering, which is in part why European powers abandoned the practice with the Declaration of Paris in 1856. So long as it continued, however, privateering called upon skillful seamen with a particular capacity for violence and for enduring danger. The commanders needed to be decisive, and above all a privateersman had to be audacious. Without audacity "he was doomed to ignominious failure."[7]

Sears qualified. At sea as in politics he was a man "of great personal intrepidity; forward in dangerous enterprises, and ready at all times to carry out the boldest measures." He commanded with success the ship *Decoy* of six guns and later the sloop *Catherine.* In 1759 he brought the *Belle Isle,* with only fourteen guns, into a bold attack on a large French sloop of twenty-four guns. Sears provided Weyman's *New York Gazette* for October 8, 1759, with an account. On the second day of pursuit he was preparing to board the French ship on the starboard quarter when

an unlucky Shot from her dismounted the Bell-Isle's Wheal, which lay'd her Decks open. They soon got a Tiller in the Cabbin, and at 7 clapp'd her aboard, when the first Lieutenant hook'd the Grappling in her Main Shrouds, and in this Condition they laid Side and Side three Hours; and altho' they frequently were upon the Ship's Gunnel, yet as often beat therefrom by Means of their Lances and Bayonets, till about Ten o'Clock the Grappling gave way, and the Sloop shear'd off, having nine Men kill'd outright, and twenty-two wounded. . . . with 7 Shot between Wind

[7] John Franklin Jameson, *Privateering and Piracy in the Colonial Period: Illustrative Documents* (New York, 1923), pp. 581–85 for the *Mars* and also 581n, ix–xiv; Edgar Stanton Maclay, *A History of American Privateers* (New York, 1899), esp. pp. 7–9, 22–25, 12; Reuben Elmore Stivers, *Privateers and Volunteers . . . 1766 to 1866* (Annapolis, 1975), p. 23. See also James G. Lydon, *Pirates, Privateers, and Profits* (Upper Saddle River, N.J., 1970), which sees New York's mid-eighteenth-century privateersmen as "the natural descendants of the city's pirates of the 1690's" (p. 7).

and Water, their Spritfail Yard and Flying Jibb Boom gone, scarce a Shroud to support the Mast, two nine-pound Shot in the Bolsprit, and both Sails and Rigging shot to Pieces, . . . Sears tho't it best to lay by and repair, intending to be at her again in the Afternoon, but a violent Gale . . . forced him to sea. . . .

Two years later Sears was shipwrecked on Sable Island, but saved his crew and himself. "The prestige of these exploits," according to one account, "gave him a great moral ascendancy."[8] His success at the privateering business was no doubt equally important to his reputation among seamen. By age twenty-nine Sears had accumulated a fortune in excess of £2,500, significantly more than the £1,640 his father had left at his death in 1754. And his ascent had only begun. By the time the peace of Paris was signed in 1763 he had made the great leap from captain to merchant, investing in vessels trading along the North American coast, Madeira, and the West Indies. In the early years of the Anglo-American conflict he was prominent in New York's mercantile community and a member of the newly formed Chamber of Commerce.[9]

Times were not auspicious for such ambition. The prosperity of the French wars passed in 1760, and New York's economy was further injured by postwar British trade and currency regulations. The Revenue Acts of 1764, which imposed cumbersome requirements on commerce and disrupted established patterns of trade, came at a critical time in Sears's career. They affected all major branches of his trade and forced him to abandon that with Madeira. He was not alone, however, in these troubles. "Trade in this part of the world is come to so wretched a pass," one New York observer claimed in June 1765, "that you would imagine the plague had been here, the grass growing in most trading streets; and the best traders so far from wanting the as-

---

[8] Isaac Q. Leake, *Memoir of the Live and Times of General John Lamb* (Albany, 1857), p. 8. [John Austin] Stevens in May, *Descendants of Sares,* p. 116; but see also Jones, *History,* II, 340, which claims that Sears was accused of cowardice and "gained little honour" by the *Belle-Isle* incident. Sears's popularity among seamen supports Stevens's conclusion.

[9] May, *Descendants of Sares,* p. 76; Christen, "King Sears," pp. 17–26.

sistance of a clerk, rather want employment for themselves."
Distress became general as a result of the Currency Act of
1764, which outlawed new issues of legal-tender paper money
by colonial governments, and whose full deflationary effect
was felt in New York only after 1768 when the final issues
of old provincial currency were redeemed. Customs revenues
under British Revenue Acts of 1766 and 1767 were, moreover,
to be paid in silver, which served to remove from the country whatever hard money it possessed. As money became
scarce, debts were difficult to collect; trade was slowed, and
unemployment spread until Governor Henry Moore noted
that "many of the poorer inhabitants have been ruin'd and
all Ranks greatly impoverish'd."[10]

The requests of New York's merchants for reform in
Britain's trade laws nonetheless remained moderate. In a
controversial petition of 1767 signed by Sears the merchants
posed no objection to the right of Parliament to regulate
commerce for the good of the larger British community
and asked no exemption from trade restrictions. Instead
they called Britain to task for violating her own self-interest
as understood according to mercantilist assumptions. The
Revenue Acts of 1764 and their revision of 1766 had so
clogged colonial commerce, the New York merchants argued, as to impair their capacity to purchase British goods.
The act in fact worked to the advantage of foreign nationals
whose trade was unfettered by these "Embarrassments," and
who were paid with "money instead of manufactures" to the
"national disadvantage." The merchant petitioners sought,
in short, a more correct understanding and appreciation of
the circumstances of colonial commerce and a consistent, rational application of mercantilist principles.[11] Yet the peti-

[10] Virginia D. Harrington, *The New York Merchant on the Eve of the
Revolution* (New York, 1935), pp. 316–24, 331–37; Christen, "King Sears,"
pp. 29–30; letter from New York, June 30, 1765, in I. N. Phelps Stokes,
The Iconography of Manhattan Island, 1498–1909, IV (New York, 1922),
749; Moore to the Earl of Hillsborough, Fort George, May 14, 1768, in
E. B. O'Callaghan, ed., *Documents Relative to the Colonial History of
. . . New York (NYCD),* VIII (Albany, 1857), 72.

[11] New York merchants' petition in John Almon, ed., *A Collection of
Papers Relative to the Dispute Between Great Britain and America, 1764–
1775* (New York, 1971; orig. London, 1777), pp. 163–67; also Christen,
"King Sears," pp. 83–94.

tion greatly provoked the British, who after repealing the Stamp Act expected of colonists only gratitude and submission. Even Lord Chatham dismissed the petition as ungrateful, excessive in its pretensions, and in its arguments "most grossly fallacious and offensive," and Governor Moore was censured for forwarding the document. Only Benjamin Franklin recalled that "petitioning is not rebellion. The very nature of a petition acknowledges the power it petitions to, and the subjection of the petitioners." The submission Britain demanded of colonists was, it seemed, much more absolute—like that of slaves, as John Holt's radical *New York Journal* suggested with increasing frequency. William Smith, a New Yorker who later became a Loyalist, foresaw the future well. When Americans reflected upon their future under a hard-pressed mother country anxious to pass its financial burdens on to its colonies, then "commanding Silence in the oppressed Beast" upon which those burdens were cast, what could be expected, Smith asked, "but Discontent for a while, and in the End open Opposition."[12]

Sears served on virtually all the committees formed to resist Britain in these years. He was on committees of the Sons of Liberty and of the merchants, whose nonimportation agreements he supported from 1765 on into the war years. He was on the committee of correspondence formed at New York in December 1773 during the tea crisis. He served on the Committee of Fifty-one, formed in May 1774 to coordinate New York's response to the Port Act, and on its successor, the Committee of Sixty, charged with enforcing the Continental Association. He was on the Committee of One Hundred, which governed New York after the outbreak of war. He was elected to New York's first Provincial Congress and sat on its Committee of Safety.[13]

But the privateersman was not suited for committees. He

[12] Harrington, *New York Merchant,* pp. 331–32 (includes Chatham quotation); Verner W. Crane, ed., *Benjamin Franklin's Letters to the Press, 1758–1775* (Chapel Hill, 1950), p. 86; Smith to Robert Monckton, New York, May 30, 1765, in William H. W. Sabine, ed., *Historical Memoirs from 16 March 1763 to 9 July 1776 of William Smith* (New York, 1956), p. 29.
[13] Christen, "King Sears," *passim;* Christen, "Isaac Sears," pp. 4–10.

lacked Samuel Adams's temperament and Adams's capacity to endure prolonged discussion: action, he decided in 1765, was the best response to aggression. He never changed his mind. Sears helped organize the Military Association of the Sons of Liberty to coordinate the armed response of colonists from different provinces should the British attempt to enforce the Stamp Act with troops. He was an early advocate of nonimportation as a response to the Townshend Revenue Act of 1767, and he fought desperately to prevent the defection of New York from that agreement in 1770 after Parliament had repealed all the Townshend duties except that on tea. With his new colleague, Alexander McDougall, he insisted that the New York assembly refuse to provision royal troops within the province, as required by the Quartering Act. And he was among those radicals who wanted to follow the example of the Boston Tea Party and use force if necessary to prevent the landing of dutied East India Company tea in New York. Again with McDougall he urged Boston to "Firmness and Perseverance" against the Port Act. To avoid its strictures by paying for the tea would afford only "a temporary relief from a particular evil, which will and must end in a more general Calamity." He and McDougall also claimed credit for having "stimulated" New York's merchants to act in 1774 after news of the Boston Port Act arrived.[14]

Sears acted where others talked. It was he who took on

[14] Christen, "King Sears," pp. 53–75, 120–33, 172–97. Alexander Colden heard that Sears "publicly declared if any Merchant, or number of Merchants presumed to break through the non importation agreement till the several Provinces had agreed to do the same, he would lose his life in the attempt, or the goods imported should be burnt as soon as landed." To Anthony Todd, July 11, 1770, *NYCD*, VIII, 220. Troops: Roger J. Champagne, *Alexander McDougall and the American Revolution in New York* (Schenectady, 1975), pp. 19–35. Sears abandoned the Delancey faction in the supply conflict, and joined McDougall, a supporter of the Livingstons. Christen argues that Sears failed to bring all of his old Delanceyite supporters with him, such that competing factions of the Sons of Liberty associated with different parties in provincial politics continued into 1770. Christen, "King Sears," esp. pp. 165–67 and, on the tea dispute, 231–59. Sears and McDougall to Boston, May 15, 1774, in Stokes, *Iconography*, IV, plate 41a. See also McDougall's detailed memorandum on New York's response to the Port Act in the McDougall papers, New York Historical Society (NYHS), New York City.

the task of coercing those who undermined American resistance. He led "visits" of the Sons of Liberty in 1766 to a
merchant accused of holding stamped papers and to a ship
carrying goods imported contrary to the New York merchants' first nonimportation agreement. He also directed
popular pressure on violators of later nonimportation agreements, and in 1769 urged colonists elsewhere to "bring . . .
to condign Punishment" those who circulated false rumors
to "raise Jealousies and Distrust amongst the Colonies" so as
to undermine the commercial accords colonists had formed
"for the Preservation of their common and most essential
Rights." The nonimportation agreement of 1768–70 was
honored with particular severity in New York. Even after
the collapse of that general effort, New Yorkers succeeded
in keeping dutied tea from their shores: with the encouragement of the Sons of Liberty, McDougall later testified,
"patriotic" smugglers imported a goodly amount of that
popular product from Holland. With the reinstitution of
commercial coercion by the Continental Congress in 1774
and his appointment to New York's Committee of Inspection, Sears resumed his role as policeman of the resistance
movement, commanding a sloop that kept watch first on the
ship *James,* then on the infamous *Beulah* when they entered
New York in 1775 with goods imported contrary to the Continental Association.[15]

In these efforts Sears had the support not only of other
radical merchants, but also of the seamen and dock workers
who alone, according to General Thomas Gage, merited the
title "mob." Among such men the captains of privateers had
a particular authority, as James Duane and Robert R. Livingston discovered when they enlisted the captains' help in
putting down the Stamp Act disturbances. And Sears seems

[15] G. D. Skull, ed., *The Montresor Journals,* in *Collections of the New
York Historical Society for 1881* (New York, 1882), pp. 349, 353–54, 361;
Leake, *Lamb,* pp. 24–26; Isaac Low, Sears, Samuel Verplanck, and Thomas
Franklin, Jr., to Roger Sherman and the Committee of Merchants at New
Haven, New York, July 12, 1769, Miscellaneous Bound Manuscripts, MHS;
Arthur M. Schlesinger, *The Colonial Merchants and the American Revolu-
tion, 1763–1776* (New York, 1968; orig. 1918), p. 190; McDougall to
Robert Treat Paine, New York, June 5, 1775, Paine collection, MHS;
Champagne, *McDougall,* pp. 77–78.

to have been especially influential: in late November 1765, Captain John Montresor noted in his journal, "the Governor sent for Sears, a ringleader to preserve the peace of the city." Sears could also count on the support of those artisans who filled the ranks of the Sons of Liberty (and whose Committee of Mechanics gradually replaced the Sons of Liberty as a separate entity in New York politics after 1774). On occasion the interests of merchants, seamen, and artisans (or of special interest groups within those larger categories) conflicted, but firm economic bonds also linked them together. In a commercial center such as New York, as the historian Alfred F. Young observes, "the interests of most craftsmen inevitably rose or fell with the foreign trade which determined the prosperity of the city as a whole." "We live by one another," a newspaper writer of 1767 noted, and so "must all feel the misfortunes that attend a general decay of business, and declension of industry." Or, as "Axe and Hammer" reminded his fellow "Leather Aprons" in an electoral broadside of 1769, "it is trade . . . that supports our families, as many a Man can testify." The concerns that bound these insurgent forces in New York were announced in the slogans they adopted—"Liberty, Property, and No Stamps" or, as they inscribed on Liberty Pole in 1770, "Liberty and Property."[16]

The resistance movement in New York also contained a larger contingent of future Loyalists than elsewhere, and therefore remained far less militant than many other coastal cities. It would do no good to propose any martial measures

[16] Gage to Secretary Conway, December 21, 1765, in Clarence Edwin Carter, ed., *The Correspondence of General Thomas Gage . . . 1763-1775* (New Haven, 1931), I, 79, and see also 70-71; Livingston to Monckton, November 8, 1765, *The Aspinwall Papers,* in *Collections of the Massachusetts Historical Society,* 4th Ser., X (Boston, 1871), 563; Scull, ed., *Montresor Journals,* p. 27; Memorandum, May 23, 1774, McDougall papers; Young, *The Democratic Republicans of New York: The Origins, 1763-1797* (Chapel Hill, 1967), p. 100; "Conciliator," in *New York Journal (NYJ),* October 15, 1767; broadside in Stokes, *Iconography,* IV, 791. Slogans: Christen, "King Sears," pp. 44-45 (citing the *New York Gazette and Weekly Post Boy* for November 28, 1765); Leake, *Lamb,* p. 59. In 1770 the Delanceyite group called itself the "Friends to Liberty and Trade." *NYJ,* March 22, 1770.

"at present, in our City," McDougall wrote Boston on February 9, 1775. "Sure I am, we shall be the last of the Provinces to the Northward of Georgia, that will appeal to the Sword." The following November Dr. Thomas Young wrote from Newport that military companies were being formed in New England "and a great ambition runs thro all ranks to become skillful in the use of arms. For God's sake," he urged, "endeavor to stir up some such thing in New York!" Still there was no response. But in the spring of 1775, as reports arrived that the King had declared the Americans rebels and issued a commission for the arrest of prominent colonial leaders, that New Englanders were excluded from trade with Britain, Ireland, and the British West Indies and from the Newfoundland fisheries, and that large numbers of royal troops were en route "to dragoon the British Colonies into a surrender of their liberty and property,"[17] Sears and his radical contingent found it increasingly difficult to remain strictly under the authority of the laggard Committee of Sixty. That committee refused even to prohibit the exportation of supplies to British troops at Boston and merely encouraged New Yorkers to "withhold such supplies . . . till we have assurances that nothing hostile is intended against us." The old Sons of Liberty caucused in the taverns, then called a series of public meetings at Liberty Pole in April 1775 to stimulate more vigorous action. Two merchants were condemned as enemies to American freedom for having long supplied the British army at Boston; two others similarly accused were "visited" by a committee that they might answer for their conduct. Sears characteristically moved that "every man should provide himself with four-and-twenty rounds." When the city's regular magistrates arrested him, "Sears, the King" was "rescued at the Jail door," as the Loyalist Samuel Auchmuty recorded, by a "rascally Whig mob" that paraded him through the town "with colours flying, . . . through the *Fly, Wall-street,* and *Broadway*" before delivering him to his assembled supporters at

[17] McDougall letter of February 9, 1775, McDougall papers; Young to Lamb, Newport, November 19, 1775, Lamb papers, NYHS; *NYJ,* April 13 and 20, 1775.

Liberty Pole. "Our Magistrates," Auchmuty complained, "have not the spirit of a louse."[18]

Within a matter of days the news of Lexington and Concord threw the town into a greater crisis. "It is impossible fully to describe the agitated State of the Town," William Smith wrote. "At all corners People inquisitive for News— Tales of all Kinds invented, believed, denied, discredited. . . . The taverns filled with Publicans at Night" and "Little Business done in the Day." While others watched the pandemonium, Sears took control: the old "Whig mob" forced the unloading of ships in the harbor destined for Boston, then raided the arsenal at City Hall, seizing about 600 muskets, bayonets, and cartridge boxes. "These arms," Marinus Willett recalled, "were distributed among the most active of the Citizens who formed themselves into a Voluntary Corps and assumed the Government of the City." A few days later Sears led 360 armed men to the home of the customs collector, demanded keys to the customs house, and closed the port. By these decisive actions the New York–to–Boston supply line was cut and the authority of the Continental Association was upheld. In the meantime the city was policed by members of the Military Association of the City of New York, newly organized "to defend their Liberty, Property, and Country," whose patrols were organized from Sears's home, and who inscribed in their otherwise spare records the patriotic words

America the illustrious
Liberty and Property America.[19]

Of lowly birth, upwardly mobile, Sears had much in common with other leaders of the New York Sons of Liberty. John Lamb and Alexander McDougall, who with Sears were

[18] Peter Force, ed., *American Archives,* 4th Ser., II (Washington, 1839), 282–86, 347–50; *NYJ,* April 13, 1775.

[19] Sabine, ed., *Smith Memoirs,* p. 222; Christen, "King Sears," pp. 318–31; "Colonel Marinus Willett's Narrative," in *New York City During the*

the most prominent New York radicals, were also first- or second-generation New Yorkers trying to make their way up in life through the world of business. Anthony Lamb, John's father, was convicted of burglary in his native England, according to Thomas Jones, then sent to America rather than executed because he was still "a lad." Once in the New World the elder Lamb became a skilled optician and a manufacturer of optical instruments. But if Lamb's father was "an honest, just, upright man, and as a mechanic . . . universally esteemed," a "useful member of society," his son found the "humble life of a mechanic suited not his taste." He was ambitious; he "longed to be a gentleman," Jones charged, and so abandoned the occupation of his father and became a merchant.[20]

Alexander McDougall arrived in America with his parents and two brothers in 1738 when he was six years old. The family had joined some 170 Scottish Highlanders assembled by a Captain Lachlin Campbell, who hoped to settle them (with the financial help of the New York assembly) as his tenants on a large grant of land in the upper Hudson Valley. Many immigrants had, however, paid their own passageway on the expectation that they would become freeholders. They protested; Campbell's plans collapsed, and in the confusion Ronald McDougall decided instead to become a dairy farmer on Manhattan. He prospered, and in time became one of the province's leading milk dealers (not just "a poor industrious milkman" as Jones claimed). Young Alexander may have "trudged about the town with the pails upon his back, dealing out milk to his father's customers," and he was for a while apprenticed to a tailor. But he succumbed to the call of the sea, advanced like Sears to commanding small sloops in the 1750s, made a modest fortune as a privateer dur-

American Revolution, pp. 53–65, esp. 54–55; Stokes, *Iconography*, IV, 884, and, for "Prospectus of Military Association and Signatures of Charter members, 1775," pl. 45; *Collections of the New York Historical Society for 1915* (New York, 1916), p. 509. See also McDougall's memorandum on the meetings of April 1775 in the McDougall papers, which makes clear how hesitant the Committee of Sixty was to assume additional power after the news of war arrived from Massachusetts.

[20] Jones, *History*, II, 342; Leake, *Lamb*, pp. 9–10.

ing the Seven Years' War, and soon became an investor and trader on his own account.[21]

Sears's manners and habits seem, however, to have been shaped far more by the quarterdeck than were those of his political fellows. Though Lamb lacked a classical education, he "was well versed in the belle-lettre knowledge of his day," according to his biographer, and spoke both German, the native language of his mother, and French, which served him well during the revolutionary war. He was also "a fluent speaker, and a forcible and ready writer," gifts lacking to Sears, who composed no elegant speeches, broadsides, or essays, and whose surviving letters are mainly business correspondence, crisp and to the point, or the work of a joint effort signed (and probably written) by others along with him. McDougall was more like Lamb in this regard. Jones had little time for any of the Sons of Liberty, but credited McDougall with "a pretty good genius" as well as "extreme" ambition. "By dint of application," Jones wrote, McDougall "obtained some knowledge in literature," which facilitated his intimacy with persons of higher status, particularly with the Livingston family, which McDougall supported in provincial politics. John Adams found McDougall "a very sensible man, and an open one," with "none of the mean cunning which disgraces so many of my countrymen"—a comment that corroborates New Yorkers' criticism of the New Englanders and suggests that Adams, like Gerardus Beekman, considered New England a country apart.[22]

Adams was also impressed by the opulence he found in New York ("rich plate, a very large silver coffee-pot, a very large silver tea pot, napkins of the very finest materials") and by the city itself, with "streets . . . vastly more regular and elegant than those in Boston, and . . . houses more grand," but not by its aristocracy. "I have not seen one real gentleman, one well-bred man, since I came to town," he noted after being received by several members of New York's elite on his way to the Continental Congress in 1774. The

[21] Jones, *History,* I, 24–26; Champagne, *McDougall,* pp. 5–6.
[22] Leake, *Lamb,* p. 10; Jones, *History,* I, 26; Charles F. Adams, ed., *The Works of John Adams,* II (Boston, 1850), 345.

upper ranks of New York society remained nonetheless difficult to enter. There were those found who McDougall's clothes too outlandish, his conversation too profuse, his tastes those of a seaman who preferred rum to wine. Sears was still more unacceptable. Even after the revolutionary war, when he lived at a fashionable address, "rolled about in his coach and four," and ate like a gentleman at three, he remained "a person of small abilities and no education" who, Jones reported with some satisfaction, was "little noticed by the present leaders."[23]

Sears, Lamb, and McDougall found great opportunities in prerevolutionary New York politics. They were ambitious at a time when politics had become the preeminent activity of public life, a pastime by which the obscure might rise to positions of power and prominence.[24] By reason of their past and their present they could, moreover, fill a necessary and distinctive role in the city: they played the role of brokers, mediating between the various social and economic groups that made up the community. As merchants they could and did confer with the best of their neighbors. At the same time they had strong bonds with the city's middle and lower orders. McDougall shared Sears's authority with the seamen, for he, too, had been a successful captain of privateers. Lamb, as the son of a prominent mechanic, provided a natural link with the town's artisans (and perhaps also through his mother with its Germans, though that connection seems to have been of lesser importance). He served on the Committee of Mechanics and, according to his biographer, once composed a handbill signed "A Plebeian" and perhaps also another signed "A Mechanic."[25] The significance of these men for the elite depended in fact almost entirely upon their influence with "the people," whose power and politics were being defined in the revolutionary period. That influence, exercised by Sears, Lamb, and McDougall in part by virtue

[23] Ibid., pp. 349, 347; Champagne, McDougall, p. 10; Jones, History, II, 341; dinner invitations from Sears in the S. B. Webb papers, Sterling Memorial Library, Yale University, New Haven, Connecticut.

[24] Patricia U. Bonomi, A Factious People: Politics and Society in Colonial New York (New York, 1971), pp. 279–86.

[25] Memorandum, May 23, 1774, McDougall papers; Leake, Lamb, p. 11n.

of their earlier lives, was also therefore very carefully cultivated.

The democratic politics of New York were far less developed in the 1760s and 1770s than were those of Boston because New York was governed by a municipal corporation, not a town meeting. Under the terms of the Montgomery Charter of 1731 the city's mayor, recorder, town clerk, treasurer, and most other municipal officers were named by the governor-in-council. The Common Council, which passed municipal ordinances, consisted of the mayor, recorder, and the city's aldermen, who were elected *viva voce* within the various wards. The electorate also chose a set of assistants and several minor officials (assessors, collectors, constables) as well as a city vestry to collect poor rates and care for paupers, but it had no central and direct role in government as at Boston. The people met in New York not at a Faneuil Hall, but in the Fields—in the open—summoned often by persons without official authority.[26]

Boston had developed an institutionalized system for the management of its democratic politics. It had, of course, its Green Dragon Tavern, its Salutation Arms; it had a Monday Night Club, a Loyal Nine, and a full set of other social clubs and masonic lodges where, as in other American cities, politics often became the topic of conversation. But it also had an established caucus system which linked artisans and other groups within the town, and coordinated support for measures that would come before the Town Meeting. On Manhattan during the final years of the colonial period, political affiliations had instead to be worked out by political brokers at Bardin's, Francis Lewis's, Montagne's, Vanderwater's, or similar taverns that appear regularly in the narratives of revolutionary New York and that had long been rallying places for the politically minded. There, a disgruntled correspondent of James Rivington's Loyalist *New York Gazetteer* complained, "inconsiderate people" congregated, giving "not the least attention to their several occupations," but instead "talk politicks, get drunk, damn King,

[26] Oscar T. Barck, Jr., *New York City During the War for Independence* (New York, 1931), pp. 12–13; Bonomi, *Factious People,* pp. 32, 37.

Ministers, and Taxes; and vow they will follow any measure proposed to them by their demagogues, however repugnant to religion, reason, and common sense."[27]

The tavern culture of New York, which rivaled all other colonial cities in the number of its drinking houses, fitted well and perhaps shaped its style of discourse, which John Adams found different from that in New England. "At their entertainments there is no conversation that is agreeable," he noted. "There is no modesty, no attention to one another. They talk very loud, very fast, and altogether. If they ask you a question, before you can utter three words of your answer, they will break out upon you again, and talk away." Taverns offered their own distinctive ways of overcoming dissidence and forming group loyalties. One argument at Drake's in early 1775, which fortunately spilled over into the press, provides a glimpse of that process. In the course of an increasingly heated exchange John Case, an old man of Loyalist leanings, announced that if given the chance he would fight for the King against the Americans. Did Sears then threaten him with a gridiron, as Rivington's paper claimed? Or did the assembled patriots exercise restraint, refraining even from rough language, as deponents in Holt's *New York Journal* insisted? According to the latter, Case was placed "in Coventry": his former companions were obliged under the forfeiture of a nip of toddy to shun his company. Old Case took his state in good spirit and called for some wine, which he drank while trying to trick people into speaking to him, calling out, " 'I'll catch one of you in your nip.' "[28] But no doubt ostracism was a powerful weapon in the good-fellowship of a tavern.

Sears, Lamb, and McDougall frequented the taverns, making and confirming affiliations, mixing drink and politics. For a time McDougall may himself have kept a sailor's "Slop-Shop," and in 1770 the Sons of Liberty acquired one of their own. After learning that a rival faction had reserved Montagne's, a favorite haunt, to celebrate the anniversary

---

[27] "Bellisarius" in *Rivington's New York Gazetteer*, March 9, 1775.
[28] Adams, ed., *Works of John Adams*, II, 353; "A Friend to Constitutional Liberty," *NYJ*, February 2, 1775.

of the Stamp Act's repeal, Sears, McDougall and nine other men of substance put up £630 for a public house on Broadway near Liberty Pole, which they renamed Hampden Hall. But above all there was Drake's, the alehouse near Beekman's Slip on the East River owned by Sears's father-in-law and patronized, according to Jones, by "sailors, boatmen, and vagabonds." It was there the Sons of Liberty signed their protest against New York's abandonment of nonimportation in 1770 (and many of its 225 signatories signed with a mark). There, too, the Sons met with William Goddard in 1774 to discuss plans for a new "Continental Post"; and there "the most Zealous partisans in the cause of Liberty" assembled, Marinus Willett recalled, as the colonists slipped into war in the spring of 1775.[29]

The taverns and their politicians were inevitably drawn into the street brawls between British soldiers and colonials endemic to New York in the depression years. The British regulars supplemented their low pay by taking jobs throughout the city, accepting recompense below that demanded by local workers, who were already plagued by unemployment. To add to the discontent New York's legislature agreed on December 15, 1769, to supply British troops within the colony in accordance with Parliament's Quartering Act of 1765. The following day, McDougall responded with his notorious broadside "To the Betrayed Inhabitants of the City and Colony of New York." To support a military force "kept here, not to protect but to enslave us," McDougall argued, was a betrayal of the "liberties of the people." Two other broadsides of December by "A Plebeian" and "A Son of Liberty" (probably John Lamb), and another of January signed "Brutus" (perhaps McDougall), argued that the assembly's action would exacerbate economic problems caused by Britain's revenue acts and by the shortsighted decisions of local employers. "Is it not enough," "Brutus" asked, "that you pay Taxes and Billeting Money to support the Soldiers, and a Poor Tax, to maintain many of their Whores and Bas-

[29] Jones, *History,* I, 25; II, 340; Champagne, *McDougall,* p. 30; White, *Beekmans of New York,* pp. 433–35; Christen, "King Sears," pp. 163–64, 197 and n; Memorandum, May 28, 1774, McDougall papers; "Willett's Narrative," p. 61.

tards in the Workhouse, without giving them the Employment of the Poor, who you must support if you don't employ, which adds greatly to swell your Poor Tax?" To employ such "Enemies of Liberty" would "bring on . . . the just Reproaches of the Poor." Meanwhile British soldiers made a concerted effort to destroy the town's Liberty Pole, which was protected by Sears, McDougall, and a group of artisans and workers gathered at Montagne's. When the redcoats finally succeeded in the early hours of January 17, they carefully deposited the pole's sawed-off pieces on the closed tavern's doorstep. That afternoon the people rallied again and resolved against employing "any Soldier, on any Terms whatever." But even as they gathered in the Fields, the *New York Journal* reported, "a number of sailors went along the docks, and turn'd ashore all the soldiers they found at work on board the vessels, and obliged such as were at work in stores, to quit it." Soldiers and civilians (led by Sears) engaged again a few days later in a violent street battle that history remembers as the "Battle of Golden Hill."[30]

By seizing upon events in these ways Sears and his fellow radicals linked the hardships of the city's workers to the broad constitutional issues of the day. They were quick also to grasp the symbolic meaning of these episodes. After the assembly arrested McDougall for his December broadside, he was publicly celebrated as the "Wilkes of America" (John Wilkes having suffered persecution by Parliament for his famous "Number Forty-Five North Briton"). The soldiers' destruction of the Liberty Pole was an obvious gift to radical politicians, who responded by erecting a new and better pole —an eighty-foot mast, encased for two-thirds of its length in iron, which was drawn from the North River shipyards by six horses in a procession of flagbearers, musicians and Liberty boys. These elaborate rituals were New York's way of

[30] Lee R. Boyer, "Lobster Backs, Liberty Boys, and Laborers in the Streets; New York's Golden Hill and Nassau Street Riots," *The New York Historical Society Quarterly* (*NYHSQ*), LVII (1973), 280–308; *NYJ Supplement,* March 1, 1770, and May 10, 1770, where Sears specifically noted his agreement with McDougall on the constitutional issue. McDougall's broadside quoted in Champagne, *McDougall,* p. 19. McDougall was probably "Brutus" since he used the pseudonym "Marcus Brutus" in a letter to Samuel Adams, January 29, 1775, McDougall papers.

cultivating a sense of common commitment, her equivalent of Boston's annual memorials to its own "Massacre" of 1770. The militant alliance of January 1770 was, moreover, formalized five years later, when storekeepers, butchers, and craftsmen joined Sears and other old Sons of Liberty of more highly ranked occupations in forming the Military Association of the City of New York.[31]

Other more material considerations cemented the political ties that bound Sears and his fellow radical leaders to their followers. Where available, patronage was used to good effect. Sears, for example, nominated Daniel Dunscomb, an influential cooper who would later become a leader of the Committee of Mechanics, to be New York's first inspector of Pot and Pearl Ash, a lucrative position which Sears was himself later pressed to accept.[32]

Administering to the needs of the poor was another way of winning popular support. The Sons' constituency was by no means confined to the poor—many mechanics were men of substance, and radical merchants continued to be politically active. Still, the number of impoverished New Yorkers increased in the late 1760s, and hard times, as Charleston's Christopher Gadsden noted, were felt with particular severity by a city's working people. The poor in America, Gadsden added, were better off than those in Europe because they faced no danger of starvation. The gardens of rural Manhattan or the pigs that still roamed the city's streets were sources of sustenance, and the plentiful oyster beds along Manhattan and Long Island provided food for the digging. "People of all ranks amongst us in general prefer them to any other kind of food," one observer noted; "they continue good eight months in the year, and are for two months longer the daily food of our poor."[33] Distress was nonetheless real; and where relief was dispensed, Sears and

[31] Champagne, *McDougall*, p. 28; *NYJ*, February 8, 1770; McDougall's list of persons to whom muskets were issued on July 8, 1775, McDougall papers.

[32] Sears letter, *NYJ*, May 10, 1770.

[33] Gadsden in *South Carolina Gazette*, November 9, 1769, reprinted in Richard Walsh, *Charleston's Sons of Liberty* (Columbia, S.C., 1959), pp. 53–54; Singleton, *Social New York*, p. 350.

the Sons of Liberty were active, solidifying their bonds with the impoverished.

The radicals' favored paper, Holt's *New York Journal,* had long taken on the cause of the poor, attacking building codes that increased the cost of living or complaining of the high price of milk. And it reminded people that they had "a Right to be heard, and attended to . . . even by the highest Powers" where their interest was at stake. Sears was able to adjust the burdens of the poor in a more immediate way during 1768–70 when he served as a tax assessor, no doubt as politically significant a position in New York as was the tax collectorship in Boston. Later he served as a vestryman, responsible for distributing outdoor relief in Montgomerie Ward, which, he claimed, had "near as many Poor as all the other Wards together." He and William Denning, a fellow vestryman, were criticized in 1773 for the large amounts of money they spent. They justified their expenditures by emphasizing the need they had witnessed, and condemned proposals that each ward be responsible only for its own poor. All New Yorkers, above all those in wards with "no real Poor in them," must contribute to relief, they insisted. The same sensitivity explains why the Sons of Liberty erected their new Liberty Pole on land contiguous to the poorhouse. They also sent the leftovers from their annual banquets on the anniversary of the Stamp Act's repeal "to the New Gaol to be distributed among prisoners" in 1769 and again in 1770, when they added two barrels of beer to the scraps from their feast. In those years the jail was filled with prisoners for debt, joined in 1770 by that hero of liberty, McDougall.[34]

The elite of New York politics were alarmed by so concerted an effort to influence the government on the part of persons who were not members of the traditional govern-

[34] *NYJ,* March 19, 1767 ("T"), March 23, 1769, and March 29, 1770; *Minutes of the Common Council of the City of New York, January 31, 1766, to December 23, 1773* (New York, 1905), pp. 128, 184; *New York Gazette and Weekly Mercury,* March 15 and 22, 1773. On the increase of poor relief in New York in these years see Nash, "Urban Wealth and Poverty," table 4, p. 557; on New York's backward record on poor relief, see Bridenbaugh, *Cities in Revolt,* pp. 324–25.

ing class. "The mob begin to think and to reason," Gouverneur Morris noted in an often-cited letter of May 20, 1774. "Poor reptiles! It is with them a vernal morning; they are struggling to cast off their winter's slough, they bask in the sunshine, and ere noon they will bite." In the city's mass meetings his fellow citizens contended, Morris reported, "about the future forms of our government, whether it should be founded upon aristocratic or democratic principles." And he foresaw "with fear and trembling, that if the disputes with Great Britain continue," there would be a farewell to aristocracy, and "we shall be under the worst of all possible dominions . . . the domination of a riotous mob."[35] Such fears were not without reason, for the mobilization of the people in revolutionary New York was part of a larger process by which the social bases of political power were permanently altered in America, though to different extents and at differing speeds from place to place.[36]

In retrospect, however, the radicals' respect for a hierarchical social order and the moderation of their demands for change seem striking. In 1765 the Sons of Liberty specifically endorsed a social system in which the various ranks of men enjoyed the "Rights, Privileges, and Honours justly due to them in their respective Stations in a regular Subordination." Ten years later leaders of the Sons of Liberty were still marked by their habits of social deference. For example, when Marinus Willett set out to seize the spare arms British soldiers hoped to take with them when they evacuated New York after Lexington and Concord, he found himself opposed by Gouverneur Morris, a Whig but Willett's social superior. Willett was, as he said, "stagard." Had he not been encouraged by another New Yorker of rank equal to Morris, the deferential Willett could not have persisted. His own "Zeal

[35] Morris to John Penn, May 20, 1774, in Merrill Jensen, ed., *English Historical Documents,* IX (New York, 1964), 860–63.

[36] See the work of Jackson T. Main, particularly his "Government by the People: The American Revolution and the Democratization of the Legislatures," *William and Mary Quarterly,* 3d Ser., XXIII (1966), 391–407. Also Richard Ryerson, *The Revolution Has Now Begun: The Radical Committees of Philadelphia, 1765–1776* (Philadelphia, 1978).

and Enthusiasm" were not enough.[37] As for Sears, he did not share Samuel Adams's fundamental confidence in popular judgment. He believed instead that leaders shaped the people's behavior: at times in fact he resembled the British in their disrespect for the popular sources of American resistance, and in their conviction that once the American ringleaders were seized all colonial "rebellion" would disappear. If Loyalist leaders on Long Island were captured, Sears suggested in November 1775, "many of the midling and lower Class of People, now under the influence of such persons, wou'd become espousers of their Country's cause."[38]

New York's common people, moreover, were apparently uninterested in any more formalized democratic role in city government. Conservatives repeatedly insisted that important decisions such as the election of delegates to the Continental Congress should be made in regular written polls of the city rather than by the voice votes of large public meetings. In that way electors with the right to vote could be distinguished from "the rabble, which may always be collected by the pagentry of a flag" or the sound of "a drum and fife." During the mass meeting of May 19, 1774—that which aroused Morris's fears for the future—Sears suggested that the new Committee of Fifty (later Fifty-one) be elected by a poll which "every man whose Liberties were concerned" would be allowed to sign, not only the regular freeholders and freemen. His proposal failed, however, for lack of support among his own followers. Tradesmen present reminded Sears that "as they were working for others they would [lose] their days work if they tarried any Longer." That so many of Sears's followers were not among the city's lawful voters was probably itself a measure of their apathy, for the suffrage requirements were relatively generous in New York, where a special decree had long allowed even the poor to claim their freedom "gratis." Like their European counter-

[37] Sons of Liberty in *New York Gazette,* November 28, 1765, cited in Christen, "King Sears," pp. 48–49; "Willett's Narrative," pp. 63–64.

[38] Sears to Roger Sherman, Eliphalet Dyer, and Silas Deane, New Haven, November 28, 1775, in G. H. Hollister, *The History of Connecticut,* II (Hartford, 1857), 241n.

parts, New York's populace was less interested in the franchise than in being heard and heeded by officials of greater social standing. Its sometimes abject submission to its betters was, however, shocking to a New Englander like John Hancock, who learned how different were the ways of New Yorkers from those of his countrymen while on his way to the Continental Congress in May 1775. When he arrived at New York, Hancock wrote his fiancée, the people wanted to remove the horses from his carriage and pull it through the streets themselves, an act common in the deferential countries of Europe. He tried to dissuade the crowd, since he "would not have had [that] taken place upon any consideration, not being fond of such Parade." In the end his coach was saved from that "disagreeable occurrence" only by the intercession of local gentlemen who led the procession.[39]

Certainly there was little in these events to justify Morris's intimations of violent social revolution. Instead the popular politics of revolutionary New York suggested something far more familiar in the history of Manhattan. New York's popular leaders had been born to unprivileged parents, but were upwardly mobile, gaining public prominence by speaking for the lower and middling orders from which they had emerged. They cemented ties with working people by promoting their special needs, by patronage, by assuming a prominent role in the distribution of poor relief. Still they were in their own way autocrats, harboring a certain skepticism about popular judgment, believing more in the influence of strong leaders than in the wisdom of the people. The rank and file of their following was held in place, moreover, as much by deeply engrained habits of deference as by any

[39] "Impartiall," *Rivington's New York Gazetteer*, March 9, 1775; Memorandum, May 19, 1774, McDougall papers; Staughton Lynd, "The Mechanics in New York Politics, 1774–1788," *Labor History*, V (1964), esp. 229. Franchise: Milton Klein's "Democracy and Politics in Colonial New York" (1959), in Klein, *The Politics of Diversity: Essays in the History of Colonial New York* (Port Washington, N.Y., 1974), pp. 21–22, 24; Staughton Lynd and Alfred F. Young, "After Carl Becker: The Mechanics and New York City Politics, 1774–1801," *Labor History*, V (1964), esp. 221–23. Hancock to Dorothy Quincy, New York, May 7, 1775, in Stokes, *Iconography*, IV, 983.

expectations of reward. Here were the marks of a popular political system that would characterize New York on into the twentieth century, and would in its own way ultimately undercut patrician dominance of the city—a system associated with the name of Tammany Hall.

The role Sears and the Sons of Liberty played and the tactics they adopted were further determined by the peculiar breadth of the resistance movement in New York. Substantial merchants and heirs of old landed families, whose Bay Colony equivalents would more likely have been found in the Loyalist coterie of Thomas Hutchinson, were in New York ready members of the nonimportation associations, the "Fifty-one," the "Sixty," the "One Hundred," the extralegal committees that came to constitute the revolutionary government of that city. They did not need Crown connections for their well-being; landed proprietorship, as in Virginia, and the respect of a deferential people buttressed their position even without London. With time it became clear that American independence was nonetheless beyond what many of them could accept; but in the early years of the Anglo-American conflict, redress, not separation, was the issue. These conservative New Yorkers perceived the conflict in Whig terms just as did their colleagues who became revolutionaries, and their disaffection for British policy was real enough. The difference between those poles of the resistance movement was one of means not ends, such that moderate Whigs' participation in New York's committee government led to repeated inaction and delay, particularly as the colonies approached their crisis of allegiance. Sears and McDougall responded to news of the Boston Port Act with a detailed scheme of economic retaliation against Britain while the city's official committee of correspondence merely bemoaned the dilemmas of such critical times. Hesitation in 1774 predicted a later unwillingness to prevent townsmen from supplying the British troops at Boston or to institute measures for military preparedness.[40]

---

[40] Note Governor Francis Bernard's comparison of Massachusetts and New York in a letter to Lord Barrington, Boston, February 7, 1768: both colonies were "liable to be harrast by the Spirit of Jealousy of and Opposition to Government," but "in N York that Spirit actuates Men of Rank

The participation of moderates also meant that New York's committees were no gatherings of like-minded men, as was the Boston committee of correspondence. Instead they represented a range of political views, among which the Sons of Liberty and the Committee of Mechanics spoke for the most extreme. Since they stood for only a portion of the community, the Liberty boys could not assume a separate authority founded upon the sovereignty of the people so readily as was done elsewhere. Thus McDougall wrote Boston on December 13, 1773, that a committee of correspondence would have been formed at New York long before "but we waited for an accession of more respectable Members. The Zealous Friends of the Common Cause are not ignorant of the importance of a uniformity of conduct in this Struggle, and will use their utmost endeavors to adopt your measures, but I cannot yet assure you that we shall succeed." The radicals also shared the respect of their English and American contemporaries for the rule of law, and were hesitant to act without the sanction of some more regularly constituted body. Even the Military Association they formed in April 1775 cited a provincial militia statute as its justification for being.[41]

Because McDougall's "Zealous friends of liberty" were only part of the resistance movement in New York, their mass meetings were rarely considered extralegal town meetings, as were those that assumed considerable governmental authority in Charleston, South Carolina.[42] Instead they acted

and Ability, in Massachusetts it works only with Men of Middling or low Rank; in the Latter the Govr has the generality of respectable Men on his Side; in the former they are more generally against Government." Edward Channing, ed., *The Barrington-Bernard Correspondence, Harvard Historical Studies,* XVII (Cambridge 1912), 142. Sears and McDougall to Boston, May 15, 1774, and New York Committee of Correspondence to Boston, May 23, 1774, in Stokes, *Iconography,* IV, pls. 41a and 42.

[41] McDougall letter in Boston Committee of Correspondence papers, photostats, MHS; "Prospectus of the Military Association," Stokes, *Iconography,* IV, pl. 45. Lynd, "The Mechanics in New York Politics," is the best account of the mechanics' politics, but Lynd gives little attention to the close ties between Sears, Lamb, and McDougall and the Committee of Mechanics.

[42] Pauline Maier, "The Charleston Mob and the Evolution of Popular Politics in Revolutionary South Carolina, 1765–1783," *Perspectives in American History,* IV (1970), 182–84.

like party conventions, defining the popular political position, adopting measures for its implementation. In 1765 the people met in the Fields to instruct the city's assembly representatives how to respond to the Stamp Act. Another such meeting, with John Lamb as chairman, was held on December 18, 1769, to condemn the assembly's decision to supply British soldiers within the province; ten days later the people met again to endorse a bill for voting by ballot. On both occasions committees including Sears were appointed to carry the meeting's resolves to the city's representatives. Meetings similar in function were called on into the mid-1770s.[43]

Always the goal of Sears and his allies was to move the entire community toward a closer accord with the radical position. In that effort the example and advice of more forward colonies was of great political utility. The weakness of the Sons' position at home therefore served to reinforce their nationalist inclinations. In 1765 the New York Sons of Liberty organized an intercolonial resistance movement, formally linking their organization with others to the northeast of New York, and later to its south. In 1770 they opposed any unilateral abrogation by New York of the colonists' nonimportation agreement, arguing that as the welfare of all the colonies was involved, the association could not be abrogated "in justice or Honor" except by *common Consent.* Then as later Sears, Lamb, McDougall, and their colleagues carried on a correspondence with radicals elsewhere, particularly at Boston, finding support and encouragement that was lacking nearer home. Letters and news from Boston, moreover, gave the radicals leverage in New York. On December 7, 1773, an "express" from the north arrived, bringing the Bostonians'

---

[43] Jesse Lemisch, "New York's Petitions and Resolves of December 1765: Liberals vs. Radicals," *NYHSQ*, XLIX (1965), 313–26; Christen, "King Sears," 140–42, 147. On July 6, 1774, another "numerous meeting of the inhabitants of the city of *New-York*, convened in the Fields by public advertisement" met, presided over by McDougall, and passed several resolutions on how New York should proceed in the current crisis. Force, ed., *American Archives*, 4th Ser., I (Washington, 1837), 312–13. The Committee of Fifty-one censured those responsible; Sears, McDougall and others defended the people's right to assemble and resigned from the Committee. See ibid., pp. 313–15, and Champagne, *McDougall*, pp. 61–62.

resolves that dutied East India Company tea was not to be landed in their town. The militancy of New York's Liberty boys suddenly increased. News of the Boston Tea Party led even Governor William Tryon to abandon his "sanguine Hopes that Temperate measures might have been manifested in the Conduct of the Body of the People of this Province on the arrival of the Tea."[44]

Logically, the Sons of Liberty were strong supporters of the Continental Congress, confident that the pressure of other colonies would hasten New York along the road the other provinces were traveling with greater speed. McDougall played unofficial host to delegates from Massachusetts, New Hampshire, and Connecticut as they passed through New York in August 1774, and John Adams's diary shows that he met Sears, Lamb, and their fellow Son of Liberty Hugh Hughes along with more socially eminent New Yorkers. On his trip to Congress the following May, John Hancock recorded that he "went to Capt. Sears's (the King here) and Lodged." In such encounters reasons of politics were wedded to those of personal ambition, for if McDougall and Sears were unacceptable in the more exalted societies of provincial New York, they were received as brothers by men of highest rank in the emergent nation.[45]

Above all, however, the radicals' capacity to affect the direction of New York depended upon their power to restrain the people. Sears had helped impose peace on the city during the Stamp Act turmoil of November 1765. Similarly, ten years later the wife of Robert Murray, who provoked public outrage by landing imported goods from the *Beulah* contrary to the Continental Association, asked Sears and Mc-

<hr>

[44] Hampden Hall protest, July 25, 1770, McDougall papers and *NYJ*, August 2, 1770; Sabine, ed., *Smith Memoirs*, p. 157, and Force, ed., *American Archives*, 4th Ser., I, 255n; Tryon to Dartmouth, January 3, 1774, *NYCD*, VIII, 408. McDougall's memorandum on the maneuverings of 1774, McDougall papers, also indicates that Sears repeatedly tried to use letters from Boston for leverage in New York political meetings.

[45] Champagne, *McDougall*, pp. 67–68; Adams, ed., *Works of John Adams*, II, 345–55; Hancock in Stokes, *Iconography*, IV, 983. Sears and McDougall called for a Continental Congress in their letter to Boston of May 15, 1774, in ibid., pl. 41a. The *Boston Gazette*, May 23, 1774, reprinted the letter with no mention of the Congress, which the Bostonians were not yet ready to advocate.

Dougall to use their "influence with the people" on behalf of her husband. "Our citizens were so enraged," McDougall reported thereafter, ". . . that it was with great difficulty they were prevailed upon not to banish them." Again in April 1775 Smith recorded that Sears and McDougall had proven "useful" in preventing the people from searching the house of Ralph Thurman, who was suspected of supplying the British army at Boston. The weakness of ordinary government was unmistakable in April 1775, first when Sears's followers rescued him from the jailhouse door, and then again when he assumed governmental power after receiving news of Lexington and Concord. Mayor Whitehead Hicks acknowledged that "the Magistratic Authority was gone."[46]

In such circumstances "respectable" citizens concerned for their security and control of the city could not ignore Sears and his colleagues. They were despite themselves locked into a politics of accommodation, which forced them to adopt ever more extreme positions or yield all authority to those whom Gouverneur Morris called "the heads of the mobility." In the crisis of April 1775, Smith noted, the "better Sort" were astonished by the course of events and called for the new revolutionary Committee of One Hundred because they had come to "dread Sears's Train of armed Men," and saw in that new association a way to end "the Field business" and reestablish "Peace and moderation." "Our Cause of Liberty gains fast here," Peter Vandervoort reported in late April; "the People begin to Unite and those we deemed Tories before now come out hearty in the Cause, and I judge some out of fear." Observers talked of Sears's hot temper, of his acting "with the Pride of a Dictator." But he readily yielded his authority to the One Hundred, demonstrating that he sought not personal power but political change. Popular force in New York was a powerful tactic in a long-term effort to radicalize the city that had demanded of radical politicians a persistence and patience beyond that in colonies where friends and enemies were more clearly separated. By 1775 "the violences of such Madmen as Captain Sears"

---

[46] Christen, "King Sears," p. 303; McDougall to Josiah Quincy, Jr., New York, April 6, 1775, in Force, ed., *American Archives*, 4th Ser., II, 284; Sabine, ed., *Smith Memoirs*, pp. 220–21.

had made "proselytes to truth and reason" of many who had once been outspoken in their opposition to the Congress and the American cause.[47]

The new harmony was frail and, as Vandervoort understood, would not survive the presence of a strong British army. Nor was New York's revolutionary government up to the "spirited measures" advocated by the "warm friends" of liberty. They would have prevented the embarkation of British soldiers from New York after Lexington and Concord, taken more aggressive measures to seize arms and ammunition, and seized Governor William Tryon but for the "D . . md Torris" who "pretended to Say it would be best to Lett him alone a little longer." It would have been easy to make prisoners of the soldiers, Willett thought, "but the Idea of a Compromise with the British Government pervaded our council." "We are all asleep," Sears complained in July 1775, "and I fear shall be so until our hands are tied here." In particular, if Loyalists were not disarmed and moved to the interior during the winter of 1775–76 he predicted that half the people of the city and province of New York would be ready to take up arms against the United States by the following spring.[48]

Sears took his seat on the New York Provincial Congress, and assumed responsibility for locating military supplies, for arranging naval surveillance of any ships coming westward toward the Atlantic coast, for erecting fortifications on the high banks of the Hudson, and for preventing colonists from supplying the British army and navy. Sears's success in blocking supplies to His Majesty's ship *Asia* angered Vice-Admiral Samuel Graves, who instructed that ship's captain to "fire upon the House of that Traitor, [Isaac] Sears . . .

[47] Ibid., pp. 220, 223. Vandervoort to Nathaniel Shaw, Jr., New York, April 28, 1775, in William B. Clark (Vols. I-IV) and William James Morgan (Vols. V-VII), eds., *Naval Documents of the American Revolution* (Washington, 1964–76), I, 241; Dr. John Jones to James Duane, December 7, 1775, quoted in Christen, "King Sears," p. 348.

[48] "Willett's Narrative," pp. 65, 57; Simeon Sellick quoted in Clark, ed., *Naval Documents,* III, 559; Sears to Silas Deane, New York, July 8, 1775, in *Collections of the Connecticut Historical Society,* II (Hartford, 1870), 279; Sears to Sherman, Dyer, and Deane, New Haven, November 28, 1775, in Hollister, *History of Connecticut,* II, 241n.

and beat it down, to convince the Inhabitants you will put your Threats into Execution." Three days later, on September 13, 1775, Graves included Sears on a brief list of "the most active Leaders and Abettors of the Rebellion" who were to be seized and confined by the British—an honor General Gage had bestowed on Hancock and Adams the previous year. A report later reached Connecticut that all members of the New York Congress except Sears and McDougall were "Friends to government," that the Congress "would manage their plans in favor of the ministry, were it not for said Sears and McDougal," that the regiments raised in New York by the Provincial Congress were "only for an outside Show" and "were mostly ministerial men, both officers and soldiers," and that the said Congress "would never have made any Opposition, to ministerial measures had it not been for Connecticut"—in whose opposition efforts Sears had by then become deeply involved.[49]

He was in New Haven in July 1775, then again in August, and seems never to have taken up his seat in New York's second Provincial Congress. A British report of October 1775 indicated that Sears had sold his Manhattan home and moved to Connecticut. His patience had apparently run out, and the urgency of the situation determined his course. But Sears abandoned New York only to save it from the enemy, for which he found more extensive and active support in the land of his childhood than in his adopted home. As there were "not Spirited and Leading men enough in N. York to undertake such a Business," he gathered together a corps of a hundred Connecticut volunteers in November 1775 and marched to Manhattan, seizing prisoners along the way, wrecked the presses and carried off the type of James Riving-

---

[49] Records of the New York Provincial Congress and Graves's letters to Captain George Vandeput of the *Asia* from Boston, September 10 and 13, 1775, in Clark, ed., *Naval Documents,* I, 1174, 1206, 1295; II, 40, 71, 87. See also extract of a letter from London, July 8, 1775, in Force, ed., *American Archives,* 4th Ser., II, 1607: if the Americans submit "sixty of you are to be hanged in *Philadelphia,* and the same number in *New-York;* five hundred Pounds is offered for Captain Sears's head in particular—a secret order." Report of a special meeting of the Committee of Inspection for New Milford, Connecticut, May 17, 1776, in Connecticut Archives, Revolutionary War Series 1, V, 394, in the Connecticut State Library (CSL), Hartford.

ton (which Sears thought would "be a great means of putting an end to the Tory Faction there, for his press hath been . . . the very life and Soul of it"), then "faced and wheeled to the left and marched out of Town to the tune of *Yankee Doodle.*"[50]

The raid caused a furor, as Sears had anticipated. He had drawn upon longstanding hostilities toward New York in gathering Connecticut volunteers for his expedition, but that same tradition of conflict exacerbated New York's resentment at the violation of its jurisdiction. Governor Jonathan Trumbull and the Connecticut assembly found New York's protests easy to answer. Since "the head or leader of the whole transaction was a respectable member of your city and Congress . . . and who belongs to and is amenable to your jurisdiction alone," Trumbull wrote the New York Provincial Congress, ". . . the affair cannot be considered as an intrusion of our people into your Province, but as a violence or disorder happening among yourselves."[51] The hostility awakened by the raid had more lasting consequences for Sears. It lost him a command in the new Continental Navy, an appointment he wanted badly.[52]

He sought the Continental Congress's official sanction for a further and more ambitious assembly of Connecticut volunteers to take charge of the Loyalist problem, and received from General Charles Lee—who understood, like Sears, that

[50] Absences from New York: Sears to Silas Deane, New Haven, July 10, 1775, in Clark, ed., *Naval Documents,* I, 852–54; Sears to Peter Van Brugh Livingston, August 18, 1775, Emmet Collection, No. 6922, Manuscripts and Archives Division, New York Public Library, Astor, Lenox and Tilden Foundations (NYPL), New York City; Christen, "Isaac Sears," p. 17; Graves to Philip Stevens, Boston, November 2, 1775, in Clark, ed., *Naval Documents,* II, 857. Loyalists: Sears to Sherman, Dyer, and Deane, New Haven, November 28, 1775, in Hollister, *History of Connecticut,* II, 241n; and account in Christen, "Isaac Sears," p. 23.

[51] Trumbull's letter, June 10, 1776, and related documents in *Journals of the Provincial Congress . . . of New York,* I, 210, 213, 346, 491–92.

[52] William Smith's account in Clark, ed., *Naval Documents,* III, 1113. Sears's reputation also suffered, Smith suggests, because in a discussion of whether New York City should be burned to save it from the enemy, Sears volunteered that "he should not regard his own House tho' it was worth several thousand Pounds." It was later learned "that he had none there nor an Ounce of any moveable Property." Sears had been first on John Adams's list of candidates for naval commands, which was compiled in November 1775. Ibid., II, 1162.

form had to be dispensed with when the enemy was at the door—an appointment as assistant adjutant general with the rank of lieutenant colonel for an expedition to New York in early 1776. The title could "have no bad consequences," Lee explained to Washington; "the man was much tickled, and it added spurs to his head." Under Lee's command Sears went about the business of rounding up enemy sympathizers on Long Island. "Yesterday afternoon I . . . tendered the oath to four of the Grate Torries, which they Swallowed as hard as if it was a four pound Shot that they were trying to Git down," he reported in March 1776. He promised to "ketch the gratest part of the ringledors" who were "a set of Villins" most of whom were "wateing for soport and intend to take up arms against us." If by the late winter of 1776 New York was "pretty well Secured," Connecticut's Eliphalet Dyer reported to Samuel Adams, it was "much owing to that Crazy Capt. Sears which Y[ork] Delegates would affect to Call him."[53]

Sears attempted without success to secure his commission on a permanent basis, and was forced after the Battle of Long Island to return to civilian life. He expressed some puzzlement that active, experienced men like himself and his Connecticut partner, David Waterbury, were not promoted before others, but displayed no enduring bitterness. It was often the case, he noted, that "when a Man has done the most he gets the least reward. It is not for the Lucre of gain that I want the Command of a Squadron in the American Navy," he explained in November 1775, "but it is because I know myself capable of the Station, and because I think I can do my Country more Service in that department than in any other—the Congress's not thinking proper to fix that Honor

[53] Sears to Sherman, Dyer, and Deane, New Haven, November 28, 1775, in Hollister, History of Connecticut, II, 241n; Lee to Washington, New York, February 14, 1776, in Force, ed., American Archives, 4th Ser., IV (Washington 1843), 1145 (Lee admitted he had no authority to make the appointment, but argued "it can have no bad consequences" and added that Sears was "a creature of much spirit and publick virtue, and ought to have his back clapped"); Sears to Lee, Jamaica, New York, March 7, 1776, Miscellaneous Sears manuscripts, NYHS; Dyer to Adams, Lebanon, Connecticut, February 27, 1776, Samuel Adams papers, NYPL; Christen, "Isaac Sears," pp. 24–29.

upon me, will by no means make me inactive in the Cause
we are all engaged in." His highest ambition, he wrote General Schuyler in March 1776, was "in Som Capaisty to make
my Service acceptable to my Country in the present important Strugle."[54]

As a merchant in Boston, where he took up residence in
the later war years, Sears purchased provisions for the American army. He also fought desperately against "Jobbers,
Monopolizers, and Torries" and for price regulation in the
conviction that further inflation would make it impossible
to support an army on the field. He attempted to organize
an intercolonial association to raise hard money for Washington's use in recruiting soldiers. He was not averse to taking an occasional more direct part in the war effort: should
the comte d'Estaing need any advice on maneuvering his
ships up Long Island Sound, he would serve whenever
called upon, Sears told General Gates in 1779, but he was
"not to be treated in the Character of a *Pilot*."[55]

His greatest service to his country may, however, have
been in building and sponsoring a fleet of privateers. In
late 1775 and 1776 Sears advised the Connecticut assembly on
the suitability of vessels for its state navy and helped outfit
ships that would serve as privateers within the Connecticut
fleet. Sears and his son-in-law, Pascal Smith, also acquired on
their own account, according to his biographer, principal
title to forty privateers and shares in several more.[56] Such
ships were critical to the American victory. They interfered
with Britain's capacity to supply its army (for example only
eight of forty British transports sent to Boston during the

[54] Sears to Sherman, Dyer, and Deane, New Haven, November 28, 1775,
in Hollister, *History of Connecticut,* II, 241n; to Schuyler, New York,
March 14, 1776, Miscellaneous Sears manuscripts.

[55] Christen, "Isaac Sears," pp. 29–46; Sears to Gates, Boston, September
1779, and Jamaica Plain, Massachusetts, November 2, 1779, Gates papers,
NYHS, box 12 (microfilm roll 6), nos. 144 and 296; Sears to Greene, Boston, October 25, 1780, New York City miscellaneous manuscripts, NYHS.
More of Sears's business correspondence is in the Knox collection, MHS.

[56] Sears and David Waterbury to the Connecticut Assembly, from New
Haven, December 19, 1775, related documents, and accounts in Connecticut
Archives, Revolutionary War Ser. 1, I, 365, 366, 367a, 368; IX, 21b, 54,
61a, 73a; XXV, 528; also Revolutionary War Ser. 2, IV, 2; Christen, "Isaac
Sears," p. 37.

winter of 1775–76 reached their destination), and whatever military supplies they seized from the enemy enriched the American arsenal. Attacks on enemy commerce were equally significant. "By abstaining from Trade ourselves, while we distress that of our enemy's," the Continental Congress's Committee of Secret Correspondence explained to Silas Deane in August 1776, "we expect to Make their Men of war weary of their unprofitable and hopeless Cruises, and their Merchants Sick of a Contest in which so much is Risk'd and Nothing gained." Insurance rates on British commercial voyages to the West Indies jumped when news arrived of ships lost to the provincials, and some underwriters refused to issue policies because of the "vast number of privateers" out to intercept homeward-bound vessels. The audacious privateers even carried the war to the enemy's door: an American privateer encountered off Torbay ("mounting twelve Carriage Guns, spread a great deal of Canvas, full of Men, and . . . painted Black") caused surprise in July 1776, but the appearance of such vessels in British waters became all the more frequent after 1777 when they won access to French domestic ports. Their exploits helped win the revolutionary war where it was won—in English domestic politics. For they convinced merchants and so helped convince Parliament that the war cost more than it was worth, that to replace the army Cornwallis lost at Yorktown would be to throw good money after bad.[57]

From the success of his privateers, Sears came in these years to be known as a man of immense estate, and in the houses he occupied Sears acquired the public signs of rank he might otherwise have won in the military. At Boston he lived for a time in the Tremont Street home of a former colonial governor, and then he inhabited the Loring family mansion at "Jamaica" in suburban Roxbury. On his return to Man-

<hr />

[57] Eric Robson, *The American Revolution in Its Political and Military Aspects, 1763–1783* (New York, 1955), p. 103 (some of the 1775–76 British supply ships were swept to the West Indies). Committee to Deane, Philadelphia, August 7, 1776; notices from the London *Public Advertiser* for July 15 and 29, 1776; and letter, Plymouth, July 28, 1776, in Morgan, ed., *Naval Documents,* VI, 103, 476, 512; Stivers, *Privateers and Volunteers,* p. 26.

hattan Sears paid £500 per month for "one of the finest houses in the city" at 1 Broadway, a princely place that had served as General Henry Clinton's headquarters during the British occupation.[58] But even in the final decade of his life Sears retained the taste for action that colored his younger years. During the revolutionary war he sometimes ignored his friends' pleas that it was not "his present duty to put himself in the way of being killed or wounded," and took command of armed ships, helping drive off or take enemy vessels in the Massachusetts Bay. He died in October 1786 much as he had lived—at sea, of a fever and "flux" contracted in Batavia while on a great adventure, the opening of American trade with China—and was buried on an island in Canton Harbor.[59]

⋙⋘

Isaac Sears, the captain of privateers, was an American of an early and enduring type. His predecessors included Elizabethan sea-dogs who carried the English flag to America and beyond, such as that half-pirate, half-servant of the Crown Sir Frances Drake, or Captain John Smith, the adventuring, upwardly mobile, comically arrogant, self-appointed commander of Jamestown. Ambitious, resourceful, self-confident, unafraid of violence, impatient of restraint and government yet patriotic to a fault, their traits would in a later day, when a no longer colonial people pushed beyond the Appalachians, be invested upon the western hero. In the eighteenth century, however, such Americans went east, on a ship, and above all upon a privateer.

They were troublesome fellows for persons committed to a more conventional order, such as Alexander Hamilton, who condemned Sears's raid on Rivington for its disregard of superior revolutionary authority, or the commander of the American army who extended to the militiamen of the

---

[58] Christen, "Isaac Sears," pp. 48–50; Jones, *History*, II, 341.

[59] William Gordon to Washington, August 30, 1781, *Proceedings of the Massachusetts Historical Society, 1929–1930*, LXIII (Boston, 1831), 458–59; May, *Descendants of Sares*, pp. 118, 117.

sea that disdain with which he regarded the headstrong, unruly militiamen of the land. "Our rascally privateersmen go on at the old rate," Washington fumed from Cambridge in November 1775, "mutinying if they cannot do as they please."[60] There was indeed a rugged independence in privateering since "each ship was a free lance," at liberty to sail the seas as she chose without any "central organization or concert of movement." And the rage for privateering took on such epidemic proportions during the revolutionary war that it seriously undercut efforts to establish a regular Continental Navy. Seamen preferred to ship out on privateers; and when a Continental warship was finally manned and put to sea, it often acted as had the privateers on which its officers and crew had served, preferring to search for prizes rather than participate in the less profitable maneuvers of marine warfare. Once French naval power entered the war, the effort to build an American navy was all but abandoned. By one calculation the number of commissioned ships in the Continental Navy dropped from twenty-one to seven between 1778 and 1782, while the number of privateers increased from 115 to 323.[61]

The reason for privateering's popularity was simple, according to Captain John Paul Jones. Self-interest and self-interest alone motivates adventurers in privateering, he claimed, including among adventurers both the owners of privateers and those they employed. "And while this is the case," he went on, "unless the Private Emolument of individuals in our Navy is made Superior to that in Privateers it never can become respectable." Sailors on warships received regular wages and divided with their officers only one-third of all prize money. Commodore Esek Hopkins reported in September 1776 that he would find it very difficult to man the new American frigates *Hampden* and *Alfred* unless the Continental Congress would "make the Chance of Prize

---

[60] John C. Miller, *Alexander Hamilton and the Growth of the New Nation* (New York, 1959), pp. 17–18; Washington to Colonel Joseph Reed, Cambridge, November 20, 1775, in Clark, ed., *Naval Documents,* II, 1082.

[61] Maclay, *American Privateers,* pp. xxiv (quoted in text), 69–70; William F. Fowler, Junior, *Rebels Under Sail; The American Navy during the Revolution* (New York, 1976), pp. 13–14, 281–82; Stivers, *Privateers and Volunteers,* p. 29, for a revision of figures first compiled by Maclay.

Money as good as they get in the Privateers, which is one half and large Sums advanc'd to the People before they go to Sea." The navy also asked men to sign on for a full year, which had little appeal to the footloose privateersmen. As a result John Paul Jones urged Congress to "Enlist the Seamen during Pleasure and give them all the Prizes." Only then might navy recruiters compete with the likes of one John Dyson, who promised "Any Seaman or Landman that have an Inclination" the opportunity "to Make their Fortunes in a few Months" by signing on the ship *Washington,* a privateer being fitted out at Beverly, Massachusetts, in September 1776.[62]

That service to country should be compensated, even well paid, was utterly sensible to Isaac Sears and others of his like. The luxury of unrewarded patriotic service was reserved for more substantial Americans who could afford that species of honor. Sears sought Congressional sanction for his army of Connecticut volunteers in 1775 chiefly so the men would be paid for their efforts. Their earlier expedition against New York Loyalists, he explained, had involved considerable personal expense to its participants, more than they could or would sustain in the future. His greatest disillusionment with the Continental Congress came in 1780, when he became convinced that the Congress had failed to fulfill its financial obligations to the officers and men of the American army.[63] Sears's attitude here was much like that of the insouciant Simeon Sellick, a sea captain who helped him remove cannon from New York to Connecticut in the early summer of 1775, and who, like Sears, had wanted badly to seize Governor Tryon. In June of 1775, without authorization, Sellick sailed his sloop into Turtle Bay and seized the British military stores kept there. The timid Provincial Congress asked that his booty be returned. Sellick had other ideas. He wanted to be paid for his bravery. The Continental

[62] Jones to Robert Morris, Newport, October 17, 1776, and Hopkins to the Continental Marine Committee, Providence, September 22, 1776, in Morgan, ed., *Naval Documents,* VI, 1303, 949; Dyson broadside, American Antiquarian Society, Worcester, Massachusetts (see illustration).

[63] Sears to Sherman, Dyer, and Deane, New Haven, November 28, 1775, in Hollister, *History of Connecticut,* II, 241n; Sears to Greene, Boston, October 25, 1780, New York City Miscellaneous Manuscripts, NYHS.

"Now fitting for a Privateer," broadside, 1776.

Congress, which took a larger view of things than the Provincial Congress, and in any case needed the supplies, responded by awarding Sellick "the sum of 333 ⅓ dollars" for his "expences, trouble, and risque in taking the goods at Turtle Bay."[64]

Clearly patriotism and profit went hand in hand for men who rode ships named the *Independence,* the *America,* the

[64] Intelligence from Philadelphia in Morgan, ed., *Naval Documents,* VI, 559. Receipt for cannon received in New Haven, June 20, 1775, Connecticut Archives, Revolutionary War Ser. 1, XXXVII, 192. *Journals of the Provincial Congress . . . of New York,* I, 35, 37–38; Worthington C. Ford, ed., *Journals of the Continental Congress,* IV (Washington, 1906), 13.

Hancock, the *Putnam,* the *Washington,* the *Bunker Hill,* the *Franklin,* the *Republic.*[65] In their pursuit of fortune they helped win the American war. And where profits ceased, the privateersmen's patriotism continued. When confined in British prisons under conditions that would have sorely tried any American's commitment, merchant seamen (the lowest segment of the seafaring population) refused to escape by joining the British navy, brought pressure to bear on brothers tempted to defect (as they had on John Case at Drake's that evening in 1775), organized committees for their self-government, and even in one instance "adventured to form themselves into a republic, framed a constitution and enacted wholesome laws, with suitable penalties."[66]

The seamen's republicanism emerged in good part from the nature of their work. A privateer might be relatively free of outside direction, but its crew was governed under a rigorous chain of command essential to the disciplined teamwork of maneuvering sailing vessels and reinforced by laws for punishment of the disobedient and mutinous. The government of ships might have been a tyranny, except that seamen joined a ship and accepted its discipline voluntarily, literally "signing on" by ascribing to a written contract that defined the terms and rules of a voyage. Seamen also had considerable choice in their commanders, who were named in a voyage's articles of agreement. Even in the Continental Navy, responsibility for assembling crews rested upon captains who campaigned for recruits with broadsides appealing to Americans' ambition and patriotism, and enlisted the help of drummers and ballad singers to draw men from yet more oppressive situations:

> *All You that have bad masters,*
> *And cannot get your due,*
> *Come, come, my brave boys,*
> *And join our ship's crew.*

[65] Maclay, *American Privateers, passim.* Often the names of privateers were also used by ships in the state or Continental navies.

[66] Jesse Lemisch, "Jack Tar in the Streets: Merchant Seamen in the Politics of Revolutionary America," *William and Mary Quarterly,* 3d Ser., XXV (1968), 371–407, esp. 401–03.

Unknown officers had little success, as did those known to be cruel or unfair with their men, incompetent, or unsuccessful in taking prizes. A system in which rank derived from competence offered particular promise to the ambitious, as John Paul Jones emphasized when he promised those seamen and landsmen who might sign on the United States Ship *Ranger* that "the first Opportunity" would be embraced "to reward each one agreeable to his Merit."[67] The appeal was intrinsically republican, promising promotion by ability, for a hereditary captain was as great an absurdity as the hereditary mathematician Thomas Jefferson once cited to discredit by comparison the system of monarchy.

The seamen's republicanism has a broader significance. It suggests strongly that the "republican genius" of the United States did not lie (as traditional republican theory taught and contemporary European observers argued) in an equality of the American people. Early American republicanism assumed hierarchy, but demanded that status come from ability and effort, not ascription, and that even the lowliest subject be allowed some say over the conditions of his existence.

The privateersman's easy commitment to both self and country was fundamental to Isaac Sears's life and politics. He knew the political language of his time, and could scorn the corrupt who sacrificed their country "for the lucre of gain" as well as anyone. Where patriotism and self-interest conflicted, he endured private loss—during the nonimportation agreements, in his efforts to regulate prices at Boston during the war, and when he subscribed private funds to help Washington recruit soldiers. But the ascetic implications of an ethic of virtue warred against the worldly activism and ambition that drove him on. If poverty was to Samuel Adams an outward sign of his inner commitment, of his virtue, and so a source of pride, property was more

[67] Lemisch, "Jack Tar," p. 379, notes the legal requirement that seamen's contracts be written; and see articles of agreement for the *Mars* in Jameson, *Privateering and Piracy*, pp. 581–85, with other examples noted 581n. Fowler, *Rebels Under Sail*, pp. 284–86 (includes ballad); Jones's appeal in Stivers, *Privateers and Volunteers*, pp. 38–39.

important to Sears, for whom it was what it became for generations of later Americans, a public sign of achievement and success. For his less prosperous followers, who had perhaps the tools of their trade and a few household items, or only the rights and freedom that Sears considered a species of property, it marked a frail barrier between themselves and the poorhouse, between themselves and the condition of those black slaves with whom they mingled in the streets of New York. And of course those among them who aspired to "Work and Get Rich" needed to be certain that the returns from their industry would be securely theirs. In any case, property demanded protection against British pretensions (as a writer in the *New York Journal* summarized them) to dispose of the colonists' lives and property at pleasure and without their consent.[68]

The security of property had important economic implications for the community. John Trenchard and Thomas Gordon had argued in their popular "Cato's Letters" that populations grew and cultures developed and prospered only in free states where men could enjoy the fruits of their labor, art, and initiative. Under the "perpetual Uncertainties, or rather certain Oppressions" of despotism, "no Men will embark large Stocks and extensive Talents for Business," and so without liberty commerce and manufacturing atrophied. "Let the people alone," Gordon wrote, "and they will take care of themselves and do it best." This Whig economics found its way into the *New York Journal,* where Holt argued that even a neglect of tillage followed from arbitrary government, "which wherever it prevails, will produce similar effects." Nothing could revive a lagging economy "so long as Freedom is wanting." There were here elements of similarity with *The Wealth of Nations,* first published in 1776. Adam Smith (an Englishman who took the American side in the imperial conflict) also insisted that freedom and prosperity were linked and that the liberty allowed to private initiative served the welfare of society. He was, however, less concerned with the greed of tyrants than with the disruptive effect of trade regulations upon a market mechanism

---

[68] "An Occasional Remarker," *NYJ,* February 1, 1770.

driven by the search for profit. His glorification of ambition and profit-seeking shocked some old Whigs raised on a different public ethic.[69]

For Sears and the New Yorkers, however, there was no necessary conflict of public and private ends. A man could not reasonably be blamed, Sears argued, for "letting his private Interest have some Weight, provided it is not inconsistent with the common Interest of the Public." Certainly patriotism demanded no senseless sacrifices. Thus after he had failed to prevent New York's defection from the nonimportation agreement in 1770, Sears sent off orders for imported goods along with all the other local merchants. To do otherwise would be to reward his opponents' perfidy with the patronage of Sears's customers, and perhaps to do permanent damage to his trade in dry goods. There were, moreover, occasions aplenty where, as Sears noted, a man's immediate private interest and the public good led him "to the same choice."[70] That was true in 1770, when workingmen's resentments against British soldiers reinforced the cause of McDougall and liberty. It was true in 1773 and 1774, when in concerting opposition to the Tea and Port Acts the Sons of Liberty courted the support of tea smugglers and dry goods merchants, men who had already suffered most or who had most to lose from British regulations. And had not Sears effectively served both self and country in supplying the American army and equipping a fleet of privateers?

Confident in the material implications of liberty, New Yorkers talked less of virtue than of interest, and turned naturally toward the language of business in the business of revolution: "Stocks have risen in favor of Liberty," Mc-

---

[69] Trenchard and Gordon, *Cato's Letters* (6th ed., London, 1755), II, esp. 245, 247, 270–71; *NYJ*, November 27, 1766 (Holt's remarks in brackets with news from Rome). See also the discussion of Smith in Eric Foner, *Tom Paine and Revolutionary America* (New York, 1976), pp. 153–58.

[70] Sears, "An Advertisement," January 24, 1769, Early American Imprints, microcard 11458. See also *NYJ*, December 29, 1775: "Tho' a truly patriotic disposition would lead a man to reject every private advantage inconsistent with the good of his country, yet no man is to be supposed so disinterested, as not to include his own interest, in all his endeavours to promote that of others." Christen, "King Sears," pp. 198–203.

Dougall wrote Samuel Adams in June 1774.[71] For Sears, for McDougall and Lamb, for their followers, and in all likelihood for the merchants, artisans, and seamen elsewhere who rallied to the American cause, the revolution promised to give far more than it asked, and its rewards would be of a material as well as a spiritual sort. Liberty was good business.

[71] McDougall to Adams, June 26, 1774, Samuel Adams papers, NYPL.

CHAPTER THREE

———— ∽ ————

DR. THOMAS YOUNG
AND THE RADICALISM OF
SCIENCE AND REASON

SAMUEL ADAMS AND ISAAC SEARS personified the ways and traditions of a particular city or region; they felt at ease and worked with greatest satisfaction in some one defined place. Not Dr. Thomas Young. He contributed to the prerevolutionary politics of four different cities, none of which was his home by birth. Unlike most other early partisans of the American cause, he had been born and reared in the countryside, far removed from the centers of colonial culture. For a time he became a devoted Bostonian, and was later deeply absorbed in the democratic politics of Pennsylvania. But he remained a migrant, a man whose home was never so much in geographical space as it was among the men of like spirit he found wherever he went in America, and among others he never knew but who were, like him, part of an international eighteenth-century radical culture.

Many considerations contributed to the social message that lay at the heart of his revolutionary politics—his family background, the place in which he was raised, his religious convictions. Young was, moreover, a doctor, a participant in an occupation that remains for modern observers far more remote than the worlds of business and politics that absorbed Sears and Adams. Medicine became an established and respected profession only in the nineteenth century, and the modern medical science that supported that achievement is also far younger than either capitalism or popular govern-ment. It dates from the advances of Pasteur in the 1860s and the establishment of the germ theory of disease. Yet there was for Young and others of his age a critical link be-tween medicine and radical politics, and so his life suggests how the ideology of science, even of a science now outmoded, contributed to the establishment of a republican political system that has already survived two hundred years.

⤙∞⤚

In at least one way, Young was the reverse of Sears, who was a New Englander by birth and a New Yorker by choice. Young was a native New Yorker who migrated to New Eng-land. He came, however, not from New York City but from the Hudson Valley, where his parents settled after leaving Ireland two years before Thomas's birth in 1731. There in New York's hinterland he was raised, was apprenticed to a local doctor, and began his own medical practice, serving patients in the western reaches of Connecticut and Massa-chusetts as well as his native province. Thirty-four years old at the time of the Stamp Act crisis, he suddenly appeared in Albany as a prominent member of the local Sons of Liberty. Then in 1766 he moved to Boston. With the opening of the Anglo-American conflict, Thomas Young had become deeply involved in politics, as he would not cease to be for the final twelve years of his relatively short life; and for a man interested in popular "patriotic" politics, Boston was the place to go.[1]

He remained there eight years, becoming—almost to his surprise—an effective partisan, even a "necessary man" as

---

[1] Previous studies of Young include David Hawke, "Dr. Thomas Young —'Eternal Fisher in Troubled Waters'; Notes for a Biography," *The New York Historical Society Quarterly*, LIV (1970), 6–29, and Henry H. Edes, "Memoir of Dr. Thomas Young, 1731–1777," *Publications of the Colonial Society of Massachusetts, Transactions 1906–1907*, XI (Boston, 1910), 2–54. See also "constitution" of the Albany Sons of Liberty in *The American Historian and Quarterly Genealogical Record*, I (Schenectady, April 1876), 146–47.

one knowledgeable observer called him. "I have frequently
wished myself in other places where I thought my poor
services were more needed," he confessed in mid-1770, "but
am now satisfied no part of the globe cou'd place me in a
situation more advantageous to the common cause. On this
part of the Stage believe I will be active! I have nearly got
the hearts of my brethren and can be attended to on the most
arduous occasions."[2] Governor Thomas Hutchinson confirmed Young's boasts, including him among "the most
flaming zealots" in Boston, the "incendiaries of the lower
order," and in August 1770 specifically identified Young as
one of six or seven persons who "influence the mob" and
"threaten all who import." The previous June, "attended
by Hundreds of Men and Boys," Young had visited a store
run by the McMasters brothers, notorious transgressors of
the town's nonimportation agreement, and ordered them
to leave Boston within seventy-two hours; and again before
a nonimportation meeting on July 24, 1770, he had led a
small parade "with Three Flags Flying, Drums Beating and
a French Horn" through Boston's streets. He may well have
been the first to propose the destruction of East India Company Tea in 1773, and was a participant in the Boston Tea
Party—all of which contributed to his reputation as a "mob"
leader and a partisan of violence. But he was also known to
oppose popular force. During the rioting that preceded the
Boston Massacre, for example, Thomas Young stood on the
streets telling people to go home; and before the Boston Tea
Party he defended Francis Rotch, to whom East India Company tea had been consigned, asking townsmen to leave
Rotch's person and property unharmed. During the uprisings

---

[2] Comment of Royal Tyler as recalled by John Adams in a letter to
Benjamin Rush, Braintree, February 8, 1789, in *Old Family Letters: Copied
from the Originals for Alexander Biddle,* Ser. A (Philadelphia, 1892),
p. 30; Young to [Hugh] Hughes and [Gershom] Mott, Boston, July 26,
1770, Mss. 41556, Huntington Library, San Marino, California. I am indebted to Bruce Henry, Assistant Curator of Americana Manuscripts at the
Huntington, for calling to my attention the above and other letters by
Young that were recently added to the library's collections. See also
Henry's "Dr. Thomas Young and the Boston Committee of Correspondence" in *The Huntington Library Quarterly,* XXXIX (1976), 219–21.

of September 4, 1774, he again personally intervened to protect customs commissioner Benjamin Hallowell from some pro-American pursuers.[3]

His most important contributions to the politics of revolution may in fact have been made not in the streets but in the committeeroom. In Boston he served on a committee of the Sons of Liberty that corresponded with the English radical John Wilkes, on a committee of the nonimportation association to investigate charges against it published by John Mein, and on a series of committees of the North End Caucus—to draft instructions for those assembly candidates the caucus members would support in Town Meeting, to coordinate action with the South End Caucus, and to draft an ultimatum to the tea consignees, demanding that they resign their commissions. His most responsible posts were on committees of the Boston Town Meeting, sometimes to resolve routine problems (how should Jacob Emmons be compensated for lands taken to form a new street?), but more often of a larger political significance. He served on a committee appointed in 1768 to present the governor with a petition protesting certain acts of the customs commissioners and the King's ship *Romney* (then in Boston Harbor) and to draft an account of recent events for the town's agent in England. Later he participated on committees to vindicate the town from false charges related to the trial of soldiers involved in the Boston Massacre and to propose methods by which the Massacre could be commemorated in Boston. In 1772 he was appointed to Boston's new committee of correspondence —the single most significant position he ever held—and in 1774 to committees charged with preparing instructions for

[3] Hutchinson to Gov. Francis Bernard, August 20, 1770, in William V. Wells, *The Life and Public Services of Samuel Adams* (Boston, 1865), I, 366. Nonimportation: Hiller Zobel, *The Boston Massacre* (New York, 1970), pp. 2–3; Anne Rowe Cunningham, ed., *Letters and Diary of John Rowe, Boston Merchant* (Boston, 1903), p. 205; Christian Barnes to Elizabeth Smith, Marlborough, Mass., July 6, 1770, Christian Barnes Letterbook, Library of Congress. I am thankful to Prof. Mary Beth Norton of Cornell University for the last referrence. Massacre: L. Kinvin Wroth and Hiller B. Zobel, eds., *Legal Papers of John Adams* (Cambridge, 1965), II, 114, 142. Tea: Francis S. Drake, *Tea Leaves* (Boston, 1884), xci; Benjamin W. Labaree, *The Boston Tea Party* (New York, 1964), esp. 141. Hallowell: *Massachusetts Spy*, September 8, 1774.

Above, "A View of Part of the Town of Boston in New-England and Brittish Ships of War Landing Their Troops, 1768," engraved by Paul Revere in 1770. *Below*, "A New and Correct Plan of the Town of Boston," 1775.

Samuel Adams, painted by John Singleton Copley in 1770, when Adams served as Boston's spokesman in its efforts to have the troops removed from the town after the "Massacre."

Faneuil Hall, Boston, from *Massachusetts Magazine,* March 1789.

Samuel Adams, engraved
by Paul Revere after the
Copley portrait for the
April 1774 issue of the
Royal American Magazine.

"S. ADAMS, ESQ., Governor
of Massachusetts, 1795,"
engraving.

Right, Josiah Bartlett, painted by E. T. Billings, after John Trumbull. *Below*, "Sea Captains Carousing at Surinam," painted by John Greenwood, 1758.

Left, Richard Henry Lee, painted by Charles Willson Peale. *Below,* Stratford, the Lee family home in Westmoreland County, Virginia, photographed by C. O. Greene for the Historic Buildings Record Survey.

Above, Elizabeth Brooke Carroll
(Mrs. Charles Carroll of Annapolis),
mother of Charles Carroll of Carrollton, painted by John Wollaston.
Right, Charles Carroll of Annapolis,
father of Charles Carroll of Carrollton, painted by an unknown nineteenth-century artist after an earlier
portrait by John Wollaston.

Mary (Molly) Darnall Carroll (Mrs. Charles Carroll of Carrollton), painted by Charles Willson Peale.

Charles Carroll of Carrollton, painted by Sir Joshua Reynolds.

Charles Carroll of Carrollton, painted by Michael Laty, after Robert Field.

Charles Carroll of Carrollton as an old man, engraving.

Boston's assembly representatives and with drafting a declaration to Britain and the world prompted by the "Intolerable Acts." He also carried on an extensive private correspondence, exchanging news and advice with other colonists throughout the northern provinces. Lengthy, detailed, often eloquent, those letters support Young's claim of May 7, 1770, that "I do little else when at home than write continually,"[4] and like the no doubt tedious hours Young spent in committee meetings, testify again to the dedication revolution demands.

Young never held an important elective office. His poverty suggests perhaps that he was not of a "proper rank" to hold such a position, for he was listed on the Boston tax assessment of 1771 as having no taxable property; but if so, Young had little sense of such a disability. His unorthodox religious convictions, his contentious and self-righteous manner, and for a time perhaps also the threat his arrival posed to other local doctors served as far more potent limitations upon his career. Even his appointment to the committee of correspondence sparked controversy. "Don't it look quite ridiculous," one opponent argued, "for a Set of *Puritans,* deeply concerned for their religious as well as civil privileges," to set up "Atheists or Deists, men of profligate manners and profane tongues" as public leaders?[5] Wherever he went opponents described him in almost identical terms. Soon after his arrival in Boston, Dr. Joseph Warren regretted the addition of a new word to Bostonians' language— "Youngism"—which, Warren claimed, served as a synonym

[4] Young to John Wilkes, Boston, September 6, 1769, in *Proceedings of the Massachusetts Historical Society for 1913–14,* XLVII (Boston, 1914), 209; "Proceedings of the North End Caucus," in Elbridge H. Goss, *The Life of Paul Revere* (Boston, 1891), II, esp. 636, 637, 638, 642–43, 644; *A Report of the Record Commissioners of the City of Boston,* XVI (Boston, 1886), 253–55; XVIII (Boston, 1887), 47, 51, 53–54, 169, 183; Young to Hughes, Mss. 41551, Huntington Library. Other significant collections of Young's correspondence have been located at the Massachusetts Historical Society (MHS), the Historical Society of Pennsylvania (HSP), and the New York Historical Society (NYHS).

[5] "Boston Tax Lists, 1771," from Massachusetts Archives, Vol. 132, State House, Boston, on microfilm at the Harvard University Library; Aaron Davis, Jr., from the *Boston News Letter,* November 26, 1772, in Edes, "Young," p. 20.

for "inaccuracy, malevolence, bad grammar, and nonsense," for "Self-conceit, vain-baiting, and invincible impudence," for "quackery, ignorance, . . . boorishness and impertinent loquacity." Others called him "a firebrand, an eternal Fisher in Troubled Waters, . . . a Scourge, a Pestilence, a Judgement," a man of "unparallel'd impudence" who was so vain as to think that anyone who expressed distaste for Young's character thereby wounded his country. Later Simon Pease noted the arrival in Newport of the "infamous Dr. Young" and regretted "that such a Fellow Shou'd get footing anywhere," and Philadelphia's Edward Shippen, Jr., called Young "a bawling New England Man . . . of noisy Fame." Young confessed a "freedom and impetuosity of speech even to a degree of rashness," but argued that those traits deserved charity however much they offended good breeding. "Such open minded undesigning fellows," he wrote, "are never likely to injure a community, being generally disposed to allow others all that freedom of thought and action they do impatiently suffer abridgment in themselves."[6]

His "impetuosity of speech" was at times impolitic. Those who sought absolute power, he believed, could justly be put to death. He founded his position upon a passage from Locke's *Second Treatise of Government,* which he cited in an essay published in the *Boston Evening Post* for November 9, 1767, then used again in addressing a Town Meeting of September 12, 1768, which had been called to decide how Boston should react to the anticipated arrival of British troops. Governor Francis Bernard charged that Young (whom he described as "very profligate and abandoned") took his position so far that he had to be silenced by his own party, and in response Young acknowledged that he had been "checked." "I said," he recalled, "that to have laws framed for us to which our consent was never so much as

[6] Warren as "Philo Physic" in *Boston Gazette,* July 6, 1767; comments by Timothy Ruggles as recalled by John Adams in a letter to Benjamin Rush, Braintree, February 8, 1789, in *Old Family Letters,* p. 30; Dr. Miles Whitworth in *Boston Gazette,* April 27, 1767; Aaron Davis, Jr., cited in Edes, "Young," p. 18; Simon Pease to Joshua Winslow, Newport, November 3, 1774, Winslow Papers, MHS; Edward Shippen, Jr., to Jasper Yeates, Philadelphia, May 23, 1776, Balch Papers, HSP; Young in *Boston Evening Post,* March 18, 1771.

pretended necessary, and taxes, with an indefinite number of officers to extort them; and all these, imposed with armed force, was an evident subjecting us to the absolute power . . . mentioned by Mr. Locke." Young was told, however, "that this was no time for haranguing on liberty in general terms," and "that Mr. Locke was open to every one, and none here scrupled the truth of his doctrine: but that the present exigency required a proposal of measures for our conduct" that would, it seems, be more practical and less sanguinary than Young's argument implied. Even after this reprimand, however, Young was drawn to extreme positions. In January 1770, during a heated debate over whether or not it would be "high treason" for nonimportation supporters to visit the sons of Governor Hutchinson, who threatened to break the nonimportation agreement, Young argued, according to an unsympathetic observer, "that such people as counteracted the general measures should be depriv'd of existence, and that it was high time for people to take the Govermt into their own hands to whom it properly belonged."[7]

But soon Young modified his ways and adopted (so far as he was able) the political methods of "the great Mr. [Samuel] Adams," as he once called his mentor, urging upon others the need for "patience as well as [for]titude," for "a soft and gentle, but positively determined conduct" as best suited for success in "popular affairs, as too much vigour only stirs up and fixes resentments." Unity, he learned, was critical to success, and it demanded restraint. "We have told

[7] Young derived his position from paragraph 17 of chapter III in Locke's *Second Treatise:* "he who attempts to get another man into his absolute power does thereby put himself into a state of war with him; it being understood as a declaration of a design upon his life; for I have reason to conclude that he who would get me into his power without my consent would use me as he pleased when he got me there, and destroy me too when he had a fancy to it," and so it would be "lawful for me . . . to kill him if I can. . . ." Young's article in the *Boston Evening Post* (*BEP*) was signed "Libermoriturus." The identification here of newspaper essays signed "Probus," "Britano-Americanus," or "Libermoriturus" as by Young is based upon his acknowledgment of those pseudonyms in a letter to Dr. Thomas Williams, 1768, Gratz Collection, HSP. On the Town Meeting, see Young in *BEP*, September 11, 1769; also *A Report of the Record Commissioners of the City of Boston*, XVIII, 259–64. "Journal of Transactions at Boston," Sparks Manuscripts X, Papers Relating to New England, III, f. 56, Houghton Library, Harvard University.

you till we are sick of repeating it that divisions and destruction are inseparable companions," he wrote the New York Son of Liberty Hugh Hughes in one of his own less patient moods. The raising of a great popular movement was an "arduous enterprize" in which "the motions must be slow . . . and determined. We need not spill the blood even of mistaken enemies," he observed in 1772, "if we can otherwise reduce them to reason, and make them our friends." Should the conflict nonetheless end in blows, "we can lose nothing by defering the combat till our forces are well disciplin'd and all mankind possessed with the justice of our cause." The goal that had been Adams's "every wish, . . . every sigh, for years past" was achieved, Young understood, in September 1774 when a patriotic crowd of perhaps four thousand persons stood in Cambridge for three hours "in the scorching sun of the hottest day we have had this summer," remaining so quiet that "not a whisper" prevented the voice of old Judge Samuel Danforth from being heard by the entire group. "Such patient endurance," Young told Adams, "is certainly a principal ingredient in the composition of that character emphatically styled a good soldier." In reply Adams, repeating like a good teacher the lesson he wanted to be remembered, wrote of "that Patience which you have often heard one say is characteristick of the Patriot."[8]

As he learned the ways of its politics, Young sang the praises of Boston. His affection for the town was never steady and profound like that of Adams, whose family had lived there for generations. Instead he experienced the excitement of a convert or discoverer who had only recently chanced upon its virtues. And he held Boston up as an example to colonists elsewhere, particularly in New York, with an insensitivity fortunately shared by few native Bostonians. "Often have I wished the deliberations of the people in your City could be conducted in the manner as ours are in this,"

---

[8] Young to Hughes, Boston, March 2, January 29, June 24, March 22, 1770, Mss. 41549, 41548, 41553, and 41550, Huntington Library; Young to Hughes, December 21, 1772, Miscellaneous Bound Manuscripts, MHS; to Adams, September 4, 1774, Frothingham correspondence, MHS; Adams to Young, Philadelphia, October [17], 1774, in Harry A. Cushing, ed., *The Writings of Samuel Adams,* III (New York, 1907), 163.

he wrote Hughes in March 1770. Faneuil Hall, home of the Boston Town Meeting, was for him "a noble School where the meanest citizen ratable at £20 beside the poll, may deliver his sentiments and give his suffrage in very important matters, as freely as the greatest Lord in the Land! Here men may be trained up for the Senate, for the field, for any department in the state where manly prudence and address are required." In Boston "elevated stations" were open "to every one whose capacity integrity and diligence in the affairs of his country attracts the public attention. These avenues my friends," Young wrote the New Yorkers, "I lament are shut to you. . . ." And again, "I thank my Creator" for making me a Bostonian. Despite the corruptions of a few, "there is no people under heaven so much to be depen[ded upon]. They are a wise, a social, and humble people: full of . . . charity and sincerity. A haughty coxcomb wou'd be despised, a tyrant abhorred among them." And still again, "there is not a community on earth to which I wou'd wish a translation of my Rights in hopes of their better security. We abound with midling men! Our greatest personages are not above a laudable concern for the welfare of the meanest. . . . Never were the body of a people more knowing and less corrupt. Many common tradesmen in this town display the wisdom and eloquence of Athenian Senators. . . ."[9]

There was purpose in his boastings. By insisting upon the virtue of Boston in these letters of 1770, Young hoped to counteract reports that Boston merchants were secretly violating the nonimportation agreement. But his words had deep personal meaning as well. Soon after his arrival in 1766, Young wrote a correspondent that he was "settled perhaps for life" in Boston "if the people please me"; and his years there brought concrete satisfactions. He had first gone up the Hudson Valley to Albany hoping "the toil would be less and the profits greater" there than had been his lot as a country doctor; but it was in Boston that his practice flourished. There, too, the thirst for fame that he once acknowledged was in some measure satisfied: he felt honored when

[9] Young to Hughes, Boston, March 22, June 24, and May 17, 1770, Mss. 41550, 41553, and 41552, Huntington Library.

rumors arrived that "Adams, Cushing, Brattle, Molineux, Young, Hancock, Cooper &c." would be arrested and sent to England. From the prospect of 1770 "an opportunity of displaying our political talents before the British Legislature," and that at public expense, did not seem disagreeable.[10]

Reality was more harsh. With the occupation of Boston in 1774 Young found himself in physical danger. Two British officers attacked him in the street one evening. He caught a glimpse of them beforehand, Young recalled, and so saved his life by moving his head to the side so their weapon brushed past his temple and crushed against his shoulder. The British fled, leaving Young for dead; he was carried home "all bloody," according to his brother, and thereafter his wife, Mary Winegar Young, so feared for him that whenever he left home at night she cried until he returned. Then abruptly he left Boston. Fragmentary notes from a letter he sent Samuel Adams on September 10, 1774, announced that his situation had become "calamitous," that terror had so deranged his wife that "she took a bed and appeared as inanimate as a corpse," such that he felt obliged "to seek an asylum for her." "I can in this place serve the common cause of America as effectually as I have done in any part of it," he wrote from Newport the following December; the "friends of liberty" there had already received him kindly. But in 1775 the threat of arrest again drove him on, this time to Philadelphia, where he quickly settled in with Timothy Matlack, James Cannon, Christopher Marshall, and Thomas Paine—with the most radical element of Pennsylvania's revolutionary politics.[11]

Would Young have remained in Boston had no "calami-

[10] Young to John Wendell, Boston, November 23, and December 15, 1766, photostat collection, MHS; Young to Hughes, Boston, September 15, 1770, Miscellaneous Bound Manuscripts, MHS.

[11] Joseph Young's memoir in Edes, "Young," pp. 27, 36–39; Young to Adams in Frothingham correspondence, MHS; Young letter to Boston, Newport, December 10, 1774, from the *Gazetteer and New Daily Advertiser,* January 19, 1775, in Margaret Wheeler Willard, ed., *Letters on the American Revolution, 1774–1776* (Boston and New York, 1925), p. 33, where Young again cited as reasons for his departure his wife's "distress of mind" and the state of his "LARGE FAMILY OF HELPLESS CHILDREN, in a place where I had NOT ONE relation or acquaintance of above EIGHT YEARS STANDING."

tous" events occurred? Probably not. He was afflicted with an intense restlessness that pushed him from place to place. Before moving to Albany, Young had visited the West Indies; he may have made a brief visit to North Carolina in 1771, during the Regulator conflicts there; and even before General Thomas Gage's soldiers prompted his exodus from Boston, Young wrote Adams that he had "much inclination to become an inhabitant of West Florida."[12] Not even the value he ascribed to Boston's democracy, its equality, the opportunities it offered men of humble birth but distinguished ability, was of New England growth. Boston appealed to Young because it approached ideals he had absorbed long before arriving there, ideals he had defined against the very different world of his childhood and the still earlier homeland of his parents, and that would continue to be the basis of his revolutionary creed wherever he went. Young's cause had never been that of Massachusetts, but of America and mankind, and so could be served on many battlefields.

Migration was for Thomas Young a family tradition that had shaped the lives of his parents and of their ancestors before them. His grandmother through both parents (his mother and father were first cousins) was Margaret Clinton Parks, daughter of Sir William Clinton, an officer in the army of Charles I who fled to France and Spain during the Cromwellian period, later visited Scotland, where he found a wife, and finally settled his family in Northern Ireland. The Clintons, Parkses, and other interrelated families lived near Belfast until about 1700, when they moved south to County Longford. There they took up neighboring tracts on land that had probably been granted to William's son, James Clinton, for military service on behalf of William III. Nearly

---

[12] West Indies: George P. Anderson to Dr. Henry R. Viets, Jamaica Plain, Massachusetts, April 28, 1957, Miscellaneous Collection, MHS. On the North Carolina trip, see Hutchinson remark in Edes, "Young," pp. 28 and also 29. West Florida: Young to Adams, Boston, September 4, 1774, Frothingham correspondence, MHS

three decades later the "whole connexion" decided to move again, gathered together their families and friends, chartered a ship at Dublin, and in May 1729 set sail for America under the leadership of Colonel Charles Clinton, James's son and a cousin of the Youngs who became the founder of New York's famous Clinton family. The voyage was protracted and tragic: many died of disease and malnutrition; then in October passengers were landed not in Pennsylvania, as intended, but in Massachusetts, where they met a cold welcome, having brought smallpox with them from the Old World. Finally in 1730 the families made their way to New York, and again the Clinton, Denniston, and Young families bought adjoining farms in what one account calls "a most luxurious grass country" like the pastures of Ireland. There in February 1731, six months after his father acquired title to the property, John and Mary Young's first son, Thomas, was born in a house made of logs.[13]

The Clinton migration to America occurred in the same year that Jonathan Swift wrote his "Modest Proposal," a savage indictment of conditions in Ireland; but the exact reasons are unknown why that family joined the *"many good Protestants"* who, as Swift noted, were choosing to leave their Irish homes. Young's younger brother, Joseph, who wrote a useful memoir of his family, recorded only that it had grown "more and more dissatisfied with the government." Family members no doubt resented above all the civil disabilities suffered by dissenters once a Test Act was imposed in Ireland: after 1704 they were barred from the army and militia, from most public offices, from the teaching profession; their ministers—and so the marriages they performed—were denied official standing. It seems unlikely that Young's relatives suffered from the rack-renting that threw thousands of Irish Protestants off their lands in the early eighteenth century, as long-term leases fell due and landlords "racked up" the rents. The Clintons were probably

---

[13] Joseph Young's memoir in Edes, "Young," esp. pp. 9–12; Charles B. Moore, "Introductory Sketch of the Clinton Family of New York," *The New York Genealogical and Biographical Record (NYGBR),* XII (1881), 195–98; XIII (1882), 5–10. See also E. Wilder Spaulding, *His Excellency George Clinton, Critic of the Constitution* (New York, 1938), pp. 1–8.

themselves landlords, and their readiness to intermarry with the Youngs suggests that they, too, were of the gentry. On leaving Ireland Charles Clinton is said to have granted his County Longford lands to the earl of Granard for ninety-nine years, and he was able to pay the passageway to America for ninety-four persons.[14] The Clinton migration occurred during the second of a series of famines that sent waves of Irish Presbyterians to America, which suggests the families may have suffered straitened circumstances like those of Richard Henry Lee in Virginia later in the century as the price of provisions rose and tenants proved unable to pay their rents. But probably for them as for other "Scots-Irish," migration responded to a pull as well as a push. Stirred by the propaganda of colonizing agents as well as the reports of previous migrants, they saw in the New World an expanded opportunity to acquire freehold land and to escape religious and political disabilities. For those who were "truly ambitious," the historian of the Scots-Irish notes, America "even promised affluence and social prominence."[15]

Young's aspirations, his temperament, his habits, were consistent with his Irish Protestant background. Impetuosity "early proclaimed itself a dominant trait among many Scotch-Irish," as did restlessness. German immigrants tended to stay fixed in place once they established a new home, as did some from Ireland. But for the most part the Scots-Irish "seemed to feel a compulsion to move again and again." They were the quintessential pioneers, pushing on from the Susquehanna and Cumberland Valleys of Pennsylvania into Virginia and the Carolinas, suggesting a "psychological repugnance to making permanent homes until they had moved several times," and continuing, like Young, a pattern that began at least a century earlier in Britain itself.[16]

The Irish background of Young's politics is more difficult to trace. The Scots-Irish were characteristically committed

---

[14] Joseph Young in Edes, "Young," p. 10; James G. Leyburn, *The Scotch-Irish; A History* (Chapel Hill, 1962), pp. 160–68. See also J. C. Beckett, *Protestant Dissent in Ireland, 1687–1780* (London, 1948). Moore, "Clinton Family," *NYGBR*, XIII, 6–7.

[15] Leyburn, *The Scotch-Irish*, pp. 168–75.

[16] Ibid., p. 199.

American patriots during the revolutionary struggles, and it has become conventional to trace their antagonism toward England back to Ireland. But Thomas Young's disloyalty was not inherited; it grew in America under the impact of events. The Clintons and Youngs named the community they founded "New Britain," which suggests no hostility toward the land of their fathers; and one of Thomas's first known literary efforts is an epic poem he published in 1761 to celebrate the British victory at Quebec under General James Wolfe. There he expressed a colonist's gratitude "that our Mother Country shou'd . . . spill her most venerable Blood in our Defense." Even after the Stamp Act crisis he emphasized American loyalty and affection for Britain: "Never were a people more in love with their King, and the constitution by which he has solemnly engaged to govern them." George III was, he wrote in 1767, "the darling of America," and those Members of Parliament who supported the American pleas for their liberty and so sought to preserve the British empire he called "tutelar deities." His letters of 1769 to John Wilkes again stressed his pride in being British, his hope that British freedom would be salvaged through Wilkes or, that failing, by the efforts of Americans. So late as September 1774 he believed reconciliation possible "if George the third will receive us as free and loyal subjects, on the terms James and Charles first stipulated with our predecessors." Otherwise, he wrote Samuel Adams, "the laws of God, of nature and nations oblige us to cast about for safety." By May 1776, however, he found the corruption in Britain so noisome that he "panted" to be "dissevered" lest America suffer *"destruction* from the contagion," and rejected the British constitution for a republic, "the only rational government that ever was established among mankind."[17]

The sympathies for the unprivileged and hostilities toward

[17] Poem in Hawke, "Young," p. 10; Young as "Sobrius," *BEP,* September 14, 1767; Young to Wilkes, esp. July 6 and August 3, 1769, *Proceedings of the Massachusetts Historical Society for 1913–14,* XLVII (Boston, 1914), 202–03, 207–08; to Adams, Boston, September 4, 1774, Frothingham correspondence, MHS; as "Elector," *Pennsylvania Gazette,* May 14, 1776. Young is identified as "Elector" in Hawke, "Young," p. 25, n. 41.

the landed rich that came to characterize Young's life and politics may also have been more American than Irish in origin. His family made its home in a frontier area of Ulster County, New York, an enclave of small farmers of Scots-Irish, English, Dutch, Huguenot, and Palatine origin situated near the great baronies of Dutchess, Westchester, and Albany counties. In this new world, with no poor Catholic peasantry beneath them, the Clintons would become democrats in contrast to what Joseph Young called the "assuming family of Livingston."[18] Historically, however, the Clintons were much like the great landed families of New York. Both had been rewarded with land for loyal service to the Crown in the late seventeenth or early eighteenth century. But one family's grant had been in Ireland, now left behind; the other's lands were in New York and still occupied.

According to his brother, Thomas Young's first personal confrontation with the rich came when he was a schoolboy. A "pompous young man" upbraided him for making mischief, saying "since Providence has denied you the capacity or talents to acquire any useful knowledge, you should not interrupt those who have both the inclination and capacity to learn; besides I shall have a great estate to manage, which will require all the knowledge I can gain to manage it, and support my rank. But if you can gain a knowledge of pounds, shillings and pence, it is all you will ever have occasion for." Little Tommy answered that "before the end of six weeks I will be qualified to teach you" and, his brother claimed, made good his promise. "From that hour he quit wild pranks and commenced the attentive student."[19] The anecdote may suggest more of 1807, when Joseph Young committed it to paper, than of the 1730s. It resembles what became the standard American success story, with its emphasis upon the power of determination and work over pretension and laziness: even its cadences are like those of "The Little Engine that Could," a late-nineteenth-century story that adapted an older American folk tale to the tastes of a

[18] Spaulding, *George Clinton*, p. 10; Joseph Young in Edes, "Young," pp. 11–12.
[19] In Edes, "Young," pp. 12–13.

railroad age. But in its values, and in the antagonisms it assumes between Young and the rich, the story suggests much about Thomas Young's adult life, for he seemed always to carry on a vendetta against landed wealth, particularly that of New York, and to associate himself with its enemies.

He married into a family of Palatines, a people who had been driven from their German homeland early in the eighteenth century and sent to America through the beneficence of Queen Anne. Their resentment of New York's landed elite went back to 1714 when five well-connected New Yorkers acquired a royal patent to lands in Schoharie that had been purchased from the Indians and settled with great pain by a group of Palatines, who were then asked to purchase, lease, or vacate lands they thought already theirs. Palatine resentments also stemmed, the Swedish traveler Peter Kalm suggested, from the general unwillingness of New York's landowners to sell their vast unimproved tracts even at a high price. Anxious to own the land they farmed, the Palatines recommended that German immigrants bypass New York for Pennsylvania, to which they turned in great numbers. Young also lived and practiced medicine in western Connecticut and nearby sections of New York during the 1750s, when agrarian disturbances occurred there much like those of the "Great Rebellion" of 1766.[20] In these years he was a close friend of the like-minded Ethan Allen and, equally important, supported the claims of Colonel John Henry Lydius to nearly a million acres of land in what is today Vermont but was then claimed by New York and New

[20] Walter Allen Knittle, *Early Eighteenth-Century Palatine Emigration* (Philadelphia, 1937), esp. pp. 188–205, 210–12 (includes Kalm); Newton Reed, *Early History of Amenia* (Amenia, N.Y., 1875), pp. 16–18; Edes, "Young," pp. 14–15; Staughton Lynd, "The Tenant Rising of 1766," in Lynd, *Anti-Federalism in Dutchess County, New York: A Study of Democracy and Class Conflict in the Revolutionary Era* (Chicago, 1962), esp. pp. 44–45; also Matt Bushnell Jones, *Vermont in the Making, 1750–1777* (Cambridge, 1939), pp. 281–82; and Irving Mark, *Agrarian Conflicts in Colonial New York* (New York, 1940), pp. 107–15. The interpretation of New York's agrarian disturbances presented here is, however, that of Sung Bok Kim in his careful study, *Landlord and Tenant in Colonial New York; Manorial Society, 1664–1775* (Chapel Hill, 1978), pp. 281–415.

Hampshire. Lydius's title depended upon a grant from the Indians and had been confirmed, his partisans asserted (with questionable accuracy), by Massachusetts's Governor William Shirley on the authority of the Crown. In an effort to settle the land, Lydius granted out several townships, Young claimed, on moderate terms—five shillings sterling rent per hundred acres of improvable land, first payable twenty years from the date of lease. But the government of New York contested the title, inspired by "the great landjobbers of New York" who wanted to "share in the profits."[21]

Young's colleagues in defending Lydius were, according to his brother, "wealthy men," which suggests that he was more interested in joining than fighting the rich—that, like his Irish ancestors, he sought to gain title to land, not to defend the landless. Similarly, the participants in New York's agrarian uprisings of the 1750s and 1760s were not a jacquerie but "petty landed bourgeois" who wanted title to their lands. The language of opposition was nonetheless laden with social antagonism. In a pamphlet Young wrote in 1764, *Some Reflections on the Disputes Between New York, New Hampshire, and Col. John Henry Lydius,* he identified the cause of Lydius with that of humble settlers, pitting them together against Lydius's "envious monopolizing enemies" in New York. Those avaricious land barons, Young charged, kept

---

[21] "Philodicaios" (Thomas Young), *Some Reflections on the Dispute Between New York, New Hampshire, and Col. John Henry Lydius* (New Haven, 1764); Edes, "Young," pp. 15–16, 26. On Lydius, see Jones, *Vermont in the Making,* pp. 142–48; and Mark, *Agrarian Conflicts,* p. 39. The terms Young attributed to Lydius compare favorably with those of New York's manorial landowners. Lydius's rental rate translates to 6d./10 acres, less than that provided by Kim for the period 1760–69 at Cortlandt Manor (4d./acre) and considerably less than that at Livingston Manor (1s. 7d./acre). Rent deferrals were common, but ranged from nine months to twelve years in the manors studied by Kim. The amount of delay reflected the time necessary to develop virgin land to the point where it could support a family as well as outside rental payments. Kim, *Landlord and Tenant,* esp. pp. 196, 172. It is noteworthy that Joseph Young singled out the name of Livingston as "assuming." Livingston Manor, whose rental rates were highest, was located across the Hudson River from Ulster County, where the Young family settled. Also Robert Livingston, Jr. (probably the son of the manor's founder) had been one of the original five patentees of the lands that included the Palatine settlements in Schoharie. Knittle, *Early Palatine Emigration,* p. 202.

"thousands of acres of excellent soil in wilderness, waiting till the industry of others round them raise their lands to three, four, or more pounds per acre." Who, he asked, "that has the most superficial acquaintance with the country, can esteem the buyer of such lands any other than a slave during life?" That the low charges prescribed by Lydius and the state of New Hampshire, whose rights Young also supported, "should be disagreeable objects of such gentlemen's contemplation, we think nothing marvellous at all." "We, the common people," have freely lavished blood and treasure for liberty and property, the "Household Gods of Englishmen," Young argued in the rhetorical highpoint of his pamphlet and perhaps of his life, and now "want lands to exercise the arts of peace upon, at such rates as we can promise ourselves some recompence to our labours thereon," not as a reward for services but as "undoubted rights."[22]

But was Lydius any less a "monopolizer" who hoped for long-term speculative profits than were his opponents? Young's presumption to speak for the "common people" might seem to come straight out of Ireland, from those Scots-Irish dispossessed of lands they had improved by landlords who imposed rents so high their tenants could hope to win no profit from their future labors, so high they could be paid only by Irish Catholics inured to abject poverty. But the Youngs and Clintons had not been dispossessed; and Young's argument was limited in its implications—it went no further than to promote the cause of good landlords over bad. Yet for him—as for Ethan Allen, who would later strangely invoke Locke's argument that the land belonged to its cultivators to defend territorial claims more extensive than any man could work—the land issue had farflung implications. The very foundations of government were at stake. Only while "authority manifests a desire of equally protecting the rights and privileges of all his Majesty's liege subjects, indiscriminately," could it "justly expect to be loved and reverenced." All honest men should espouse Lydius's cause, for "if we fall . . . they may very naturally expect to

---

[22] Joseph Young in Edes, "Young," p. 26; Kim, *Landlord and Tenant,* esp. pp. 344, 415; Thomas Young, *Some Reflections,* pp. 11, 12, 15.

share the general ruin": "Tear Indian Title to pieces and tear the country to pieces!"[23]

Lydius lost his doubtful case, but Young continued to develop his argument against legal privilege, leaving the war between monopolists behind, taking on ever more radically equalitarian positions, and defending oppressed persons whose fate involved his private material interests in no immediate way. Boston appealed to him because it was free of New York's "accursed aristocracy" that closed the avenues of upward mobility to men of modest estate but great ability. The power of that elite had also "ruined" New York's constitution: "such ample dominion in the hands of a few, and abject dependence in the condition of so many are evils pregnant with innumerable others," Young claimed, and he demanded reform not just of government but of property-holding patterns. "Entails should be broken as often as possible, and partition of estates encouraged."[24] He sided with the insurgents during New York's agrarian uprisings of 1766, and considered their suppression part of a long-term effort to expropriate the cultivator. "The Earth is the Lords, and the fullness thereof," Young wrote. "But N. York Gentlemen, have for about a Century pretty strong disputed his Title and seem resolved that neither he nor his Creatures shall have any share in the premises unless on the terms of being their servants forever." Soon the sea would be "patented out to a Company," and how could a man make a living if "forbidden to trespass either on the Land or Water?" Even the rights of the Crown were involved: "A King was never designed more than as general Trustee of the Rights of the People," and so would be "very ill advised to ever grant extensive monopolies to any." If, for example, the fishery were restrained (as Britain would do a decade later), then "farewell forever to friendship with a Nation, of such infatuated partiality."[25]

[23] Ibid., pp. 17, 19; Darline Shapiro, "Ethan Allen: Philosopher-Theologian to a Generation of American Revolutionaries," *William and Mary Quarterly,* 3d Ser., XXI (1964), 236–55, esp. 241–48.
[24] Young to Hughes, Boston, March 22 and January 29, 1770, Mss. 41550 and 41548, Huntington Library.
[25] Young to John Wendell, Boston, December 15, 1766, photostat, MHS.

Once Britain seemed to side with "monopolizers," it naturally fell heir to Young's home-grown antagonisms. But his cause was never independence alone. In the course of his campaign against privilege Young had become a confirmed democrat, a revolutionary who demanded social and political change of a profound sort. Where "the upper part of a nation . . . have the authority of government solely in their hands," he wrote, its members "will always be for keeping the low people under." Danger to the body politic came above all from an "encrease of property" in the hands of men who became "haughty and imperious," "cruel and oppressive," considering themselves "above the law." And so Young insisted that "people of the lower ranks" share in government. Even kings were but trustees for the people whose dependence upon their subjects could "never be too great."[26] For him the central problem of government was how to limit the sway of the rich and powerful. As a result Young never shared the widespread enthusiasm for Britain's eighteenth-century "balanced" constitution, which confirmed preserves of power for the King and lords as well as the people. Instead he looked back to the Saxons, who "considered every man alike as he came out of the hands of his maker—riches with them, constitutionally considered, gave no power or authority over the poorest person in the state." Every householder "liable to pay his shot and bear his lot, might consent to every law that was made for his observance." Only then, he argued, was the "English constitution in its original purity," before the Norman invader destroyed "as many of the free customs of the people as he possibly could," and slowly introduced "that infernal system of ruling by a *few dependent favourites,* who would readily agree to divide the spoils of the lower class between the supreme robber and his banditti of feudal lords."[27]

Against the threat of wealth and privilege, Young exalted the people, particularly the lower orders (which, incidentally, provided the bulk of his medical patients). It was "those

[26] Young in *BEP* as "Sobrius," September 15, 1767; "Britano-Americanus," September 23, 1767; "Libermoriturus," November 9, 1767.

[27] Young as "Elector," *Pennsylvania Gazette,* May 15, 1776; also as "Libermoriturus," *BEP,* November 9, 1767.

worthy members of society," the tradesmen, along with "the yeomanry in our Country towns" who he believed would "form the revolution of the other ranks of Citizens" in the Anglo-American conflict; and upon these the new political order would be built. Measured against this democratic ideal, even Boston had room for improvement. While there, Young wished for a new legislative hall large enough so "all that chose to attend" could witness the assembly's deliberations and so more easily call their representatives to account.[28]

But it was in Philadelphia, where he arrived in the midst of the revolutionary crisis, that Young found the greatest opportunity to work for concrete political change. There he quickly fell in with a coterie of radicals who were, like himself, men of at best modest wealth and often outsiders as well —recent arrivals to the city, renegade Quakers, persons who had never exercised significant political influence in the past but who drew upon the support of artisans in a campaign for both independence and a more equalitarian regime. Young had strengths in Pennsylvania politics that were all but irrelevant in Massachusetts: during the course of their campaign to overturn the colonial assembly and found a far different provincial government, radicals sent Young to the immigrant communities at Lancaster and York, where his family background provided an entree with the Scots-Irish and his fluency in German facilitated appeals to the Pennsylvania "Dutch" (i.e., Deutsch, or German). Among his Philadelphia colleagues, moreover, Young found independent support for even his most extreme proposals. With James Cannon he urged an extension of the franchise to all taxpayers and militiamen and argued that power should no longer be accorded "over-grown rich Men" who, as Cannon feared, would be "too apt to be framing Distinctions in Society, because they will reap the Benefits of such Distinctions." From this strain of radical equalitarianism emerged a proposal that the new Pennsylvania Declaration of Rights state "that an enormous Proportion of Property vested in a few Individuals is dangerous to the Rights, and destructive

[28] Young to John Lamb, June 19, 1774, Lamb papers, NYHS; to John Wendell, Boston, November 23, 1766, photostat, MHS.

of the Common Happiness of Mankind," and that "every free State hath a Right by its Laws to discourage the Possession of such Property." That clause was rejected by the Pennsylvania convention, but Young became nonetheless a strong supporter of the state's constitution of 1776, which he later recommended to Vermonters as a model of government. By providing for a unicameral legislature and a weak executive council, all of whose members were elected annually and subject to provisions for rotation in office, by eliminating property qualifications for office and extending the franchise to all male taxpayers who had reached the age of twenty-one, the Pennsylvania constitution abandoned the complex model of Britain's government and earned its reputation as the most severely democratic of the revolutionary era.[29]

Young's sympathies were never confined to the urban "lower orders"; they continued to include those rural Americans who were fighting an uphill battle in their quest for land. Even while deeply involved with Philadelphia radicalism, he supported the cause of Connecticut settlers who were attempting to settle the Wyoming Valley of Pennsylvania despite that state's effort to dispossess them. Indeed, the causes seemed to him identical: both were set against privileged persons who believed "liberty the peculium of Men of some rank," who sought to "continue themselves and *favorites* in power, and make and execute what laws they please, frame new expeditions to Wyoming, and saddle *nonelectors* with all the expense." This, he argued, was "the system of Lord and Vassal, of *principal and dependent,*" of pri-

[29] Eric Foner, *Tom Paine and Revolutionary America* (New York, 1976), esp. pp. 109, 125–26, 129–30 for quotation by Cannon from a broadside to all military Associators which was issued by the Committee of Privates, June 26, 1776, and 131–34 for the proposed provision for the Pennsylvania Declaration of Rights. On Young's missions to Lancaster and York, see Edward Shippen, Jr., to Jasper Yeates, Philadelphia, May 23, 1776, Balch papers, HSP; and William Duane, ed., *Extracts from the Diary of Christopher Marshall* (Albany, 1877), p. 74, for entry of May 30, 1776. On these communities see Leyburn, *The Scotch-Irish,* pp. 196–200. And on Pennsylvania revolutionary politics see also Richard Alan Ryerson, *The Revolution Is Now Begun: The Radical Committees of Philadelphia, 1765–1776* (Philadelphia, 1978).

vate advantage and public loss that the new order should eliminate.[30]

Finally, he supported the efforts of his old friend Ethan Allen and the inhabitants of Vermont (a name Young invented) in their "struggle with the New York Monopolizers." Having "taken the minds of several leading Members in the Honourable the Continental Congress," he assured Vermonters in a circular of April 11, 1777, that they could easily break off from New York and become an independent state. "You have nothing to do but send attested copies of the Recommendation to take up government to every township in your district," he wrote, "and invite all your freeholders and inhabitants to meet in their respective townships and choose members for a General Convention . . . to choose Delegates for the General Congress, a Committee of Safety, and to form a Constitution for your State." Would Vermont's delegates be admitted to the Continental Congress? Organize fairly and try, he urged, "and I will ensure you success at the risk of my reputation as a man of honour or common sense. Indeed, they can by no means refuse you! You have as good a right to choose how you will be governed, and by whom, as they had."[31]

His argument was strong on logic but short on wisdom. New York was unwilling to countenance "this Attempt to dismember our State" on the part of its "revolted Subjects," as the province's Congressional delegates put it; and New York's support was critical to the American cause. As a result Congress rejected the Vermonters' plea, explaining that it had been created to defend the separate states against Great Britain, not to "recommend or countenance any thing injurious" to their "rights and jurisdictions." Nor could Vermont's effort to secede from New York "derive . . . countenance or justification from the act of Congress declaring the United States to be independent of the Crown of Great Britain, nor from any other act or resolution of Congress." In effect, the winning of independence and the establish-

---

[30] Young as "Elector," *Pennsylvania Gazette,* May 15, 1776.
[31] "To the Inhabitants of Vermont," in Edes, "Young," pp. 44–45.

ment of the republic demanded that Congress declare limits upon the "right of the people to alter or abolish their government," which Jefferson had eloquently asserted and the United States had officially approved not yet a year before.[32]

Congress's harshest words were reserved for Young, whose circular was condemned as derogatory to the honor of Congress in its presumption to speak for its members. Not even Samuel Adams, who had defended Young against critics in Boston and whom Young had continued to consult in Philadelphia, seems to have come to the support of his disciple, whose inveterate impetuosity had threatened American unity. What opposition emerged to Young's censure was inspired, it seems, far more by questions of circumstance and good taste than by those of policy and justice. For six days earlier, on June 24, 1777, Thomas Young had died of a "virulent fever" while serving the American cause as senior surgeon in a military hospital, leaving his sickly wife and six poverty-stricken children to the charity of his countrymen.[33]

Young's hostility toward New York's "aristocracy" and the old British empire was but part of a larger struggle that transfused his life. He took upon himself the task of opposing all inherited doctrines and institutions that were to him "irrational," and always had difficulty curbing his tongue in denouncing beliefs that others held sacred. An indictment for blasphemy, issued in Dutchess County during 1756, for

[32] New York Congressional delegates to the President of the New York Convention, Philadelphia, April 22, 1777; James Duane to Robert R. Livingston, June 28 and July 1, 1777; and New York delegates to the New York Council of Safety, Philadelphia, July 2, 1777, in Edmund C. Burnett, ed., *Letters of Members of the Continental Congress,* II (Washington, 1923), 336, 389–90, 395, 296; Worthington C. Ford, ed., *Journals of the Continental Congress,* VIII (Washington, 1907), 509–13.

[33] Adams to Lee, Philadelphia, June 26, 1777, in Burnett, ed., *Letters,* II, 388–89; death notice from Boston's *Independent Chronicle,* July 17, 1777, in Frothingham correspondence, MHS. Also Edes, "Young," pp. 44–50.

example, announced his religious iconoclasm. Thomas Young, physician and a previous resident of Crum Elbow precinct, the charge proclaimed, did "speak and publish these wicked false Blasphemious Words concerning the said Christian Religion (to wit) Jesus Christ was a knave and a fool . . . and that he the said Thomas Young then and there declared"—lest there be any misidentification—that "the said Jesus Christ of whom he then and there spoke was born of the Virgin Mary." In later years he retreated from the more offensive of such assertions, proclaiming his "most sincere attachment to the interest of the protestant religion," at least in "contradistinction" to that of Rome, whose "errors and superstitions," including the "damnable doctrines of *implicit faith, passive obedience and non resistance*" he promised to "oppose til death." But his Christianity was at best radically unorthodox.[34]

Young was a deist, not an atheist, although to many more traditional colonists the two were all but identical. He had in the 1750s collaborated with Ethan Allen in writing an early draft of the most important of all American deistic tracts, *Reason, The Only Oracle of Man; Or A Compendious System of Natural Religion,* known more simply as *The Oracles of Reason* or *Ethan Allen's Bible,* which Allen finally published without credit to Young in 1784. One scholar has concluded that Allen composed fewer than one hundred of the *Oracles'* four hundred and seventy-seven pages. In newspaper essays written while he was in Boston, Young personally affirmed several fundamental deistic tenets. Men, he wrote, could know God through nature. "Our beneficent Creator" had in fact imprinted a "Revelation of his eternal wisdom, unlimited power, and unspeakable goodness, upon every atom of the Universe"; and His word was clear and consistent, "for infinite wisdom admits of no variation or shadow of turning, neither can a divine revelation admit of a doubt, ambiguity or obscurity." The Scriptures were full of "many glorious things," but they were clearly at best a

---

[34] Henry Nobel MacCracken, *Old Dutchess Forever!* (New York, 1956), pp. 321–22; Young in *BEP,* March 18, 1771.

subordinate form of revelation, to be believed or disbelieved according to how well their teachings accorded with nature.[35]

All this had political meaning. To Young, the God of Nature and Nature's God was, in short, a republican. He was "no *respecter of persons,* ceremonies, or modes of worship," but looked "at the heart," accepting "worship which is afforded to him in spirit and truth." Acts of justice, humanity, and charity were, moreover, equally acceptable "whether performed by a Jew or a Samaritan" to a God who rewarded men not by rank, race, or other inherited distinction, but according to their works. Here lay another foundation of Young's revolutionary commitment, for his deism was evangelical, pushing him out into the world, demanding change for the good of God's creature, man. There was, the *Oracles of Reason* proclaimed, "an indispensable obligation on the philosophic friends of human nature, unanimously to exert themselves in every lawful, wise, and prudent method, to endeavour to reclaim mankind from . . . ignorance and delusion," enlightening men as to the true nature of God and morality, which would greatly serve "their happiness and well being." And so the creed Young himself publicly professed in 1771: "God, delighting in the well being of all his creatures, requires of me the improvement of all the talents he has favored me with for the promotion of that great end," he wrote, "and . . . my neglect or refusal herein subjects me to his righteous displeasure."[36]

Young's religious commitment to the cause of human welfare reinforced other decisions that shaped his life, above all that to enter the world of medicine. For if fever, the leading killer of the eighteenth century, was a "general foe to human happiness," as he once observed, those who fought it and other similar afflictions were clearly soldiers in the cause of mankind. Young's interest in medicine began early in

[35] George Pomeroy Anderson, "Who Wrote 'Ethan Allen's Bible'?," *New England Quarterly,* X (1937), 685–96; *Reason, The Only Oracle of Man* (New York, 1836; original 1784), p. 9; Young in *BEP,* August 27, 1770, and March 18, 1771.
[36] Young in *BEP,* August 27, 1770, and March 18, 1771; *Reason, The Only Oracle of Man,* p. 1.

childhood, well before he left any evidence of religious icon-oclasm. Were he offered a chance to rule the world on con-dition that he abandon the "study of physic," he once told his brother, he would spurn the proposal. His aspiration to prac-tice medicine shaped Young's early education. He learned to read from his grandmother, "a good English scholar," learned to cipher from his father, "a tolerable arithmeti-cian," attended a school four miles from home for a brief time, and drew on the linguistic abilities of a local minister. But he remained largely self-taught, taking it upon himself to study languages relevant to medicine (Latin and Greek, French and German), and developed an "indefatigable" in-terest in botany, since so many remedies for disease were then derived from plants. Finally at age seventeen Young began a two-year apprenticeship under a local doctor, John Kit-terman, which concluded his formal education and allowed him to enter the adult world, a "physician" in his own right.[37]

Medicine was a logical life choice for the able children of immigrants who lacked social rank. Thomas Young's brother Joseph followed him into medical practice; and of the four sons of his cousin Charles Clinton, who had emi-grated from Ireland with Young's parents, two became doc-tors and two entered occupations with similar advantages for the upwardly mobile—politics and the military.[38] But medi-cine was not a prestigious profession in the age of the American Revolution. It was in fact not yet a profession. In the large urban centers of England and Scotland, "physi-cians" merited a certain honor. Generally university men, gentlemen, and scholars, they were distinguished from the lesser apothecaries, who dispensed drugs, and from surgeons, the lowest of all, since they worked with their hands. Such distinctions failed to cross the Atlantic, however. In the colonies, as in the English countryside, there was but one category of medical men, who were most often nearer to the apothecaries and surgeons of London or Edinburgh than to those cities' "physicians." The elaborate system of cer-

[37] Young in *The Royal American Magazine,* April 1774, p. 129; Joseph Young's "Memoir" in Edes, "Young," pp. 12-14.
[38] Spaulding, *George Clinton,* pp. 6-9.

tification that regulated entrance into the English medical profession was also absent in America. As a result nothing prevented "unqualified" aspirants from claiming the title of "doctor," reserved in British cities for physicians alone. Some progress had been made: as Richard Shryock noted two decades ago, "a dawning enlightenment in medicine paralleled the quite different Great Awakening in religion during the middle decades of the eighteenth century." But a 150-year struggle to define and upgrade the practice of medicine, to transform a marginal occupation into an established profession, was then only beginning. Local medical societies that sought to distinguish qualified personnel through licensing regulations and to impose harmony within the profession by voluntary regulation of competition began to proliferate only after the revolutionary war. They remained unsuccessful until well into the nineteenth century.[39]

Young was actively interested in this effort to establish medicine as a respected profession. A set of detailed medical essays he published in the *Boston Evening Post* in late 1769 and early 1770 was specifically addressed to this end. It sought to show "every plain honest country gentleman and judicious citizen, that reading Culpeper's English Physical enlarged, or even Hutchins' Almanack improved, will not furnish a man with these articles of knowledge." In short, self-help would not do; the public needed trained doctors. His articles might serve, moreover, to win support for the founding of "a college of Physicians" at Boston and perhaps also "a competent library for the instruction of youth in the several branches of Anatomy, Surgery, Midwifery and Medicine; all to be under such regulations as to the wisdom of the legislature should seem meet."[40] But since such regulations were far in the future, doctors were left to establish lines of competence and respectability informally, sometimes in scurrilous public disputes that were only in part from a "competition for business and money," as Philadelphia's Dr. Ben-

[39] Richard Shryock, *Medicine and Society in America, 1660–1860* (New York, 1960), esp. pp. 2–21, 31.

[40] Quotations from Young in *BEP*, December 25, 1769, and February 26, 1770. Other essays in the series were published in the *BEP* for January 1, 8, 15, and 22, 1770.

jamin Rush once claimed. The acrimony of medical disputes (opponents were called mountebanks, fools, madmen, "petulent Jackanapes," "cloaked murderers") was at base social, part of a larger effort to distinguish an elite of "gentlemen," learned physicians, from others who were at best "pretenders to physic," "ignorant Empiricks," "quacks." And so even Young's summary of medical learning, by which he hoped to advance the practice of medicine in general, awoke criticism. His extensive treatises on the nature of health and disease, on the classification of disorders of the body's "solids" and "humors," had revived, an opponent charged, "the long and justly rejected corpuscularian, chymical and other fanatico philosophical systems, and blended them into one confused chaos."[41]

Young's medicine was not, however, far different from that of his critics, or from that of eighteenth-century doctors more generally. The practice of "physic" was heavily influenced by the previous century's advances in what is now called physics, or mechanics. Only after mastering the principles of "natural philosophy," Young argued, should young medical students turn toward the study of anatomy. The body was essentially a "material system . . . subject to the laws of nature," a machine whose "principles, powers, and laws of motion" must be known to workmen "charged with the care of keeping it in due order." Young once even referred to the human body as a "pneumatico hydraulic engine." Health and disease were understood above all in terms of the physical attributes of the body's "solids" and its liquids or "humors," their "principles of motion."[42]

These statements suggest that Young was not, as his critics occasionally charged, simply an ignorant "Empirick," prescribing remedies from uninformed private observations of disease. He cited the authorities of eighteenth-century medicine—Pitcairne, Sydenham, Haller, Whytt, Pringle, and

---

[41] Rush quoted in Shryock, *Medicine and Society,* p. 32. The terms of opprobrium were used in the course of a dispute over Young and his medical practice that raged in the *BEP* and *Boston Gazette* between April and June 1767. Quotation from "Timetes," *BEP,* February 19, 1770.

[42] Young in *BEP,* December 25, 1769; and *Royal American Magazine* for February 1774, pp. 47–48.

above all the "great Boerhaave."[43] But he never attended a university and never mastered the works he named: there was a superficiality to his learning, a confusion in his formulations that, with his bombastic manner, exasperated more cultivated readers. When accused in 1767 of quoting authorities he had never read carefully, Young responded ingenuously that he perhaps possessed neither "ability nor inclination to read authors in whole or in part," and later opened himself to ridicule for a casual reference to Harvey's famous work on the circulation of the blood as that of a late author "whose name I have lost in much and multifarious reading." In the end, his ignorance of formal medical learning was of little concern to him, for he lacked confidence that the established *"Institutions of Physic"* told all there was to know, or even what was most important, and urged young physicians to rely instead upon their own observations so medicine would be advanced.[44] Yet his practice remained the product of prior assumptions as well as practical experience. He accepted an explanation of body heat from a medical essay published in Edinburgh, for example, not just because it proved "beneficial in practice" but also because it was "most simple" and so "consonant to nature." In an age of fevers, that theory took on a critical importance. It provided the basis for Young's treatment of diseases so dissimilar as smallpox and rickets, and also for his politics.[45]

Physical warmth, Young taught, depended upon the "tendency of all substances to a separation of their component parts when shut up in a close place and duly moistened." In short, the body operated like a compost heap of fresh hay from which "a great heat arises," leading to "its near, or perhaps total putrefaction." If so, temperature was determined by the speed of digestion. Foods putrefied even

---

[43] See esp. Young's essays in *BEP,* April 20, 1767, and December 25, 1769. For a general account of eighteenth-century medicine, see Lester S. King, *The Medical World of the Eighteenth Century* (Chicago, 1958).

[44] *BEP,* June 1, 1767, and December 25, 1769.

[45] *Royal American Magazine,* February 1774, p. 47. For his treatment of rickets see ibid., September 1774, pp. 239–40. On smallpox, see Young to Henry Ward, Philadelphia, March 27 [26], 1776, in Bernard Knollenberg, ed., *Correspondence of Governor Samuel Ward, May 1775–March 1776* (Princeton, 1952), pp. 201–04.

in a healthy body, and unless "either assimilated to the living parts, or cast out of the system in a reasonable time they become violently noxious." Should the process for some reason be obstructed the body's warmth would increase and the "acrid matter" might make its way into the blood. More often it remained in the digestive tract, demanding the administration of purgatives. Young first reached this conclusion after a "violent fever" he had suffered in 1758, and from which he had saved himself, he believed, only by cathartics: "had all the ill conditioned matter resembling semiputrid gall, juice of the liver, &c. remained till it had acquired a much greater degree of putrefaction," he claimed, "it would have poisoned every drop of fluids, if not *melted down* the solid parts of the body." Long experience, involving even advanced cases, convinced him of the efficacy of bleeding, "puking," and above all the administration of purges followed finally by a "COOLING and composing regime." Continually he argued the danger of hesitation. "A mistaken fear of weakening the patient by purging off humors running into the last stages of putrefaction," he claimed, "has deterred many from giving their patients some chance of recovery, when the neglect of it left none at all." Young's approach was, he thought, far preferable to other prevailing treatments for fever, including the "cruel method of blistering from crown to ancle" on the theory that disease must be terminated through the skin. Such practices were continued, he claimed, only through a thoughtless adherence to the *"tradition of the fathers."*[46]

Between 1765 and his death twelve years later, Young may well have written more on medicine than on politics, but those subjects were closely linked. Like other medical "systematists" throughout the western world, and like many deists, Young believed that all natural truth could be reduced to a few basic principles. For doctors, this meant that what are today recognized as fundamentally different diseases were instead similar disorders that could be treated in

---

[46] *Royal American Magazine* for February, March, and April 1774, pp. 47–48, 98–100, 129–31, and for March 1775, pp. 89–90; Young in *Pennsylvania Gazette,* July 26, 1775.

similar ways. Its implications went beyond medicine, however, because natural truth was not confined by eighteenth-
century writers to what the twentieth century defines as the
sphere of nature and science. Young, for example, once referred to "eloquence, history, and politics" as branches of
"science in general." As a result the science of human nature
—the basis of political science—was subject to the same fundamental rules or truths as were all other sciences.[47] If doctors like Young spoke of the human body as a machine, so
also enlightened political writers constantly referred to governments as machines; and both were subject to governing
"principles of motion." Indeed, both the human body and
the body politic were subject to a common threat—"putrefaction" or, in politics, a "corruption" that Young, as much
as any Calvinist, found a normal part of human nature. Disease in politics as in persons could be induced scientifically
from its symptoms—that of England, for example, could be
diagnosed from the threats to freedom in America, Ireland,
the West Indies, even England itself. And so in September
1769 Young naturally invoked medical theory and terminology in discussing Britain's political disorder. "We long to
hear of some paroxisms among you that may forward a
crisis of the lingering disease," Young wrote John Wilkes,
the English radical whom he and other radical colonists
considered a close ally in their struggle for liberty. "Such
corrupt humors hanging so long on the vitals threaten the
utter extinction of the animal heat."[48]

If diseases of the body and of the polity were alike, so, too,
were their cures. In 1769 "paroxisms" seemed sufficient to

[47] Young to Hughes, Boston, May 7, 1770, Mss. 41551, Huntington Library. For the concept described here see the opening section ("The
Design") of Alexander Pope's *Essay on Man:* "the science of human
nature is, like all other sciences, reduced to a few clear Points: there are
not many certain truths in this world." Young was a great admirer of
Pope, whom he enthusiastically recommended to Abigail Dwight in a
letter of February 13, 1767, in the Sedgwick II papers, MHS. Among
medical men, Benjamin Rush professed a unitary theory of disease much
like Young's. See Donald J. D'Elia, "Benjamin Rush, Philosopher of the
American Revolution," *Transactions of the American Philosophical Society,* New Ser., LXIV, part 5 (Philadelphia, 1974), esp. 73, 99–100.
[48] Young to Wilkes, *Proceedings of the Massachusetts Historical Society,*
XLVII, 210.

purge Britain's "corrupt humors," but seven years later they were clearly inadequate; and Young understood independence as a necessary means of separating America from the "contagion" of British corruption. It was an extreme remedy perhaps, but a fitting one for Young to prescribe, since he had spent his medical career teaching that the greatest danger to survival lay in hesitation, in delaying "heroic" remedies that alone could save the patient. God's truth, moreover, was incompatible with "doubt, ambiguity, or obscurity," which manifested at best man's inability or unwillingness to perceive and accept that truth. Convinced that by reason and observation he knew the principles of nature and their application in current circumstances, Young acted with a certainty and confidence that some called impudence, but others understood in different terms. Science, in short, provided Young with what New England tradition gave Samuel Adams—that "sternness of stuff" John Adams found so essential for a revolutionary leader.[49]

As the colonial cause increasingly brought into focus his equalitarianism, his evangelical devotion to mankind, and his medical and scientific convictions, Young seems to have abandoned whatever ambitions for wealth he might once have had, surrendering material self-interest to the cause in which he was engaged. Like Samuel Adams, he came to accept poverty with pride. "Few there be," he commented to his friend Hugh Hughes, "who can bear the fatigue necessary to make the great man in easy circumstances." *To make the great man:* that was his ultimate aspiration. Martyrs lived their lives neglected, he once noted, but could hope to die revered. And so he urged New Yorkers to "fight the good fight, to hold fast the faith, and endure unto the end," confident that their present afflictions would earn a "far more exceeding and eternal wright of glory"[50]—a reward that was in the end denied him by posterity and by his own generation as well.

Despite his emphasis upon the common people and his

[49] Young in *BEP,* August 27, 1770.
[50] To Hughes, May 17, January 29, and March 2, 1770, Mss. 41552, 41548, and 41549, Huntington Library.

hostility toward great wealth, despite his praise of poverty, Young was in the end no leveler, as he demonstrated in fighting for the establishment of medicine as an elite profession. In the heady atmosphere of the mid-1770s he was willing to explain fevers and fluxes in terms of "common sense," but he refused to abandon the technical terms of medicine. These were expressions of precision, the marks of learning. There could be no democracy here: until someone invented "a vocabulary of medical terms as concise and particular as the one in use," he wrote, "we must be indulged in writing *Hypochondria* in Physic as well as *Hypothenuse* in Mathematics." He once dismissed hierarchy as a form of superstition, but the hierarchy he condemned was that of the old order. With the Revolution, he argued, recognition and power should be restricted to men of "capacity and integrity in public affairs," to men of ability who would be obliged to "fall into the common mass of the people every year" so they would "be sensible of their need of the popular good will to sustain their political importance." Privilege and authority would, in short, no longer be the province of those who, like colonial New York's "dirty pultroons" or England's aristocracy, had been born into wealth and power or had acquired it through the help of the state. But rank would not be destroyed. It would simply be relocated—in a republican meritocracy, to which the able sons of poor and rich would have equal access.[51]

⬦

A first-generation American without claim to respectability or fortune, a man marked by natural impatience and tumidity, a persistent transient possessed of unconventional religious views and a controversial practitioner of medicine, Thomas Young was very much a part of his mid-eighteenth-century world. Some of his traits can be explained by his Scots-Irish background; others were nurtured in the dis-

[51] Young to "Agricultor," *BEP*, March 28, 1774; and "To the Inhabitants of Vermont" in Edes, "Young," p. 45.

tinctive social and political culture of the Hudson Valley.
Above all as a doctor, Young shared in what may well have
been a radical profession or proto-profession. The names of
other doctors active in the American cause come quickly to
mind—Boston's Joseph Warren, for example, or Philadelphia's Benjamin Rush, the preeminent American physician of his day. Historians of medicine suggest these were
but the vanguard of an army of doctor-patriots: twenty-two
doctors sat in the Massachusetts Provincial Congress of 1774–
75, eleven died at Bunker Hill, five signed the Declaration
of Independence, and nearly 12,000 were involved in the
American revolutionary war. Later doctors "more than any
other profession leaned toward Jeffersonian ideas," and in
that political enthusiasm joined the members of other occupations which "appeared least 'respectable,' and most mobile." There were of course Loyalist doctors: among those
who filed claims with the British government for losses suffered as a result of their loyalty to the Crown, doctors
outnumbered persons from all other professional groups.
Loyalist doctors were, however, perceived at the time as un-
characteristic of their profession as a whole—so much so, in
fact, as to awaken Rush's suspicion. The "physician who is
not a Republican," he told his students, "holds principles,
that call in question his knowledge of the principles of medicine." In short, a "Tory" doctor was probably a bad doctor.[52]

But why? Because the principles of "heroic" medicine
shared by Young and Rush so logically led their proponents
from the battle against putrefaction in humans to that
against corruption in politics? For some, perhaps; but no
specific medical system seems to have defined the politics of
radical physicians. Young's demand that doctors intervene
dramatically in the processes of nature for the good of their

[52] G. Marks and W. K. Beatty, *The Story of Medicine in America* (New
York, 1973), pp. 117, 516–17, 530–31; Francis R. Packard, *History of
Medicine in the United States* (New York, 1963), p. 118; David Hackett
Fischer, *The Revolution of American Conservatism: The Federalist Party
in the Era of Jeffersonian Democracy* (New York, 1965), p. 208; Wallace
Brown, *The King's Friends: The Composition and Motives of the American
Loyalist Claimants* (Providence, 1965), p. 264; Rush, "Lectures on Pathol-
ogy. Influence of Government on Health," quoted in D'Elia, "Benjamin
Rush," p. 74.

patients contradicted his religious affirmation of nature as beneficent, as a revelation of God. There were those who disagreed with his practice—men such as New Hampshire's Josiah Bartlett, an Old Revolutionary and a signer of the Declaration of Independence whose career has some similarity to that of Young. Bartlett was an obscure country doctor interested in establishing medicine as a profession as well as organizing opposition to Britain. He held meetings of doctors in his home well before independence, and in 1791 helped found the New Hampshire Medical Society. But his medicine was founded upon a belief in nature as ally, not antagonist. He taught that the human body itself prescribed what it needed to be freed of disease, demanding water by thirst, for example, or covering by chills. "Proper Exercise, air and Diet," along with efforts "to keep the mind as Easy and Contented as possible" were "of much more Service than a multiplicity of Medicines," he advised his wife from Congress when one of their eight children was ill. This rather different approach was founded upon an empirical base much as was Young's, for Bartlett also arrived at his medical convictions during a fever he suffered in the 1750s. His trust in nature, one student has argued, carried over into his faith in democracy: the people, Bartlett believed, were best able to prescribe what was necessary for their collective health. And so again medical theory—although a different one from Young's—supported the radical content of revolutionary politics.[53]

The radicalism of many doctors may have been linked less with the systems of medicine they espoused than with their larger commitment to science and reason. Here the similarities between Young and Thomas Paine are particularly striking. Both were men of humble origin; both were

[53] I am indebted here to the unpublished work of Linda Upham Bornstein, which was done at the University of Massachusetts, Boston. Josiah to Mary Bartlett, Philadelphia, July 6, 1778, in Frank C. Mevers, ed., "The Papers of Josiah Bartlett, 1729–1795," New Hampshire Historical Society Microfilm (Concord, N.H., 1976), roll 2. Bartlett added, however, that some medicines were helpful. For a brief biography and bibliography on Bartlett, see Frank C. Mevers, ed., *Guide to the Microfilm Edition of the Papers of Josiah Bartlett, 1729–1795* (Concord, N.H., 1976), pp. 11–19.

deists; both harbored a deep hostility toward inherited privilege; both freed themselves from a distinct geographical base, moving on to support their cause wherever it seemed to be advancing and in need of help—Young from the Hudson Valley to Albany, to Boston, to Newport and Philadelphia, and Paine from England to America and France. In later years Paine claimed that the "natural bent of his mind had always been to science," not politics, which he had long considered a form of "Jockeyship"; but again, his science and politics were closely connected. Paine's radicalism, according to Eric Foner, began well before he came to America, among those English "religious Dissenters and self-educated artisans and shopkeepers, many of whom leaned toward Deism," and who attended the lectures of itinerant popularizers of science. For such men popular Newtonianism, with its suggestion that society as well as nature could be reduced to a science and that all human institutions must be judged against reason, easily bred conflict with an established system ordered by precedent rather than by logic. Paine's interest in science introduced him to "articulate critics of English government" such as Benjamin Franklin, who was partly responsible for his migration to America. For Paine in England, then, as for Young in America, science proved "a breeding ground for radical politics."[54]

Nor were the revolutionary implications of science and reason confined to Anglo-American culture. Nowhere were the frustrations of the bright and able so eloquently expressed as by the hero of "The Marriage of Figaro," a French play of the 1780s by Beaumarchais, himself an early supporter of the American Revolution. Figaro had studied chemistry, pharmacy, and surgery, but his low birth blocked all efforts to advance himself until he was left to live by the lowly, semimedical occupation of a barber-surgeon. "What have you done to deserve so many things?" he asks his noble master, then answers: "You took the trouble to get born!" If the French Revolution was "already almost full-blown in

<hr>

[54] Paine, "Age of Reason," in Philip S. Foner, ed., *The Complete Writings of Thomas Paine* (New York, 1969), II, 496; Eric Foner, *Paine*, pp. 6–7.

Figaro," as Crane Brinton argued,[55] it was because he had many real-life analogues. There was an "important but generally unappreciated connection between political radicalism and the frustrated ambitions of many would-be Newtons and Voltaires of prerevolutionary Paris." Future revolutionary leaders like Jacques-Pierre Brissot, Jean-Louis Carra, and Jean-Paul Marat were strongly attracted to science and participated in the cults of Mesmerist popular science, whose teachings were then hardly less creditable than Young's on medicine. In reason and scientific truth, Robert Darnton argues, such men found the basis for a profoundly radical critique of the standing order, for a plea that society no longer advance men for "savoir faire," as Figaro put it, but for "savoir"—knowledge, intelligence, ability.[56]

That Young participated in this effort is remarkable, given his prolonged isolation from the centers of Atlantic culture. He lived and worked for over thirty years in the countryside before moving to more cosmopolitan colonial cities. Yet he knew that his age was one of science and reason, understood their liberating force, and infused them into religious and medical beliefs that themselves shaped his evolving politics. Thus hostility toward New York's landed aristocracy fed not just hate and resentment, but the vision of a new republican world liberated from the errors of the past—a vision that joined him to a far larger revolutionary world of the eighteenth century.

[55] Quotations from Crane Brinton, *The Anatomy of Revolution* (rev. ed., New York, 1957), pp. 67–68.

[56] Robert Darnton, *Mesmerism and the End of the Enlightenment in France* (Cambridge, 1968), pp. 91–95, 110–11, and *passim*.

INTERLUDE

---∞---

*From the Letters of Josiah
and Mary Bartlett
of Kingston, New Hampshire
1775-1778*

In the New Hampshire Historical Society,
Concord, New Hampshire

The Bartlett papers are available on microfilm. See Frank C. Mevers, ed., "The Papers of Josiah Bartlett, 1729–1795," New Hampshire Historical Society Microfilm (Concord, New Hampshire, 1976). The letters used here were from the first and second of seven rolls. Some of the letters have also been reprinted (along with several others not used here) in Frank C. Mevers, ed., *The Papers of Josiah Bartlett* (Hanover, N.H., 1979).

Doctor Bartlett left home
for Congress,
eleven days away,
on the fourth of September, 1775.

"at present the Greatest uneasiness I have
is leaving my family for So long a time
But Shall Endeavor to make my Self
as Easy as possible
and Return as Soon as I Can,"
perhaps by the beginning of November,
when I "hope to find you all in Good health. . . .
Capt Calef will frequently Call
to See how you Do
and will be ready to assist you"
     (Woburn, Massachusetts, September 5, 1775)

"nothing will Give me So much Uneasiness as to hear
any of you are Dangerously Sick in my absence
But I hope & trust kind Providence
will bring us all togather again in Safety:"
          (Philadelphia, September 16, 1775)

". . . I have been Inoculated for the Small Pox
and am almost Got well of it
I had it very favorable
not above 20 Pock or thereabout
Tho I was Confined by the fever
to the House 5 or 6 Days

It is 4 weeks this Day Since I left Kingstown
and have not heard from you Since I Saw you
I want very much to hear from you
Tho I know you have the same almighty preserver
in my absences—
as soon as I Can you may be sure
I Shall Return with great pleasure
The Living in So Grand a City
without the pleasure of a free Country air
is not very agreable to me"

To

Mrs Mary Bartlett

Kingston

New Hampshire

Oc^t 2nd 1775

"I am pleased to hear . . . that Ezra is Better=
I have been Concerned about that poor Child . . .
you will See in the newspaper all the publick news:
I want to be informed of Sundry things from you=
whither Levi has been to School Since I left home=
whither we are like to have a Gramer School with us this fall=
whither the womans School Goes on=
whither you are like to Settle a minister now I am absent=
whither Judkins has finished Glazing the House
and a number of other Questions which I must omit
till I have oppertunity to ask them by word of mouth. . . .
Remember my Love to all the Children in particular
and let them Know that I Dayly think of them
and hope when I Return I Shall have the pleasure
to hear of their Good Behavior=
. . . assist George's family if they should be in need=
Remember me to all that ask after me=
and may the Supreme Disposer of all Events
in Due time put an End to the troubles of america
& Settle her Liberties on a Solid foundation=
and may I have the pleasure to Return in health
and find you & the rest of the family well—"
          (Philadelphia, October 11, 1775)

"I had the pleasure this morning
to Receive yours of the 13th of this month
informing me that you & the Rest of my family were well
altho Molly & Ezra had been Sick. . . .
I am by the Goodness of God in a Good State of health;
have got my Strength
and have not So much of the Headach as usual=
am in hopes I Shall be at home Sometime in December. . . .

"Last Sunday Mʳ Randolph Member of Congress from Virginia
& late President of the Congress was taken at table
with an Apoplexy & Died in a few hours
and was yesterday Buried attended by the Congress,
the Assembly of this Province,
the minister of all Denominations in this City,
3 Regiments Consisting of about 2000 men in their Regimentals
with Drums muffled &c and it is thought
12 or 15 thousand other Inhabitants;
in Short it is supposed to be
much the Greatest funeral that Ever was in America
    . . . take particular Care to lay in wood
    and other necessaries for winter
    and if in want of money
    apply for that money due from the Town. . . ."
                    (Philadelphia, October 25, 1775)

"I Cant help writing by Every opertunity
to let you know that I am well
for if hearing from me gives you & my Children
half the Satisfaction that hearing from you & them Does me
I Shall not think much of the trouble of writing
I have been now above 2 months from home
& had but 2 Letters from you
Tho I have wrote you 7 or 8 before this
I hope you and the family are all in Good health:
If I was within 100 miles
So as to Come home once in a month or two
& See you and Return
I Should be very Glad
but must tarry till the Congress rises
and as there is So much Business before us,
I know not when that will be"
                    (Philadelphia, November 6, 1775)

"Strange my letters are So long Coming to you. . . .
I hope you have Received Several more of my letters
as I have for Some Constantly wrote to you Every week
I Received Polly's Letter and am Glad
She has thought So much of me
as to write to me=
. . . I am Sorry to hear the Town is Still Devided
about ministerial affairs
My present hope is that I Shall be at home
in 4 or 5 weeks from this time
and that I Shall find you
& my family
& all friends
well

In haste I Remain yours &c
Josiah Bartlett"
(Philadelphia, November 27, 1775)

To

Mrs Mary Bartlett

Kingstown
Newhampshire

post free)
J Bartlett)
N:Hampsh^r)

No one would suspect I had the Small Pox by my looks
"have but a few pock in my face & them So Small
as not to be Seen unless Carefully looked for
. . . Some news of Governor Dunmores Behavior in Virginia
will I See Detain me here longer
than I was in hopes of, However Still hope
I Shall be able to Set out from hence by Christmas
if not sooner:
of this one thing you may be assured
that as soon as I can return with propriety
I shall immediately set out,
for I am Sure you Cannot be more Desirous of Seing me
than I am of Seeing you & the family
But as providence has Called me here
I Cannot Return
(and I Believe you would not Desire I should)
till the Business will permit me to Do it with honor.
. . . as to my afairs at home

I must leave them to your Direction til my return
hope if you want any advice or assistance
the Neighbor⁸ will not be backward
Give peter a particular Charge
to take good Care of the Cattle
& not to waste the hay.
and Encourage him to behave well till my Return.
. . . Remember my love to all the Children:
I think a good Deal of them all, particularly poor Ezra;
hope he is as well as when I left you
otherwise think you would have wrote to me
I Believe the account of the rising in England
is not to be Depended on=
    the weather here is Cold
    & the ground froze"
        (Philadelphia, December 4, 1775)

"am Sorry to inform you
that I Cannot return to you at present.
So much Business lays before the Congress;
I fear it wont rise for Some time,
when it Does rise,
one Delegate from Each Colony must tarry
to transact the Publick Business in the recess,
So that I think I Shall not be able to return
till towards Spring:
. . . I hope all will turn out for the best,
who Knows but that if I had Set out this very Severe weather
it might have been the means of my Death
and So hinder my being Ever able to See you,
. . . this Day being Christmas the Congress Did not Set,
So I had an oppertunity to ride
about 6 or 7 miles out of town in a Sley
yesterday and the Day before we had a Severe
    Cold Storm of Snow
which is now about Six inches Deep=
Desire Capt Calef to look me out a good faithful Steady hand
& hire him for me for 9 months or a year
to assist in my farming Business. . . .
                JB:"
      (Philadelphia, December 25, 1775)

"I fear I Shall not hear from you for Some time,
as you have looked for me home
and I Suppose not wrote to me,
but I hope from this time . . . till my Return
you will write to me Every week:
. . . if you have any School I Should be Glad
to have Levi attend it as much as Possible
if not let Mr Hills or Dr Gale write him some Copies
and let him write
I hope he will take Care to get as much Learning as possible
and not Idle away his time now he is young
So as to be a Great Dunce when he Grows up=
let me Know particularly how Ezra is="
                    (Philadelphia, January 1, 1776)

"Let peter take Good Care to lay in a Stock of wood . . .
& to take Good Care of the Stock of Cattle
if you want Hay or Corn I would have it be Bought Seasonably
for it is likely Corn will be Dearer next Spring and Summer
than this winter
. . . let Good Care be taken when the Snow goes off
      in the Spring
to keep up the fences round the mowing Ground
Especially the Hunton Meadow
& to Keep the Cattle off the winter Rye
take Care to Save Seed Corn
. . . I have sent by George the following articles viz
      Chints for 3 Gowns
         one for you, one for Polly & one for Lois
I hope they will Suit you
tho I am generally unlucky on that account=
      five Black Handkerch^s,
         one for you & one for Each of my 4 oldest Daughters
      a Quire of paper if I Can Stow it in the Bags
      2 papers of pins
      150 needles
I Desire to Send
      7 p^r Silver Sleeve Buttons
         for you to Give to Such of the Children
         as have none,
         to remember me by."
                (undated; probably Philadelphia, January 1, 1776)

"when I have a little time to Set Down & think of home
I Seem as if I Could hardly Content my Self
to tarry here any longer
I want much to hear from you & the family
but much more to See you
. . . I have wrote to our Convention
to Send another Delegate here in my Stead
as Soon as he Comes here
I Shall prepare to return home"
            (Philadelphia, January 8, 1776)

"Yours of the 6th Inst: I Received the 22nd
. . . it gave me great pleasure to hear
you & my family were well the 6th of this month;
I hope you & they Still Continue So.
I am by the favor of kind providence
in health at this time:
I have been lately a little troubled
with a pain in my head,
owing I Suppose to my being So long Confined
without any Bodily Exercise:
as the Days Grow longer I Design Every Day
. . . to ride or walk an hour or two;
. . . At four the Congress Comonly rise,
Dine by 5, walk till Six,
then on a Committee till 8, 9, or 10:
this is Comonly my Business Every Day—"
            (Philadelphia, January 24, 1776)

"I heaving an oppertynity to Send a Letter
by Coll^el Whippel which I expect will be the Last
I Shall Sent to you as I expect
you will Set out for home
as Soon as he arrives at phaledelphia. . . .
I hope you will prepare your Self for your Journey
both for your health & for your Defence. . . .
I would advise you not to take your Jorney to tegous
. . . if you have a mind I Should Send a man to meet you
as far as Cambrige watertown or Connecticut
if you Can write & Describe the time when
& place where he Shall meet you

I will endevour to Send aman
I hope these Lins will find you in good health
. . . my Self & the rest of the family
by the favour of Devine Providance
are very Comfortably at this time"
                    (Kingston, February 9, 1776)

"Yours of the 2n^d Inst: I Rec^d this morning
and with pleasure . . . I think it a great favor,
that So large a family, Should be blessed with health,
for So long a time,
. . . if life and health permit, I hope to be at home
before the middle of april,
for as Soon as the going is any thing like,
I Design to Come home,
Even if I Should be obliged to return again to this City
after a Short Stay with you.

"When I read at the Close of your letter,
an account of the Death of my good friend, John Wadleigh,
it very Sensible affected me,
as I had received no account of his being worse
than when I left home;
I had really a great value for him, and think the Town
. . . have met with a great loss in his Death;
I Cant help Calling to mind, the many hours,
pleasant Conversation I have had with him,
and tho' he had Some Sentiments Different from mine,
yet I really Loved & Esteemed him,
and I Despise the Bigot,
who Can have no Esteem or friendship for any man,
whose religious opinions are Different from his own.

"This Day Dr Smith of this City Delivered a funeral Oration
to the Memory of General Montgomery and the other Brave men,
who fell in the attack on Quebeck;
. . . The Solemnity of the Ocasion,
with the news of the Death of my friend Wadleigh,
or Something Else,
Seems to have Setled my Spirits at least a peg too low.
I know that troubles & Disappointments,
are the Common lot of all men,
and that the Supreme Disposer of all Events, Can,

and I really believe, will,
over rule all things for the best,
that is my greatest Comfort
when things Seem to look with a Dark and Dismal Countenance,
Either of a publick or private nature.

". . . it is now very Cold for this place
tho not Equal to Some in Newhampshire."
(Philadelphia, February 19, 1776)

"These Lines Leave me & the Rest of the family well;
I hope & trust they will find You in Good health—
the Day You Left Kingstown no Rain;
Wednsday Clowdy forenoon & the afternoon very rainy;
thursday a Clear & Pleasant Day;
Friday Clear & warm forenoon
& Smart thunder Shower In the afternoon;
this Day fine & Pleasant thus far. . . .
Lieu Pearson is a Live & I think he is Some Better*
. . . he walked across the Room Without help Yesterday;
the hiccups holds him Yet By Spells;
that Disorder in his face Proves to be
the Saintanthony's fire
it has Spread to the other Side of his face
& he is blind With that Eye"
(Kingston, May 11, 1776
8 o'clock in the morning)

". . . I hope by this time You have arrived
as far as Philadelphia in health & without Difficulty
& may You be kept from all Evil, tho I hear
Some British Lords have Laid a Plan
to attack Philadelphia by Land
if Impracticable by Sea. . . .
Lieu* Pearson is Better of all His Disorders. . . .
no Deaths in this Parish Except the widow fowler
who was buried last Sunday
their has been near 30 Persons Sick with the Canker
& all like to Recover. . . .

warm Rains & Shines by turns . . .
has Brought the peach trees
Cherry and other Plumb trees in full Blossom—
apple trees Begining to Blossom
they Do not appear to Bloom
So thick as they Did Last Year—
we have almost Done Plantain"

May 17th 1776   NP Trees

TO

Josiah Bartlett Esqr
A Member of Congress
Philadelphia

Recd June 1st
1776

"Yesterday afternoon I arrived here in good health
after a very fatigueing Journey:
. . . I went by Norwich & New London to Newhaven;
went to meeting Sunday afternoon at Brandford . . .
on monday rode from Newhaven to Horseneck . . .
I got to New York on tuesday. . . .
The account of the Roebuck & Liverpool men of war
Coming up Deleware within 30 miles of this City
& the Engagement of the Philadelphia Gondalos with them
you will no Doubt See in the newspapers
the Gondalos had much the advantage of the men of war
& obliged them to Sheer off;
when the men of war were Coming up
the people here were much frighted
& many of them Sent out their goods into the Country:

"The Congress have Sent out a General Recommendation
to all the Colonies to take up
a new form of Government—

"You Desired me to write, you
how much forwarder the Spring was this way than with us;
The people all the way as I Came
Complain of the Backwardness of the Spring

till this week:
At the South part of Connecticut last monday
the apple trees were in full Blossom
peachtrees & Cherry trees out of Blossom:
from New York to this City the trees all out of the Blossom
& Cherries of Some Bigness
the winter Rye Eared out to its full heighth
However the people all the way were planting Indian Corn. . . .

"Tell Mrs Burbank that the Regiment her Son is in
was Encamped at Some Distance from New York
So that I Could not See him but I Saw a Captain
that Belonged to the same Encampment
. . . & he promised me to find him out & give him the letter
The Company where Mr Flaggs Son is
was Stationed at Stratton Island
four or five mile from New York
but I took the best Care to Convey it to him"
                    (Philadelphia, May 18, 1776)

"I have heard from You but once Since You left home;
the time Seameth Long;
I hope You have not forgot to write to me=
I hope You are Well & in Good health—
I expect to hear from you in a Short time;
my Self & the Rest of the family are very well
at this time. . . .
there has been no funeral in the town this week. . . .
it is a fine Growing Season tho Cool—
Lieu^t Pearson walks abroad with a Staff
tho he is weak Yet. . . .
        nothing Strange among us—"
                (Kingston, May 29, 1776)

"a Child of Jacob Peasleys
was buried last Sunday
it Died a Consumption=
the weather Uncommon Cold for the Season
a Great frost the night of the 30th of may
Did Some Damage among Beans & other tender [*plants*]

we have Scarce left of our winter Cloathing=
had Plenty of rains the week Past=
Yesterday the . . . alarm men met upon the Plain
& Chose their off[icers]"
                    (Kingston, June 7, 1776)

". . . my self and the rest of the family
that is at home are all in good health
Polly is gone to see Levi at newbury
I hope they are both well,
        and you at a distance. . . .
the People in general are more healthy
no funaral this week. . . .
I and the People among us Saw an account
of the ingagements of the Roebuck
        and liverpool men of war with the Gondaloes
but we did not know they were so near Philadelphia
you gave us an account of great Chains
        being Drawn a crost the river Deleware
and it is a mistry to us how they got up the river
I Shall be glad if you can write to me how it was
the frost with us the last of may was very Great
it froze Ice upon the water
it cut Down beans Pumkins Cucumbers and Such. . . .
indian corn very bacward among us
begining to weed
worms have not eat very much corn
yet. . . .
by the leave of divine Providence
nothing Strange among us
the children all remember
their Duty to you"
                    (Kingston, June 10, 1776)

"My Dear Son
    I send this with my love to you
    . . . your mother has wrote to me
    that she hears you are well and like being at School
    I hope you will take Care to behave
    So as to have the good will of your Master

    & School mates
that I may have the pleasure
to hear . . . that you make a wise improvement
    of your time
to gain learning that the Cost I am at for you
may not be in vain

"You have now an oppertunity
to gain learning & to fit your Self
for whatever Station in life
it may please God to place you
If you now neglect the price put into your hands
You will have Cause to repent it all your Days;

"that you may remember that all favors & Blessings
Come from the Supreme father of all,
who is good to all . . .
and that God will take you under his holy protection
    is the ardent prayer of your affectionate
        father
        Josiah Bartlett"
    (Philadelpia, June 17, 1776)

"I Can with Pleasure Inform You
that myself & the Rest of the family are Comfortable
tho Sally has been very Poorly
She was taken Last Sunday with a fever & Purgin
which Lasted her two or three Days
but She is Better now. . . .
the weather warm and Dry
if we have not rain soon I Expect
the hay will be as Scarce as it was last year
flax in general will be exceeding Scarce
worms eat Some Places all Clear
left none
ours thin and Short
our winter rye looks very well
indian Corn Stands very well
frost nor worms has not hurt much of it
apples are Likely to be Scarce. . . .
few Straburys
the Drowth is not So Early as it was last year

no funeral in this Parish Since I wrote to you before;
in hawk joseph Sanborns wife died
She was brought to bed with a Child a thursday
and died a Saturday. . . .
and a Child of David tilton died
his family was most all Sick at a time
Eight or ten of them
I believe the rest are like to Recover. . . .
mr. moses Sweat is began a School upon the Plain . . .
he has upwards of forty Schoolars—
one mr Shaw is a Preaching in the East Parish="
                    (Kingston, June 21, 1776)

"it is a pretty healthy time in this City at present,
   but as the hot weather has Come on for about a week
   & no rain the air Seems to Stagnate,
   & if it should hold Dry, will I fear produce Sickness,
   I have for 2 or 3 Days past in the afternoon
   rode Back a mile or two.
   & the very air of the Country Seems reviving=

"as to what you mention of the Skirmish
   of the men of war & the Gondaloes;
   it was Below the Boom Batteries &c &c
   made for the Defence of this City;
   they are not above 8 miles below the City,
   as being the most Convenient place to Stop the ships.
   I am not under the least fear of their being able
   to penetrate to this place,
   So you may make your self Quite Easy about me,
   on that account.

"I am sorry to hear the frost has Done Damage with you:
   hope it has not Killed all the Beans &c
   the Corn will Commonly Grow again=
   How is the flax in General like to be;
   what are like to be the Crops of hay with you;
   how is the winter & Sumer Grain like to be &c:
   Please to write me what is like to be
   the Success of the farming Business this year=
   Mowing English Grass was finished last week here. . . .

"I have been for about a week on a Committee
of one member from Each Colony
to form a Confederation or Charter
of firm & Everlasting Union of all the United Colonies:
It is a matter of the greatest Consequence
& requires the greatest Care in forming it: . . .

"I hope Kind Providence will order all things for the best,
and if Sometimes affairs turn out
Contrary to our wishes,
we must make our Selves Easy & Contented,
as we are not Certain what is for the best"
                    (Philadelphia, June 24, 1776)

"this morning I Rec^d your Seventh Letter
and am thankful to hear you are in good health
I wish you Peace and Prosperity
*   in all your lawfull undertakeing=*
I and the Rest of the family
are by the favour of kind Providence in health
Sally is now Comfortably. . . .
I have not had So much of the headach as usal
but more of the Colick Pain
as for the farming business
I Beleive Biley and Peter maniges Prety well. . . .
inglish Corn Looks very well . . .
indian Corn Some Backward But it Grows fast now;
the weather very hot and Dry;
the worms has eat Considerabley
*   of our Corn in the new Ground;*
. . . apples very Scarce
I belive there will not be much Cyder made this year
however I hope and trust we Shall Be Provided for
as we have Been in times Past
Caried throw many trials and Difficulties
Beyond Expectation"

June 30th 1776

TO

Josiah Bartlett Esqr
member of Congress
Philadelphia

Rode 6 miles to Germantown before breakfast . . .
Went to see "the Brittish Museum So Called
it is a house Built on purpose
to preserve all the natural Coriosities
that Can be Collected from all parts of the world
as Birds, beasts, fish Shells, Snakes, plants
& a great many other Curiosities
among them there was a Shark a Crocodile a Cat fish,
a Dog fish a Sea porcupine a Creature Called a Hog in armour
2 ostrich,s Eggs which were perfectly round &
     of the Colour of Ivory
and I Guess would hold a pint & an half Each
there was a great many other Creature of a Strange make
from any thing I ever Saw before. . . ."
                    (Philadelphia, July 2, 1776)

Other curiosities: two or three tons of ice
"they use it to Cool their Liquors in the Summer
particularly punch;
fresh meat laid on it will Keep a week in the hottest weather:
another Curosity was two fish Pools for Breeding fish. . . ."
                    (undated)

Hasty pudding is here called mush.
                    (Philadelphia, September 9, 1776)

"The affair of a Conferation of the Colonies,
Independence &c is now on the Carpet
& will Soon be published I Expect=
Remember my love
to all my Children, in particular"
          (fragment, June 17, 1776)

"I hope we all Shall be kept in health
     peace & Safety;
we have the Same keeper tho we are Seperated
Yet God is every where Present=
a general time of health=
we have had a Great plenty of Rain this week=

I am in Great hopes the English Corn
will be very Good this Year—
Indian Corn Grows very fast=
I Believe hay will be better than our fears;
in Short these bountifull Rains
    has Revived the face of the earth=
. . . We have had very Sharp Lightning & heavy thunder . . .
which has Struck trees and the Ground Several times=
as the weather is much hotter with You than with us
I Shall be Glad to Know
whither You have heavy thunder & lightning there
or no—"
        (Kingston, July 6, 1776)

"our People met here for trainings & town meetings
three Days this week to List men to Go to Canada;
. . . old m^r Proctor and old Willm Collins of this town
& Several Younger men have listed;
they are to march next week I hear. . . .
I want your advice & assistance
but must make myself Contented—
. . . Peter is more Steady now than he was
when You left him Before—

". . . P S I fear the Small Pox will Spread universally
as boston is Shut up with it
& People flocking in for innoculation;
. . . the times Looks Dark and Gloom
upon the account of the wars
I belive this year will Decide the fate of america
which way it will turn God only knows
we must look to him for Direction & Protection;
Job Said tho he Slay me yet will I trust in him
    M^r thay^r Gives his Regards to You
        M B
    July 15th we are all well"
      (Kingston, July 13 and 15, 1776)

"Ezra was taken last monday in the afternoon
(after we had Dated a letter to you that we were well)
with the Canker and Scarlet fever. . . .

he is now Some better. . . .
the men among us are very backward
about Going into the war
they are not Contented with the Province bounty
our men have had a town: meeting
& have voted to raise their bounty
to fifty Dollars a man besides their wages
They are to begin their march to Day
& meet at Esqr websters at Chester
David Quimby of hawk is Captn
John Eastman Second Lieut
old m^r Proctor is Gone
m^r wheeler is a Going"
     (Kingston, July 20, 1776)

"their has been no funeral in this Parish
Since them I mentioned you
but in the East Parish M^{rs} tilton
wife of Cap^{tn} tilton
buried her only Daughter Last wednesday;
a bout four or five years old
She died with the feaver and Canker
he is Gone to Canada
heavy news to him
when he Comes to hear of it"
    (Kingston, July 29, 1776)

"m^r John Noyes Says he has been in england
& Several of the west Indie Islands
But he Says america is the only Place
for living Comfortably
if we can enjoy our Liberty
he Says Some of the people in england
is almost as Stuped as the Brute creation;
they are so Ignorant they could hardly Beleive
he was an american because, they Said
he Lookd & Spoke So much like an English man

"The people among us is very hurried
Gitting in the English harvest;
I beleive they will Chiefly finish this week;

we have cut all our Grain;
Something Late Gitting in hay;
we have not half Done
as the Grass Grew very fast of late=
Plenty of rains; the weather not very hot="
          (*Kingston, August 9, 1776*)

"*Prices of things have Been Extravagant*
molasses four & Six Pence p^r Gallon . . .
new England Rum five Shillins p^r Gallon
west India Seven & Six Pence p^r Gallon
Cotton wool four Shillins p^r pound
Bohea tea ten Shillins p^r pound
& other things in Porpotion
Mens Days work Some three Shillins
& Some four Shillins p^r Day"
          (*Kingston, August 29, 1776*)

"*help is So Scarce we Could not Git one Days work*
about Reaping upon any account & none about mowing
But what I Paid the money for=
we have almost Done haying. . . .
Our English corn is not thresh^d Yet . . .
Apples Scarse; Plumbs in the Garden Plenty. . . .

"*I Do not write this by way of Complaint*
I Believe Biley & Peter has Done as well
          as Can be expected
& other People You Know
will take Care of Self first

"*Pray Do come home before Cold weather as You Know*
my Circumstances will be Difficult in the winter
If I am alive
                    In hast from Yours &c
                    Mary Bartlett"
          (*Kingston, September 9, 1776*)

"Remember my love to all my Children . . .
I want to Know how hay is likely to be with us;

how the English Corn is like to be;
whither the worms Destroy the Indian Corn;
how the flax is like to turn out &c &c
Remember me to David Sanborn and tell him
I feel pretty Easy about my farming affairs
as long as I know he has the Care of it
Remember me to M[r] Thurston D[r] Gale Cap[t] Calef
M[r] Thayer &c &c &c"
> (York, Pennsylvania, June 21, 1778)

"I am Sorry to hear there is like to be
a Scarcity of Cider,
as I Sensibly feel the want of it here,
where there is always a Scarcity
or rather where they never use much of it,
and what is made is very inferior
to the New England Cider;
If I am not likely to make any
I hope you will purchase a few barrels
    if you Can Conveniently. . . .
as I Should be glad of a little
    (after So long fasting from it)
when I return home—

". . . the little bobed Hats for the men
are growing fast out of fashion,
the mode now is large round brims
& Cocked Nearly 3 Square,
no hats are now made in any other mode here,
So much for fashions,
for the Satisfaction of my Children—"
> (Philadelphia, August 24, 1778)

"Honord father
. . . Last night to our Great Joy
we Received Yours of the 24th and 31st of august
which Inform us You were well then. . . .
Pretty Healthy in this Parish
Tho it is Sickly in Some places round us
with the Dissentary;
H[r] Hook of Hawk Lost a Child with it Last week,

and the Revd Mr Cotton of Sandown has it very Bad;
it has Prevailed So in Some places
as to Sweep of whole families—
Aunt Ruth Bartlett call^d hear Last Sunday
& Said She Left Judith very Sick with the Dissentary
and was a Going to see Mrs Gordon
who was Sick with the Same Disorder. . . .
the Disappointment of our troops at Rhode Island
or Something Else has caus^d an amazing Rise
        of west India Goods
Sugar at Eight Shillings a pound,
& other things in proportion;
and the farmer is as bad as the merchant,
for Indian Corn is Seven Dollars p^r Pound,
Cyder 20 or 30 Dollars p^r Barrel,
Butter none under four & in Some places
        Seven Shillins p^r Pound;
in Short they that live Between the farmer and merchant
Come Poorly off. . . .
no School on the Plain,
Except a Singing School two Evenings in a week,
which Miriam Rhoda and Josiah attends—
I thank you for taking So much thought of us
as to write any thing for our amusement. . . .
I hope we Shall Soon have Peace and plenty
& every one Set under his own vine and fig tree
& none to make us afraid. . . .
                your afectionate Children

                Mary Bartlett
                Lois Bartlett"
        (*Kingston, September 26, 1778*)

"May God grant us wisdom
   to form a happy Constitution,
   as the happiness of america
   to all future Generations
   Depend on it."
        (Philadelphia, June 24, 1776)

"the General Court adjourned
        after the first week of Setting

by Reason of the Smallpox
there is I hear near two hundred
　　Innoculated . . . in Exeter. . . .

"Levi is Gone to newburys School. . . .
he Boards at Mr *Noyes:s . . .*
a Cold may Storm this week. . . .

"nothing Strange
time Goes on much as Usual with us . . .

MB
*May 28*th *1778*
TO
The Honble
　　Josiah Bartlett Esqr
　　in Congress York Town
　　　　Pensylvania"

N. B. "Poor Ezra" Bartlett, who was five years old in 1775 and 1776 when his health so worried his father, lived to become a respected physician, as did his brothers Levi and Josiah, Jr. Ezra died at age seventy-eight in 1848. His youngest sister, Hannah, who was conceived during her father's visit home in the spring of 1776, and whose coming explains the fear and distress with which Mary Bartlett anticipated the "Cold weather" of that year, was born on the thirteenth of December but died the next April. Levi Bartlett, *Genealogical and Biographical Sketches of the Bartlett Family in England and America* (Lawrence, Mass., 1876), pp. 58, 51.

Engraved certificate: John Warren, the younger brother of Joseph Warren, testifies that Levi Bartlett, the son of Josiah and Mary Bartlett, has attended his medical course, 1785.

CHAPTER FOUR

---◦∞◦---

A VIRGINIAN
AS REVOLUTIONARY:
RICHARD HENRY LEE

THE IMPRESSION OF RICHARD HENRY LEE left by his collected writings is paradoxical. He was a fourth-generation Virginian, a member of one of the Old Dominion's first families, and so resembled those Hudson Valley land barons who provoked Thomas Young's hostility. Yet he shared Young's enthusiasm for the American cause and for New England as well. In many ways, in fact, Lee seemed to be a misplaced New Englander. The person he most admired, the man with whom he shared most fully his values and aspirations, was that latter-day Puritan Samuel Adams. Lee, like Adams, continually stressed the importance to the American cause of "virtue"; a willingness to sacrifice immediate self-interest for the public good remained for him the "great Essential," a critical "spring" of the Americans' "great revolution." That value shaped Lee's style much as it shaped Adams's. His letters were stifflly formal: one biographer noted that they often read as if intended for publication. They advanced an argument, or cause, and revealed only rarely "a slight human touch." Lee's widely praised speeches were similarly disciplined—short and succinct, his points clear and deliberate—and so they contrast with those of the prolix Patrick Henry, who overwhelmed listeners with grace and eloquence, but left them unsure just what he had said. Even Lee's physical appearance was appropriate to his image as a classic patriot, "one of Plutarch's men" as both Lee and Adams were described. Here in fact he excelled his northern colleague, for while Adams was short and squat, Lee was tall and spare. He had red hair like his countryman at Monticello, but a visitor to Virginia's House of Burgesses in March 1773 was struck instead by the "aquiline nose and Roman profile" of a legislator he described as "the harmonious Richard Henry Lee."[1]

Alike in principle and manner, Adams and Lee also shared their politics. Lee supported the Continental Congress's resolves of October 1778 against "theatrical entertainments, horse racing, gaming, and such other diversions as are productive of idleness, dissipation, and a general depravity of principles and manners." There he acted, his biographer claimed, "more like a Massachusetts Puritan than a Virginia Cavalier" whose neighbors freely participated in such diversions.[2] In the heated Deane-Lee controversy that divided Congress in the late 1770s, moreover, the Lees had no firmer allies than the Old Revolutionaries of New England in their crusade against Silas Deane and the forces of corruption that he seemed to incarnate. At times Lee's affection for what he called the "eastern part of this Union" seemed almost unbounded: in 1778 he went so far as to suggest that "Eastern Pilots" were most likely to bring "the Vessel of State . . . safely and happily into port." On another occasion he confessed a hope that he might spend his final days in Massachusetts, where the people, he thought, were "wise, attentive, sober, dilligent and frugal." These preferences were not lost on Lee's enemies in Williamsburg,

---

[1] Lee to Gov. Jonathan Trumbull, Chantilly, January 22, 1780; to Henry Laurens, Chantilly, June 6, 1779; and to Thomas Jefferson, Chantilly, June 8, 1779, in James Curtis Ballagh, ed., *The Letters of Richard Henry Lee* (New York, 1970; reprint of the original from 1911 and 1914), II, 172, 62, 83; Oliver Perry Chitwood, *Richard Henry Lee: Statesman of the Revolution* (Morgantown, W. Va., 1967), pp. 223–27; Thomas Jefferson to William Wirt, Monticello, August 4, 1805, in *Pennsylvania Magazine of History and Biography*, XXXIV (1910), 390; Jefferson's comments in Charles M. Wiltse, ed., *The Papers of Daniel Webster, Correspondence*, I, *1798–1824* (Hanover, N.H., 1974), 372; Judge St. George Tucker to William Wirt in William Wirt Henry, *Patrick Henry: Life, Correspondence and Speeches*, I (New York, 1891), 163.

[2] Chitwood, *Lee*, p. 133.

who charged that in the Continental Congress he "favored New England to the injury of Virginia."[3]

But Lee was no New Englander. His revolutionary career, his values and aspirations, even his love for New England came above all from his fate as the third surviving son of a ranking Virginia family whose members were themselves at a critical historical juncture. Burdened by cultural standards and material obligations he found difficult to satisfy, Lee carried into the Anglo-American conflict contradictions of a personal character that made him perhaps the most complex of his generation of revolutionaries.

❦

By the standards of his time, and perhaps of any time, the son born to Thomas and Hannah Ludwell Lee on January 20, 1732, was extraordinarily privileged. He entered a family that had historically been distinguished by its wealth: his great-grandfather, Richard Lee "the emigrant," had begun acquiring land soon after his arrival in Virginia during the early 1640s, and by the time of his death he was the colony's largest landowner. Richard Lee's grandson, Thomas, who was Richard Henry Lee's father, was a fifth son and so received only a modest inheritance. He managed nonetheless to acquire landholdings far beyond those of his ancestor. At his death in 1750, Thomas the "empire builder," as he has been called, passed on to his descendants some 30,000 acres in the Northern Neck of Virginia, that is, the area between the Potomac and Rappahannock rivers, southeast of today's Washington.

The parents' favors were distributed unequally among their children. Thomas's wife, one descendant charged, "confined all her care and attention to her daughters and her eldest son, who was to be the head of the family, and gave

[3] Lee to James Lovell, Chantilly, June 12, 1781; to General William Whipple, Chantilly, November 29, 1778; to John Adams, Chantilly, October 8, 1779; and to Arthur Lee, Freestone, Va., February 11, 1779, in Ballagh, ed., *Lee Letters,* II, 236; I, 453; II, 155, 32–33. Lee described the arguments of his enemies in a letter to Patrick Henry, May 26, 1777, ibid., I, 300.

up her younger sons, when boys, to be fed, in great measure, by their own enterprise and exertions." Similarly, the greater part of Thomas Lee's estate, including the family homestead, Stratford in Westmoreland Country, went to the eldest son, Philip Ludwell Lee, and only the first four of Thomas's six surviving sons—Philip Ludwell, Thomas Ludwell, Richard Henry, and Francis Lightfoot—were left landed estates. The youngest two, William and Arthur, were by the terms of their father's will to be bound to some "profession or trade, so that they may learn to get their living honestly."[4]

Whatever their individual material endowments, however, all Lees acquired by birth the status and style of life appropriate to a family whose property had long marked it as one of the first in Virginia society. As a young adult, Richard Henry Lee decided to rent out many of his inherited slaves as well as his patrimonial lands in the western reaches of the Northern Neck, hoping to support his family upon the proceeds while devoting himself to governmental affairs. His home, Chantilly, was built near his birthplace in Westmoreland County upon lands leased from his elder brother. The commodious house offered a view of the Potomac that excelled Stratford's, and became a center of hospitality where a visitor in 1790 found "everything that is most excellent in fish, crabs, wild fowl, and exquisite meats" as well as "the best of liquors."[5]

Lee's standard of living exceeded that of most colonists, but so, too, did his obligations. Rental income from his property never equaled expectations; and although his own plantation produced little tobacco, as he explained to his brother William in 1769, yet he was obligated to pay a "heavy rent" for his home as well as "large public levies."

---

[4] For a succinct account of Lee family history, see Paul P. Hoffman, *Guide to the Microfilm Edition of the Lee Family Papers, 1642–1795* (Charlottesville, 1966), esp. pp. 11–15. Also Burton J. Hendrick, *The Lees of Virginia, Biography of a Family* (Boston, 1935), esp. p. 159 for quotation from Richard Henry Lee's biography of Arthur Lee, p. 89 for Thomas Lee's will, and p. 60 on his estate. Genealogical information is also available in Edmund Jennings Lee, *Lee of Virginia, 1642–1892* (Philadelphia, 1895).

[5] Account of Chantilly by Thomas Lee Shippen, September 20, 1790, in Lee, *Lee of Virginia*, p. 120.

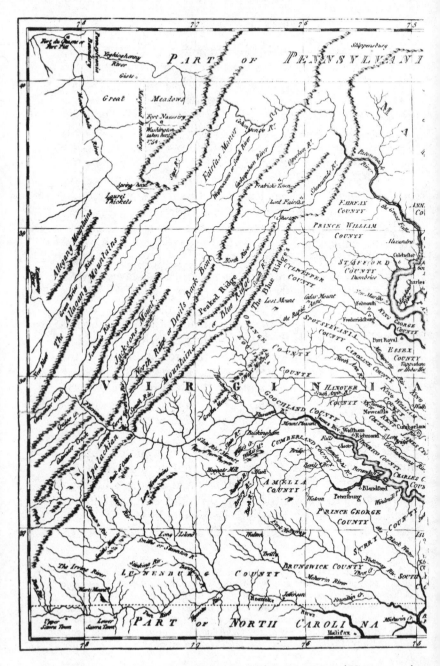

"A New and Accurate Map of Virginia, and

Part of MARYLAND and PENNSYLVANIA," 1780.

Meanwhile his family continued to grow. "Five children already, another far advanced on the stocks, with a teaming little Wife," he observed in October 1772, "are circumstances sufficiently alarming." The last of his four sons and five daughters was born in 1782, which meant that the costly obligations of educating and establishing children remained with Lee until his own death twelve years later.[6]

That duty was a particularly serious one in Virginia, where concern with maintaining family rank dominated the upper orders of society. Local tradition was, moreover, reinforced by Lee tradition. *"Ne incautus futuri"*—do not be incautious of the future—was the family motto, coupled on its crest with a squirrel holding an acorn. The "nut" previous generations had stuck away for posterity was land; and Lee's generation followed family custom by seeking large tracts in the trans-Appalachian West through the Ohio Company and Mississippi Company. But land did not obsess him: he later supported the cession of Virginia's western claims to the United States, and thought more modestly of capital endowments for his daughters and of education for his sons, who would one day inherit his own ancestral lands in Fauquier County. But even the task of educating the two eldest boys imposed severe strain on his resources. He sent Thomas and Ludwell Lee to England because he believed schooling was "much cheaper obtained" there than anywhere in America except perhaps at the College of William and Mary, which he found substandard. Thomas was to be readied for the church at the "cheapest and fittest place," Ludwell for the bar, but no more than £30 sterling per year could be spent on each for board, clothes, and instruction, Lee stressed, because that was "all . . . I can afford." The boys would have to be "very frugally clothed"—"the plainest, to be decent," he insisted, "will please me much the best."[7]

In part from necessity, then, Lee affirmed an inclination

---

[6] Richard Henry to William Lee, Williamsburg, December 17, 1769, and Lee Hall, October 23, 1772, in Ballagh, ed., *Lee Letters,* I, 39–40, 78.

[7] Hendrick, *Lees of Virginia,* p. 21. On western lands, see Lee to Samuel Adams, Chantilly, February 5, 1781, in Ballagh, ed., *Lee Letters,* II, 214–15. On his children, see Richard Henry to William Lee, Chantilly, July 12, 1772, and April 13, 1772, ibid., I, 70–72, 66.

toward Spartanism that he himself would practice during the darkest days of the revolutionary war. "Mr. Lee's fortune not being very ample and having a large family to support," a memorandum in his papers notes, he lived off payments sent him as a Continental Congressman from Virginia. To cut expenses he shopped for himself, and during a two-month period in late 1777 lived on wild pigeons which were sold for a few cents a dozen "and afforded but a scanty fare." Such sacrifice sustained the American cause, and in its way, Lee consoled himself, provided a legacy of freedom which would prove far more valuable to posterity than great nominal wealth alone.[8]

Lee's financial concerns were shared by other Tidewater Virginians who had seen their personal debts grow in the years after 1740. By the beginning of the revolutionary war, Virginians owed Great Britain more than two million pounds. Planter indebtedness resulted in part from spending habits that distinguished the eighteenth-century gentry from its American ancestors. The founding fathers of Virginia's aristocracy had arrived in the New World during the middle years of the seventeenth century, and began then to claim lands that would, they hoped, fulfill their aspirations for gentility. It was for land that the first American Lee left York County for the Northern Neck when it was still a frontier area held by Indians. But labor was needed to work the land; and planters finally found a stable source of labor in African slaves, who were imported in abundant numbers only after 1700. With black labor to work his extensive landholdings, Thomas Lee was able to break with the more modest style of his forefathers, and to build the elegant Stratford between 1725 and 1730.[9]

Time, however, proved that such family seats were built for the moment, not the ages. Though per capita wealth in the Chesapeake was probably rising in the 1760s and

[8] Memorandum and letter to Mrs. Hannah Corbin, Chantilly, March 17, 1778, ibid., I, 332n, 393.
[9] Emory G. Evans, "Planter Indebtedness and the Coming of the Revolution in Virginia," *William and Mary Quarterly* (*WMQ*), 3d Ser., XIX (1962), 511, 518–19; Bernard Bailyn, "Politics and Social Structure in Virginia," in James M. Smith, ed., *Seventeenth-Century America* (New York, 1959), pp. 90–115; Hendrick, *Lees of Virginia*, pp. 20–21, 48.

1770s, some gentlemen borrowed far more money than they could repay to sustain their lifestyle—and were able to secure credit in part because the region's economy was growing. The Tidewater was not therefore a victim simply of tobacco's capacity to "exhaust" the soil, as historians long believed. Planters practiced a primitive method of field rotation by which tobacco was grown on a plot for four years at most. Fields were then turned over to corn "as long as any will come," and thereafter abandoned to an encroaching forest from which they could be recalled after twenty years and devoted once again to tobacco. On the eve of the American Revolution the economy of the Chesapeake was, in any case, in a state of transition, as wheat culture increasingly took the place of tobacco. The change, Thomas Jefferson believed, was all for the better: the cultivation of tobacco was "productive of infinite wretchedness" while that of wheat, "besides cloathing the earth with herbage, and preserving its fertility," fed workers abundantly, required only moderate toil except at harvest time, and diffused "plenty and happiness among the people." Grain exports to Europe served to mitigate the effects of a depression in the tobacco trade during the 1760s; but income from tobacco and grain sales together failed to offset expenditures. As a result, George Washington testified in 1769, "many families are reduced, almost, if not quite, to penury and want," and estates were being sold daily for the discharge of debts. If they paid less for their purchases, planters might at least arrest the growth of indebtedness. In 1771 Richard Henry Lee was one of several Virginians who tried to found a cooperative "patriotic store" which, it was hoped, by circumventing the despised factors who served as retail agents for Scottish mercantile houses, could reduce costs by half. But the scheme failed and planters were left with a more painful solution to their financial stress—the abandonment of extravagance, a return to moderation and frugality.[10]

[10] The classic account is Avery Odelle Craven, *Soil Exhaustion as a Factor in the Agricultural History of Virginia and Maryland, 1606–1860* (Urbana, 1926), which was Vol. XXIII (March 1925) of the *University of Illinois Studies in the Social Sciences*. A more recent study, which criticizes sections of Craven's argument, is Carville V. Earle, *The Evolution of a*

Nor did the future promise much relief for Tidewater planters who foresaw increased competition from new and more fertile lands as the agricultural frontier pushed no longer northward from the James and York rivers, but west and south. To those like Lee whose home plantations were small and who were unwilling to migrate, the prospect was particularly threatening. Lee's sense that the old-settled sections were doomed lay behind his advice that brother William sell Greenspring, the historic plantation near Jamestown that William had acquired by his marriage in 1769 to Hannah Ludwell. William could invest the principal from such a sale, Richard Henry suggested, and, if need be, purchase at some later date new and better lands in another yet undefined region. Thus, too, Lee could argue in the 1790s that "the interior parts of the country with their new lands could much better afford to pay high taxes than the settlers of the exhausted lands."[11]

For four generations the Lees lived at Stratford, but in increasing duress. The effects did not hit all persons at once. In colonial cities, Christopher Gadsden once argued, artisans

---

Tidewater Settlement System; All Hallow's Parish, Maryland, 1650–1783 (Chicago, 1975). I am indebted for comments upon this section to Allan Kulikoff, who also generously allowed me to read his paper "The Rise of the Chesapeake Gentry," which he presented at the 1978 meeting of the Organization of American Historians, and a preliminary version of "The Economic Growth of the Eighteenth-Century Chesapeake Colonies," which was published in the *Journal of Economic History*, XXXIX (1979), 275–88. See also Emory G. Evans, "The Rise and Decline of the Virginia Aristocracy in the Eighteenth Century: the Nelsons," in Darrett B. Rutman, ed., *The Old Dominion* (Charlottesville, 1964), esp. pp. 67–70. Evans stresses both debt and an apparent decline in business competence among members of Virginia's mid-eighteenth-century gentry as reasons for its downfall. Jefferson's comments are in his *Notes on the State of Virginia*, ed. William Peden (Chapel Hill, 1955), pp. 166–68. Washington to George Mason, Mount Vernon, April 5, 1769, in John C. Fitzpatrick, ed., *The Writings of George Washington*, II (Washington, 1931), 501–03. Store: John Carter Matthews, "Richard Henry Lee and the American Revolution," Ph.D. dissertation, history, the University of Virginia, 1939, pp. 59–60; "Diary of Landon Carter," *WMQ*, 1st Ser., XIII (1904–05), 157–58.

[11] Lee to William Lee, Greenspring, January 25, 1778, in Ballagh, ed., *Lee Letters*, I, 382–83; Lee's speech reported in Edward S. Maclay, ed., *Journal of William Maclay, United States Senator from Pennsylvania, 1789–1791* (New York, 1890), p. 56.

and working people first felt the effects of economic stress. The equivalent group in the upper ranks of Virginia society was younger sons. Even in the best of times few of them could hope to achieve the wealth of their fathers; and their chances of downward mobility increased where families were large with several male heirs, and where the patrimonial estate was divided unequally among the children, as was true of the Lees. It was perhaps the fate of younger sons that inspired Richard Henry Lee's neighbor George Mason when he warned the federal constitutional convention that it must "provide no less carefully for the rights of the lowest than of the highest orders of citizens" because the "superior classes" would certainly within "a few years . . . distribute their posterity through the lowest classes of Society." The first of Thomas Lee's sons, Philip Ludwell Lee, was known for his arrogance: he treated "with equal disdain both negro and down-at-the-heel white man," lacked republican inclinations, and manifested "little public spirit in the face of epochal events." At the time of his death in 1775, he was, it is said, of Loyalist sympathies. The five Lee brothers active in the Revolution were all younger sons; and economic circumstance was integral to their lives and politics.[12]

With time, however, even the firstborn would feel the hurt. By the early nineteenth century Stratford's ceilings were falling in and its fields lay uncultivated, signs of a neglect and decay that rapidly ate away the outward signs of Virginia's aristocratic past. Stratford, with its two-foot-thick walls, survived nonetheless until modern restoration "returned" it to a state better in all likelihood than it had enjoyed for more than a few brief decades in the eighteenth century, if then. Meanwhile plantation lands were slowly parceled out to small wheat farmers, and most of the great planters' homesteads disappeared. "All that stands upright of that [once] imposing mansion is the kitchen chimney,"

[12] Gadsden statement, November 9, 1769, in Richard Walsh, *Charleston's Sons of Liberty, A Study of the Artisans, 1763–1789* (Columbia, S.C., 1959), pp. 53–54; Mason in James Madison's *Notes of Debates in the Federal Convention of 1787,* Adrienne Koch, ed. (New York, 1969), p. 40; Hendrick, *Lees of Virginia,* pp. 80, 87–89.

a mid-nineteenth-century traveler remarked of Chantilly. "Lee is gone, his house is in the dust, his garden a wild."[13]

Service to the public was no less an obligation of Virginia's upper order than commitment to family. From their earliest years in America the Lees were active in government. The first Richard Lee served as sheriff, as burgess, as member of the prestigious governor's council, and for a time as Governor William Berkeley's secretary of state ("the second most prominent position in Virginia"). That distinguished record was again exceeded by his grandson, Thomas, who attained the province's highest offices, serving as president of the council and, for a time, as acting governor.[14]

For Richard Henry Lee, then, public office followed naturally from station and tradition. After spending the years from 1743 to 1752 as a student at Wakefield Academy in Yorkshire, England, he returned to Stratford and continued reading in the classics and politics before becoming a justice of the peace in 1757. The following year, at age twenty-six, he first entered the House of Burgesses. Later he served in the Virginia provincial convention and in the Continental Congress, over which he presided from 1784 to 1786, and claimed a seat in the United States Senate from its first session until he retired from politics in 1792. Lee's place in history depends in good part upon his tireless service in these legislative bodies and their numerous committees. The demands imposed upon members of the Continental Congress in the late 1770s were especially straining. Lee complained in October 1777 that he scarce had time to perform one one-hundredth of his work: "My eyes fail me fast and I believe my understanding must soon follow this incessant toil." Here again he differed dramatically from his rival as

---

[13] Douglas Southall Freeman, *R. E. Lee, A Biography* (New York, 1934–35), I, 1, 11; Hendrick, *Lees of Virginia,* pp. 403–05; Craven, *Soil Exhaustion,* pp. 68, 121; account of Chantilly quoted in Lee, *Lee of Virginia,* p. 205.

[14] Hoffman, *Guide to the Lee Microfilm,* pp. 11–15.

Virginia's foremost opponent of Britain, Patrick Henry, whom Thomas Jefferson described as a lethargic legislator and committeeman, and who—a modern biography suggests —used the prominence gained by an occasional stirring speech to expand his law practice and build a fortune upon which he might establish his family's respectability.[15]

Lee had no profession beyond public service. Like Samuel Adams, he was for all practical purposes a professional politician. During times of need, he could see no way to improve his circumstances but through the public sphere— that is, by seeking ever more lucrative appointive offices. Early in his career Lee was particularly anxious to win a position on the Virginia council, whose members were better compensated than those in the House of Burgesses. In 1772, while explaining why he had "an eye to the deputy Secretarys place," he frankly avowed his financial motives, calculating for his brother William how much the secretary-ship was worth, and what part of that sum would go to the deputy. Lee even requested the post of Virginia stamp collector in a particularly embarrassing episode of 1764. Politics and government were his life; yet he lacked the quasi-religious sense of vocation that sustained Adams's similar commitment. Having pursued office in part for profit, and acutely conscious of others' avarice, he remained especially vulnerable to disillusionment. Politics, Lee remarked to a correspondent in 1791, was "generally speaking . . . the Science of fraud," and politicians were "the Professors of that Science."[16]

---

[15] Biographical information on Richard Henry Lee is drawn from Chitwood, *Lee;* Hoffman, *Guide to the Lee Microfilm,* esp. pp. 18–19; Matthews, "Lee," esp. pp. 61, 120–22, 191; and *The Dictionary of American Biography,* XI (1933), 117–20. Lee to Patrick Henry, York, Pa., October 8, 1777, in Ballagh, ed., *Lee Letters,* I, 325. On his Congressional career see also Paul Chadwick Bowers, Jr., "Richard Henry Lee and the Continental Congress: 1774-1779," Ph.D. dissertation, Duke University, 1965. On Henry, see Jefferson to William Wirt, August 4, 1805, *Pennsylvania Magazine of History and Biography,* XXXIV, 393; and also, more generally, Richard R. Beeman, *Patrick Henry, a Biography* (New York, 1974).

[16] Matthews, "Lee," p. 10, says members of the Virginia council received £600 sterling a year while burgesses earned fifteen shillings per day while the House of Burgesses was in session. Richard Henry to William Lee, Chantilly, July 12, 1772; and to Thomas Lee Shippen, Chantilly, September 21, 1791, in Ballagh, ed., *Lee Letters,* I, 72; II, 544.

Virginia politics imposed limits on the social isolation of the native aristocracy, forcing men of rank to court voters with more modest landholdings. As a burgess Lee supported measures designed to appeal to a broad constituency. In the fall of 1762, for example, he introduced a bill lowering franchise requirements, and soon thereafter brought in another for the relief of insolvent debtors. Lee's identity as a popular politician was defined, too, by his demand as a young legislator that the burgesses investigate the accounts of John Robinson, the powerful speaker of the House of Burgesses and colonial treasurer. That step had long-term implications for Lee's position in Virginia politics. As George Wythe later explained to John Adams, Robinson was "found deficient in large sums," which he had lent from the public treasury "to many of the most influential families of the country, who found themselves exposed," and who never forgave Lee.[17] But the attack on Robinson appealed to Lee's neighbors on the Northern Neck who remained too distant or too insignificant to share in the inner counsels and temptations of Williamsburg. It reinforced Lee's own self-image as a man of virtue, immune to the corruptions of power, and as the opponent of an indigenous "aristocracy" that sought to monopolize the rewards of government—in short, as a champion of the "many" against the privileged "few."

During the course of the revolutionary movement, the involvement of Virginia's upper orders with broader segments of her population became more intense as the elite assumed responsibility for mobilizing the people. Lee organized a demonstration at Montross, the Westmoreland County seat, on court day in September 1765. A carefully organized crowd exhibited, then hanged effigies of George Mercer, the Virginia stampman, and George Grenville, the British minister responsible for the Stamp Act. The event provides a splendid example of the oral and visual appeals

[17] On Virginia politics in general see Charles Sydnor, *Gentlemen Freeholders: Political Practices in Washington's Virginia* (Chapel Hill, 1952); and Rhys Isaacs, "Dramatizing the Ideology of Revolution: Popular Mobilization in Virginia, 1774 to 1776," *WMQ*, 3d Ser., XXXIII (1976), 357–85. Lee in the House of Burgesses: Matthews, "Lee," esp. pp. 11–12. Charles Francis Adams, ed., *The Works of John Adams* (Boston, 1850–56), X, 36–37.

used to mobilize the often illiterate populace of rural Virginia. Lee also initiated the Westmoreland Association of 1766, an organization of 114 militant opponents of the Stamp Act whose numbers included representatives of prominent families together with scores of more obscure persons, each of whom pledged "to obtain as many signers of the Association, as he possibly can." Then on February 28, 1766, the day after the association was formed, its members served as the nucleus of a 400-man crowd that forced Archibald Ritchie, a local Scottish merchant who had announced his willingness to clear vessels on stamped paper, to express remorse for his rash words and renounce any intention to uphold the Stamp Act. Lee and his closest political associates in the Northern Neck, including Richard Parker and Samuel Washington, organized that affair.[18]

Lee's involvement with the American cause was consistent with the identity he had assumed in Virginia politics, for he understood the colonists' cause as that of "Virtue and mankind." He was one of the first to oppose Britain's revised imperial policy. In May 1764, more than a year before the first colonial Stamp Act uprising, Lee confessed himself so "warmed" by Britain's plan to impose a stamp tax that he could hardly contain his rage. Could anyone question

---

[18] Montross: Chitwood, *Lee,* pp. 37–39; and description by John Mercer in *Virginia Gazette* (Purdie and Dixon), September 25, 1766. Westmoreland Association: Richard B. Harwell, ed., *The Committees of Safety of Westmoreland and Fincastle* . . . (Richmond, 1956), pp. 99–102; and John C. Matthews, "Two Men on a Tax: Richard Henry Lee, Archibald Ritchie, and the Stamp Act," in Rutman, ed., *The Old Dominion,* pp. 96–108. For the background of the Ritchie affair, see letters to Lee from Samuel Washington, February 22, and Richard Parker, February 23, 1766, as well as Lee's draft of the Westmoreland Association, in Paul P. Hoffman, ed., "Lee Family Papers, 1742–1795," University of Virginia Microfilm (Charlottesville, 1966), roll 1. Local feeling against Ritchie apparently ran very high. Washington found many of his neighbors "Ready at a moments Warning to Assist in any thing Destructive to [Ritchie] and his Intentions" to clear vessels on stamped paper. Ritchie "must have been mobd in the bear mentioning of such an Infamous Design" in most parts of the Northern Neck, he added. Parker agreed: "Even the women I believe would take arms if they were permitted." Before the confrontation at Leedstown occurred, Parker expressed fear that Ritchie might "arrive to such a state of despondency as to hang or drown himself and we shall be deprived of the Satisfaction of seeing the Wretch who so insolently defied his Country, mortified."

whether " 'the free possession of property, the right to be governed by laws made by our representatives, and the illegality of taxation without consent' " were "essential principles of the British constitution?" His initial response to the Townshend Revenue Act of 1767 was less certain—the law was "not perhaps, literally, a violation of our rights," he suggested in March 1768. But by 1770 his opposition had developed to the point that Parliament's exemption of the tea duty from its general repeal of the Townshend Act seemed to him only a contrivance by "vain, weak Ministers" intent on tyranny to "abuse" or mislead the Americans.[19] In this context Lee's failure to win Crown offices became understandable. Could a corrupted regime be expected to prefer members of that worthy family? Before they would find success "virtue must . . . drive vice and folly off the ground." Indeed, until British politics changed in such a way as would "enable a man of principle to ask a favor with consistency" the Lees could console themselves that their rightfulness lay behind their exclusion from favor: "we must wrap ourselves in our virtue and be contented," William Lee suggested in 1773.[20]

While William and Arthur Lee worked closely with the Wilkes movement in London, linking the cause of liberty in England with that in America through their participation and their extensive correspondence with colonists all along the Atlantic seaboard, Richard Henry fostered a sense of common plight among Americans. For him, Virginians' freedom was immediately threatened by the New York Restraining Act, the *Gaspée* commission in Rhode Island, the Boston Port Act. A prudent man, he argued, "should lend his assistance to extinguish the flames, which had invaded the house of his next door neighbour, and not coldly wait, until the flames had reached his own." The "Tyrannic Boston Port Bill" seemed to him above all "a most Violent

[19] Lee to Gen. Charles Lee, Williamsburg, July 6, 1776; to unnamed correspondent, Chantilly, May 31, 1764, and March 27, 1768; and to William Lee, Chantilly, July 7, 1770, in Ballagh, ed., *Lee Letters,* I, 206, 5–7, 27, 45–46.

[20] Lee to William Lee, Chantilly, July 9, 1770, in Ballagh, ed., *Lee Letters,* I, 52; William to Richard Henry Lee, Temple [London], February 14, 1773, Arthur Lee Papers, Houghton Library, Harvard University.

and dangerous Attem[pt] to destroy the constitutional liberty and rights of all British America," and he urged that a Continental Congress be called to devise the "most decisive" methods to secure those rights against "the Systimatic plan formed for their destruction."[21]

For Lee resistance to such measures was profoundly conservative. What might appear to some as "the overflowings of a seditious and disloyal madness," he assured Lord Shelburne in May 1769, were in reality loyal actions, representing "nothing more than a necessary and manly assertion, of social privileges founded in reason, guaranteed by the English constitution, and rendered sacred by a near two hundred years." Americans remained very "warmly attached" to Britain and wished her prosperity "with unfeigned heartiness." Independence long seemed to him unnecessary, incompatible with the purposes of even the most militant resistance. At the first Continental Congress, John Adams recalled, Lee assured New Englanders that the Americans would "infallibly carry all our points." Boston would be relieved; all of Britain's offensive acts would be repealed; "the army and fleet will be recalled, and Britain will give up her foolish project."[22]

He did not, however, shrink from evidence to the contrary. By April 1776, when the war was nearly a year old, he discussed independence not as a goal but as a fact, arguing in good Whig fashion that Britain's crimes had released Americans from the obligation of allegiance. And he went on to take, with his brothers, a most unconservative role in the constitutional debates of revolutionary Virginia. There the Lees stood battle against "a certain set of Aristocrats, for we have such monsters here," as Thomas Ludwell Lee complained on June 1, 1776, men who had delayed passage of Virginia's Bill of Rights by objecting to "the first line which declares all men to be born equally free and independent."

[21] Lee to unnamed correspondent, Chantilly, March 27, 1768; to Samuel Adams, Chantilly, February 4, 1773 (on the *Gaspée*); to Arthur Lee, Chantilly, June 26, 1774; and his resolutions of June 1774 in Ballagh, ed., *Lee Letters,* I, 26–27, 82–83, 114–18, 115n (quotations at 26, 114, 115n).

[22] Lee to Lord Shelburne, Chantilly, May 31, 1769, ibid., I, 37; Adams, ed., *Works of John Adams,* X, 278–79.

Twelve days later, on the urgings of his friends in Virginia, Richard Henry Lee left Congress to join battle against such "aristocrats" in the drafting of his home state's first constitution.[23]

Lee's views on government were not those of the self-conscious radical Thomas Paine, who would have invested all authority in an annually elected unicameral legislature. Like John Adams, Lee preferred a more complex set of institutions that would retain the governor and bicameral legislature of the colonial past, but would keep all incumbents in check by insisting upon short tenure in office. He thus ardently opposed Carter Braxton's proposal that Virginia's governors hold office on good behavior, its senators for life, which would have made those officials in effect life peers. Measured against an opponent so regressive in the context of 1776, when Americans demanded severe restraints on power and a rigid subjection of all authority to the will of the people, Lee's views could seem markedly democratic. He in fact recommended favorably the constitution Virginia adopted in June 1776, a document that reflected his views far more than Braxton's, as "very much of the democratic kind." In other ways, too, Lee approved democratic reforms the Revolution suggested, opposing all secret sessions of legislative bodies so the people could better survey their delegates, and avowing his willingness (in 1778) to approve an extension of the franchise to adult women who held lands of their own right.[24]

But if Lee was a popular leader of the American Revolution, if he helped to mobilize an insurgent people, publicly committed himself to the cause of the many over the few,

[23] Thomas Ludwell Lee to Richard Henry Lee, June 1, 1776, in Hoffman, ed., "Lee Family Papers," microfilm roll 2. For a similar reference to Virginia's "aristocrats" as those who supported Robinson, see Thomas Jefferson to William Wirt, Monticello, August 4, 1805, *Pennsylvania Magazine of History and Biography*, XXXIV, 388–89.

[24] Lee to Patrick Henry, Philadelphia, April 20, 1776; to Robert Carter Nicholas, Philadelphia, April 30, 1776; to General Charles Lee, Williamsburg, June 29, 1776; and to Hannah Corbin, Chantilly, March 17, 1778, in Ballagh, ed., *Lee Letters*, I, 179, 184, 203 (quotation), 392–94. Also Matthews, "Lee," pp. 160–63; Chitwood, *Lee*, pp. 21–22. For Braxton's plan, see Peter Force, ed., *American Archives*, 4th Ser., VI (Washington, 1846), 748–54.

and took seriously the right of even female property holders to be taxed only by representatives of their own choosing, there were distinct limits to his democracy. Where Samuel Adams was egalitarian in style—unassuming, common in manners and appearance—Lee carried himself with a dignity and perhaps even a hauteur that "seemed to the Lees only self-respect," as one of his biographers suggested. He never shared Adams's instinctual egalitarianism, Adams's faith in the ultimate good sense of the common people. Lee trusted instead patriotic men "of independent Circumstances . . . candid, temperate and sensible": these alone could serve the cause of a "regulated Liberty," free both of "the fury of a Mob" and of "the art, cunning, and industry of wicked, vicious and avaricious Men."[25] His democracy presupposed a society in which the mass of men deferred to and felt a common cause with their betters—as was the case in eighteenth-century Virginia, where white men of all ranks had pulled together under a native-born elite as the colony's slave population grew. Democratic commitment faltered once the British tried to irritate class divisions within the dominant race and indigenous groups seemed to threaten the rights of the propertied. ("The enemy affect to leave harmless the poor," Lee wrote in the low months of 1781, "and they take everything from those they call the rich.")[26] In the mid-1770s Lee urged that a rapid transition from extra-legal

[25] Matthews, "Lee," p. 399; Lee to Richard Lee Bland, Chantilly, February 5, 1794; and to Thomas Lee Shippen, Chantilly, February 12, 1794, in Ballagh, ed., *Lee Letters,* II, 564, 576.

[26] On the relative social cohesion of eighteenth-century white Virginia, see John C. Rainbolt, "The Alteration in the Relationship between Leadership and Constituents in Virginia, 1660 to 1720," *WMQ,* 3d Ser., XXVII (1970), 411–34, esp. 428–32; also Edmund S. Morgan, *American Slavery, American Freedom* (New York, 1975). There is evidence that this solidarity was shaken by religious divisions in the immediate pre-revolutionary era. See Rhys Isaacs, "The Evangelical Revolt: The Nature of the Baptists' Challenge to the Traditional Order in Virginia, 1765 to 1775," *WMQ,* 3d Ser., XXXI (1974), 345–68. Yet Lee saw white Virginians as united against Britain even before Lord Dunmore's proclamation of November 1775, which clearly drew whites together against the threat of black insurgency. See his letter to Samuel Adams, Virginia, February 4, 1775, in Ballagh, ed., *Lee Letters,* I, 127: "Among all ranks and Classes of people (a very few interested foreign Traders excepted) there appears great unanimity, and firmness of zeal in support of the American cause." But see also his letter to Arthur Lee, Epping Forest, June 4, 1781, ibid., II, 230 (quoted in text).

revolutionary government to established, regular institutions was essential for the repression of "popular commotions" and "anarchy" and so for the "preservation of society." Confronted with a set of "rude" people in the West, he favored the establishment of "strong toned government," such as that under the Northwest Ordinance of 1787, which he praised as "much more tonic than our democratic forms on the Atlantic." Two years later in the United States Senate he argued forcefully that American Presidents should be endowed with an elaborate honorific title "to keep up a proper respect"; even "the appearance of the affectation of simplicity" here seemed to him harmful. Lee "acted as a high priest through the whole of this idolatrous business," commented William Maclay, a more modern democrat who found the proposal absurd.[27]

In other ways the politics of the Lees, and particularly of Richard Henry Lee, remained clearly consistent during the great transformation from the 1760s to the 1780s. Throughout these decades they claimed the mantle of virtuous, self-sacrificing public spokesmen fighting the corrupt or privileged few. Just as Richard Henry had led the attack against Speaker John Robinson at the outset of his political career, so in the late 1770s and 1780s he and his youngest brothers repeatedly accused public servants—especially Silas Deane, Benjamin Franklin, and later Robert Morris—of mishandling public funds. The famous and embittered Deane-Lee controversy began with Arthur Lee's charges against Deane, a fellow commissioner to the court of Versailles, and continued as Deane published countercharges against the Lees, noting the number of offices they held, questioning their loyalty, suggesting to "the Free and Virtuous CITIZENS of AMERICA" that the Lees' fortune was being "raised upon the ruins of the general weal." Before the affair was over Deane as well as William and Arthur Lee were recalled from their diplomatic posts, Henry Laurens resigned as

[27] Lee to Robert Carter Nicholas, Philadelphia, April 30, 1770; to Patrick Henry, Philadelphia, April 20, 1776; to George Washington, New York, July 15, 1787; and to Col. Henry Lee, New York, July 30, 1787, in Ballagh, ed., *Lee Letters*, I, 184, 177; II, 425, 430; Maclay, ed., *Journal of William Maclay*, pp. 33, 37.

president of Congress, Thomas Paine (who, like Laurens, supported the Lees) was forced to leave his position as secretary to the Congress's committee on foreign affairs, and Congress divided into two warring factions throughout the better part of two years (1778–79).[28] The episode permanently shaped Richard Henry Lee's attitudes toward the national government and the fate of the American Revolution. Seeing themselves as quintessential patriots, the Lees identified their enemies as men who "do not 'mean the good of America'": thus Deane's support, Richard Henry Lee claimed, rested upon commercial plunder, ambition, and Toryism. When Congress failed to condemn the Lees' critics and to vindicate fully that family's honor, did it not announce to all its servants its disapproval of "real ability" and integrity? "I must confess," a distraught Richard Henry Lee wrote in October 1779, "that I entertain a bad opinion of any man who will serve Congress while such sentiments are suffered to exist in that body."[29]

A man whose democracy was so tinctured with elitism, and who remained so prone to disillusionment, could hardly ride the crest of popular revolution as did his old friend in Boston. "The love of liberty has fled from hence to France," Lee wrote in September 1789, when he expected that the Third Estate, having gained "a complete triumph over the Nobles and the Clergy," would go on calmly "to establish a Constitution much like the English." But he soon found the French Revolution intolerable. After the execution of Louis XVI, and after the Jacobins seemed to outrage "all decency and justice" by confiscating British and Dutch trading vessels, Lee decided that France's leaders (like his own enemies in America) sought not freedom but "wealth and power." That old champion of American independence then hoped "the British Lion" would "claw these fellows hand-

---

[28] Quotation from Deane's letter in the *Pennsylvania Packet,* December 5, 1778. For a particularly good account of the Deane-Lee affair, see Jack N. Rakove, *The Beginnings of National Politics: An Interpretive History of the Continental Congress* (New York, 1979).

[29] Lee to James Searle, Chantilly, July 24, 1779, Lee Family Papers (9019), University of Virginia Library, Charlottesville; to Arthur Lee, Freestone, Virginia, February 11, 1779, in Ballagh, ed., *Lee Letters,* II, 30; to James Searle, Chantilly, October 15, 1779, Haverford College.

somely for their misdoing." "I heartily wish the French as much Liberty as they can bare," he wrote in 1794, "but I do not believe that the present rulers design it for them therefore I hope that in Gods good time they will all be hanged."[30]

Lee's claim to a place in history clearly owes little to the latter stages of his public life. Like others of his generation, his career reached its peak in 1776, and more particularly in June of that year. It was then that Lee followed his own instincts as well as his state's instructions, and moved those resolutions the Continental Congress adopted on July 2, 1776, declaring that "these United Colonies are, and of right ought to be, free and independent States."

The mystery of Richard Henry Lee may well be not why he became no more radical than he did, but why he became a revolutionary at all. Certainly the basis of his commitment to the American cause was distinct from that of other Old Revolutionaries. He did not, first of all, become a revolutionary from the weight of family or local tradition, as did Samuel Adams. Lee's ancestors were not Puritans, not early participants in England's revolutionary or "Whig" tradition. They were Anglicans and Tories. His great-grandfather had laid the family's fortune in America as a supporter of the Stuarts and of their local agent, Governor William Berkeley; his grandfather continued his fealty to James II even after the Glorious Revolution of 1688, and for a time lost his position on the Virginia council for refusing to take an oath to William and Mary. Yet Richard Henry Lee readily identified himself as a Whig, and participated in a revolution that seemed to him founded upon "motives of sound whiggism."[31]

---

[30] Lee to Francis Lightfoot Lee, New York, September 13, 1789; to Thomas Lee Shippen, Chantilly, April 15, 1793, and also February 12, 1794, in Ballagh, ed., *Lee Letters,* II, 501, 556–57, 576–77.

[31] Hendricks, *Lees of Virginia,* pp. 17–18, 34, 42; Lee to Thomas Jefferson, Chantilly, July 8, 1779, in Ballagh, ed., *Lee Letters,* II, 82.

Nor did class antagonisms like those of Dr. Thomas Young fuel his radicalism. Lee's crusades against "the few" were less against a social than a moral class, against those "corrupt" persons who sought to confine power and the material rewards of office to themselves and their friends. Because Lee was an advantaged son from a landed family, similar to the New York gentry against whom Young had defined his politics, their shared fervor for the American cause is particularly intriguing.

Lee, like the New York Sons of Liberty, was acutely conscious of the economic implications of freedom. His writings reveal a concern with the simple and immediate costs of British taxation far more than do those of most other revolutionary leaders, as one might expect of a man whose straitened circumstances had long demanded careful attention in matters of finance. The peril of British taxation, he argued, was not to him alone but to all Virginians. If the Stamp Act were implemented, Lee wrote in 1766, it would probably take from his "poor Country at least fifty thousand Sterling per year," which was "twice as much as all the Taxes laid by our own Assem[bly] have ever yet amounted to, and which must ruin us all." He was less immediately affected by British trade regulations than was Isaac Sears; still, his brother William and, to a lesser extent, he himself were involved in commerce. As an educated and articulate colonist he expressed his fears for the future with clarity and precision. "To what purpose," he asked John Dickinson of Pennsylvania in 1768, do merchants toil and "people labor for wealth, if Arbitrary will, uninfluenced by reason, and urged by interest, shall reap the harvest of their diligence and industry?" Security of property was a prerequisite of entrepreneurship and so of economic growth; and the protection of property was a critical component of liberty.[32]

In later years Lee went beyond this traditional identification of liberty with prosperity, arguing that "the free nature and genius of commerce abhors and shuns restraint, and

---

[32] Lee's address, "A Virginia Planter" to the people of Virginia, 1766, in "Lee Family Papers," microfilm roll 2, where it is misdated as 1776; Lee to John Dickinson, Chantilly, November 26, 1768, in Ballagh, ed., *Lee Letters,* I, 30.

that in young commercial States, to embarrass Trade with heavy imposts or other clogs, is effectually to demolish it." Yet he never abandoned his firm commitment to liberty as above all a moral state, and developed an acute suspicion of any commercial interest. "The Spirit of Commerce is a Spirit of Avarice," he wrote in 1785, one that would seize whatever power it could "to monopolise, to engross, and to take every possible advantage." Nor had he patience for the new "liberal" theories of *laissez-faire*. He scoffed at the "Mandevilles . . . who laugh at virtue, and with vain ostentatious display of words . . . deduce from vice" or the pursuit of self-interest "the public good." Such men, he claimed, were "much fitter to be Slaves in the corrupt, rotten despotisms of Europe, than to remain citizens of young and rising republics."[33]

Ultimately it was this moral stance, this identification of family and self with the side of virtue and against the forces of selfishness and corruption, already clear in the Robinson episode, that inclined the Lees toward the colonial side in the early stages of the Anglo-American conflict. That commitment may have wavered briefly in 1764, when Lee applied for the stamp collectorship; but repeated failure to win Crown appointments only reinforced his and his brothers' conviction that the British regime was "rotten," distributing offices only to buy or reward its "tools."

To resist such rulers remained for Lee a conservative act. It was a means of preserving the British constitution, of protecting legal privileges justified by two centuries of British history. Independence by contrast imposed a radical break with the past. The inauguration of a republic, which gave revolutionary content to what was otherwise a colonial rebellion, was a yet more extreme step. It represented an effort to establish what all tradition had dismissed as utopian, a form of government that could exist only in the pure realm of thought, not in the corrupted field of human reality. Lee's willingness to go beyond resistance, to accept the revolutionary implications of events and commit himself to inde-

[33] Lee to James Monroe, Chantilly, January 5, 1784; to unnamed correspondent, New York, October 10, 1785; and to Henry Laurens, Chantilly, June 6, 1779, in ibid., II, 289, 389, 62–63.

pendence and the republic, requires special explanation. The problem of interpreting his commitment and the leadership role Virginia's Tidewater elite took in the American Revolution is like that of explaining any aristocrat's support of revolution. Privileges won by birth and advantaged positions in society would seem to make such men partisans of the established order, to immunize them from the "disease" of revolution. Yet, progressive nobles have often taken major roles in championing fundamental reform; and the participation of such men may be far from unlikely if, as in the case of Lee, they found little sustenance in the prerevolutionary world. Lee's role in the American Revolution, even the language with which he explained his political convictions, was founded, in short, upon a profound and far-reaching alienation from his native Virginia, one that began in his fundamental dislike of the colony's labor system.

Lee's political writings are marked by a repeated emphasis upon the fate of men who lost their liberty and were thereby "enslaved." The theme appears in his first writings on the Stamp Act: were Americans denied their right to be taxed only with their consent, by representatives of their own choosing, they would become "the slaves of five hundred masters," the Members of Parliament. Resistance to Britain was for him above all resistance to slavery, "which both reason and experience prove to be productive of the greatest human evils." Britain's loss of her American empire he found "a very fit consequence of the foolish and wicked attempt to reduce to slavery so many free, useful, and affectionate friends."[34] Others of course also wrote of the threat of slavery; in Whig political thought that term was a technical one, for an ultimate state of unfreedom. But for Lee the menace took on a striking literalness and urgency. If the Stamp Act were implemented, he told "The Good People of Virginia" in an address of 1766, "your wives and Children are to be [ma]de Slaves and your estates taken from you by

---

[34] Lee to unnamed correspondent, Chantilly, May 31, 1764; to James Monroe, Chantilly, January 5, 1784; and to Thomas Jefferson, Philadelphia, May 3, 1779, in ibid., I, 6; II, 287, 54.

viole[nce w]ithout your consent." And he lived to see, or believe he saw, his predictions realized. Only the "refusal of the India Company on account of the difficulty and delay" prevented the British "Villains from sending American prisoners to the East Indies for slaves," he wrote Patrick Henry in April 1777. "And that being refused, they were on the verge of sending such of them to Africa as were in England." Still some persons sought submission to these "Devils"! "For Heaven's sake," he urged, "let every nerve be strained to expel them from North America. They contaminate the air they breathe."[35]

Lee opposed black slavery well before he opposed Britain. From his earliest days in the House of Burgesses he favored imposing impediments upon the slave trade, personally introducing proposals for taxing imported slaves in both 1769 and 1774. These proposals could have been self-serving —if importation of slaves had been ended, the value of those already owned by Tidewater planters would have risen as new planters in the West were forced to purchase their labor force in a more restricted market.[36] Lee, however, went on to condemn slavery itself. That institution injured the Africans, whom he described as "fellow creatures . . . created as ourselves, and equally entitled to liberty and freedom by the great law of nature." Like his brother Arthur, who wrote at least three essays against slavery, Lee also acknowledged the danger of uprisings on the part of a people whose interests contradicted those of their owners. Men who "observed their masters possessed of a liberty denied to them"

[35] Lee as "A Virginia Planter," in "Lee Family Papers," roll 2; and to Patrick Henry, Philadelphia, April 15, 1777, in Ballagh, ed., Lee Letters, I, 275. Lee's fears had some basis in fact. See Danske Dandridge, American Prisoners of the Revolution (Charlottesville, 1911), pp. 92, 138–60.

[36] Chitwood, Lee, pp. 17–21, and Richard K. MacMaster, "Arthur Lee's 'Address on Slavery': An Aspect of Virginia's Struggle to End the Slave Trade, 1765–1774," Virginia Magazine of History and Biography, LXXX (1972), esp. 148, 151. For Gov. Francis Fauquier's interpretation of the controversy over the slave trade as one between "old settlers who have breed great quantities of slaves . . . and the rising generation who want slaves and don't care to pay the Monopolists for them at the price they have lately bore," see Matthews, "Lee," p. 6.

and to their children, he wrote, must be "natural enemies to society" and to its peace and security.[37]

To the arguments of a moralist and civil realist he added those of an economist. Here Lee's dislike of slavery was part of his larger disagreement with the course of Virginia history in the eighteenth century, when, as leading planter families rose to ever greater wealth and power on the proceeds of slave labor, white immigration dwindled, and old Virginians of European origin but modest fortune chose to leave their home colony, seeking fortunes elsewhere in America. This development, Lee argued, had not served Virginia well. "Some of our neighbouring colonies, though much later than ourselves in point of settlement, are now far beyond us in improvement," he noted. "To what . . . can we attribute this strange, this unhappy truth?" Nature had not endowed them with "superiour fertility of soil, nor do they enjoy more of the sun's cheering and enlivening influence; yet greatly have they outstript us." Lee's explanation was simple —"*that with their whites they import arts and agriculture, whilst we, with our blacks, exclude both.*" Slavery, he believed, robbed its victims of all incentive for initiative and industry, leaving only "ignorance and idleness" in its wake.[38] Other Virginians agreed—George Mason, for example, the freeholders of Hanover County, or those of Prince George County who resolved in June 1774 that "the African trade is injurious to this colony, obstructs the population of it by freemen, prevents manufacturers and other useful emigrants from Europe from settling amongst us, and occasions an annual encrease of the balance of trade against this colony."[39]

The argument ignored the disincentive Virginia's land system posed to white immigration. Tidewater planters owned much of the Old Dominion's western lands, which

[37] Lee's speech on slavery in Richard Henry Lee, *Memoir of the Life of Richard Henry Lee*, I (Philadelphia, 1825), 17–19. See also Chitwood, *Lee*, pp. 18–19; MacMaster, "Arthur Lee's 'Address on Slavery.'"

[38] Hendrick, *Lees of Virginia*, pp. 71–73; Lee speech in Lee, *Memoir of . . . Richard Henry Lee*, I, 17–18; Lee's draft (October 1774) of a Congressional address to the people of Quebec, quoted in Chitwood, *Lee*, p. 73.

[39] Citations in MacMaster, "Arthur Lee's 'Address on Slavery,'" pp. 145, 152.

meant that white immigrants to Virginia (as to parts of upstate New York) faced the prospect of becoming tenants, while elsewhere they might acquire freehold land. Moreover, while Lee and other Virginians assumed Africans were unfitted for craft occupations, white artisans in Charleston were complaining of Negro competition.[40]

More important here, Lee's argument against slavery was but one of a series of criticisms of Virginia that ranged from the grand to the trivial. The colonial government of Virginia, for example, never evoked the same sense of pride and commitment from Lee that the Massachusetts colonial "constitution" awoke in Samuel Adams. In a careful disquisition of 1766 to Arthur Lee, Richard Henry described Virginia's institutions as similar but inferior to those of Britain. Within the next decade he, like other colonists, became disillusioned with the British constitution. Even so his opinion of Virginia's government failed to improve. "However imperfect the English plan was," he wrote in May 1776, "yet our late Government in Virginia was infinitely worse." He found the College of William and Mary unsuitable for his children (too little attention was given to students' learning and morals); and not only was Virginia's economy backward compared to those of her northern neighbors, but his own home on the Northern Neck was so far from the world of affairs that he had to beg news from others "in the high road of intelligence" like Boston. To make matters still worse, the place was unhealthy. Fevers and agues endemic to the lowlands afflicted Lee throughout his life, leaving him and his family dependent upon "Peruvian" or "Jesuit Bark" that contained quinine, but was at times hard to come by in the relatively isolated reaches of northern Virginia.[41]

---

[40] On the land system in Virginia, see Willard F. Bliss, "The Rise of Tenancy in Virginia," *The Virginia Magazine of History and Biography,* LVIII (1950), 427–41. Christopher Gadsden to William Henry Drayton, Charleston, June 1, 1778, in Richard Walsh, ed., *The Writings of Christopher Gadsden* (Columbia, S.C., 1966), pp. 126–27.

[41] Lee to Arthur Lee, Chantilly, December 20, 1766; to Edmund Pendleton, May 12, 1766; to William Lee, Chantilly, July 12, 1772 (on William and Mary); to Samuel Adams, Chantilly, January 18, 1780 (on his remoteness); and to Arthur Lee, Baltimore, February 17, 1777 (on "Jesuit Bark"), in Ballagh, ed., *Lee Letters,* I, 18–22, 191, 70–71; II, 171; I, 258.

When challenged, he was hard put to "sell" Virginia. After his brother Arthur announced an intention to settle in England, Lee answered that "America . . . has a parent's claim to her descendants," particularly to "the best of her sons," who were possessed of "arts and learning," and she had "a right to insist that they shall not fix in any place, where, by so doing, they may add strength to cruel and tyrannical oppression." Was it then America, not Virginia, that claimed his patriotism so early as July 1765? Fifteen years later when events conspired to bring Arthur across the Atlantic once again, Richard Henry suggested that he settle outside his home state. "Your friends," he wrote, "think that Boston or Philadelphia will be the best Theatres for the display of your law powers. They are certainly much superior places to this country in that Line." Nor did he seek to continue the ties that bound William Lee to Virginia, but persistently advised him to sell Greenspring.[42]

What kept Richard Henry Lee in Virginia? The authority and status conferred upon him as a Lee, perhaps; habit, and the convenience of settled living arrangements. Yet his letters reveal little joy in family life. Even positive references to Chantilly suggest his thoughts were centered elsewhere: as soon as he could "quit the entertainment of my prattling fireside, when I have heard every little story and settled all points," he wrote William Whipple in 1778, "I shall pay a visit to Williamsburg where our Assembly is now sitting." Again a year later he indicated that the pleasures of home were less in what it offered than in what it lacked—"Wicked, perverse or foolish Politicians . . . whose misconduct makes us fear for the safety of the Country." For long periods of time he remained at the Continental Congress, without wife or children, yet left no evidence of the desperate need for news from home that appears repeatedly in Samuel Adams's and Josiah Bartlett's private correspondence or of the homesickness, the acute loneliness, the outspoken preference for his homeland over the several seats of Congress that charac-

---

[42] Lee to Arthur Lee, July 4, 1765, and April 24, 1780; to William Lee, Chantilly, January 8, 1771, and Greenspring, January 25, 1778, in ibid., I, 10–11; II, 177; I, 54, 382–83; Lee, *Lee of Virginia,* pp. 235–36.

terized Cornelius Harnett, a fellow Old Revolutionary from Wilmington, North Carolina. His most acute complaints were reserved for Richmond, a "filthy place" where the Virginia assembly met after independence, and whose "noxious water and air" left him ill for several days in May 1783 and impaired his health for years thereafter. He lacked George Washington's fascination with agriculture; nor was Lee attracted to the pastoral, intellectual, and artistic pastimes that drew Jefferson to Monticello. There is, moreover, no reason to think that the gay social life posterity associates with Tidewater Virginia particularly pleased him: he commended at most the "sensible social evenings" spent by the inhabitants of another plantation, Liberty Hall. When Lee threatened to retire, it was less for the attractions of home than from a disillusionment with public life—less a pull than a push. "The hasty, unpersevering, aristocratic genius of the south," he once wrote John Adams, "suits not my disposition, and is inconsistent with my ideas of what must constitute social happiness and security."[43]

As long as he remained in Virginia, however, the problems of his homeland could hardly remain external to him. He was himself too much a Virginian, too much caught up in the traditions and circumstances of that colony, to be simply an observer of its plight. Instead he remained trapped in the contradictions between his ideals or those set by his society and the conditions of his life. Lee was, for example, an opponent of slavery who owned slaves. His father left him some forty bondsmen over ten years of age in 1750, and Lee himself passed on several slaves to his own heirs four and a half decades later. During his lifetime he lived in part off the rent others paid for the use of slaves he owned. He and his brother William also participated fully in the buying and selling of Africans. "I do not see how I could *in justice to my family* refuse any advantages that might arise from

---

[43] Lee to William Whipple, Chantilly, November 29, 1768, and June 26, 1779; to R. Wormley Carter, Richmond, June 3, 1783 (on Richmond); and also to Patrick Henry, New York, February 14, 1785; to General William Whipple, Chantilly, November 29, 1778 (on social life); and to John Adams, Chantilly, October 8, 1779, in Ballagh, ed., *Lee Letters,* I, 454; II, 80–81, 282, 331; I, 454; II, 155.

the selling of them" as long as the slave trade continued, Lee explained in May 1773. A similar rationalization probably lay behind his application for the stamp distributorship in 1764—that as long as the Act was to be enforced, he might profit from it as well as another since he had a large family to support upon a small estate.[44]

How valid was such a plea? Honor in Virginia demanded "independent means," that is, wealth sufficient to free its owner from the need for outside support; and Lee himself put his trust in men of "independent circumstances." Such an "independency" was manifest, for example, in the largess of Christopher Gadsden, the Charleston merchant and revolutionary leader who claimed in later life that he had never accepted payment for public service except during his years in the Continental Congress. But even as a burgess, one critic claimed, Lee demanded every farthing of recompense due him. Still he found the cost of attending the assembly high and scrambled for better-paying jobs, pleading with increasing explicitness his familial needs. Such efforts suggested that he lacked the critical "independency." And was service to family an adequate excuse for disservice to the public? Lee could and did argue that his appointment to the Virginia council would serve at once his own and the public's best interest—an argument repeated later by William and Arthur in their quest for diplomatic posts—but his application for a position under the Stamp Act made his motives suspect. Was lust for office in the name of family perhaps just another form of corruption—like that which New Englanders charged to Thomas Hutchinson?[45]

[44] Matthews, "Lee," p. 6; Chitwood, *Lee,* p. 19. On his leasing of slaves as well as lands, see the account lists annexed to Richard Parker's letter to Lee, March 7, 1776, in "Lee Family Papers," microfilm roll 2. Lee to William Lee, May 1773, cited in Chitwood, *Lee,* p. 21 (italics mine); see also the charge of "An Enemy to Hypocrisy," *Virginia Gazette* (Purdie and Dixon), July 18, 1766.

[45] Gadsden as "A Steady Federalist," January 30, 1797, in Walsh, ed., *Gadsden Writings,* pp. 279–80; accusations of John Mercer in *Virginia Gazette* (Purdie and Dixon), September 25, 1766; Lee to William Lee, Williamsburg, December 17, 1769; and, on his pleas for offices, to James Abercrombie, Westmoreland County, August 27, 1762 ("the desire I have to do my country good service, is my only motive for this solicitation"); to William Lee, Chantilly, July 9, 1770 ("the power of checking ill, and

Lee's enemies certainly saw him as far from the virtuous ideal he affected. They wrote of him in the *Virginia Gazette* as one "Bob Booty," as the embodiment of hypocrisy; they claimed he had attacked Speaker Robinson not from disinterested principles but because he himself craved Robinson's place, and attributed Lee's attacks upon Stampman Mercer not to patriotism but to envy and disappointment, Mercer having won the office Lee had sought. This contradiction between Lee's affirmation of virtue, of disinterested sacrifice for an all-encompassing public good, and his regular endorsement of policies that would benefit primarily his family or his kind—as in his opposition to the slave trade, his effort to convince tenants to pay their rents in gold or produce rather than inflation-prone legal currency (which nearly cost him his Congressional seat in 1777), or his advocacy in the 1790s of shifting the tax burden toward new settlers in the West—accounts for the common distrust of Lee, for the violently contradictory judgments he and his brothers provoked. To his son-in-law, Charles Lee, Richard Henry Lee was "the best of men," but William Maclay had once considered him "the worst of men."[46]

Lee's actions during the demonstration he staged against Mercer in September 1765—surely among the most bizarre of the revolutionary period—suggest that he was profundly torn by the contradiction of being at once an opponent of slavery and a slave owner, a proponent of virtue and a seeker of the spoils of office. That pageant was introduced by two of Lee's slaves who carried long clubs and wore clothes modeled after those of the radical John Wilkes's followers in England. Next, according to a detailed newspaper account, appeared a "confused rabble of other Negroes, and Whites of the lowest rank," followed by a "main guard" that carried in a cart the effigies of Mercer and Grenville. Those effigies were later hung, then burned by Lee's own

---

the means of doing good" occur "oftener in our upper than in our lower house"), and July 12, 1772 (family need); and to Arthur Lee, February 24, 1775 (the public wisdom of his being appointed to the council) in Ballagh, ed., *Lee Letters,* I, 40, 1–2, 52, 72, 131.
[46] "An Enemy to Hypocrisy," *Virginia Gazette* (Purdie and Dixon), July 18, 1766; Charles Lee quoted in Chitwood, *Lee,* p. 225; Maclay, ed., *Journal of William Maclay,* p. 72.

Negroes, who appeared in their "birthday suits" to play the roles of jailers, sheriffs, constables, bailiffs, and hangman. Behind Mercer's image came Lee himself, assuming the role of "ordinary, to take his confession, and publish his last speech and dying words." Finally this motley parade "was closed by those ranks and degrees of people generally . . . known . . . by the appelation of Tag Rag and Bobtail."[47]

But the Stampman's effigy, according to two of Lee's opponents, was a thinly disguised image of Lee himself into which (to adopt modern terminology) he projected his own guilt. Lee "fabricated a meagre effigy, created after his own likeness, and inspired with his own soul." That effigy, another account explained, was "six feet, and the breadth thereof six inches (that is to say, of [Lee's] own size)."[48] In one hand it held a sign saying "MONEY is my GOD," in the other a second that proclaimed "SLAVERY I LOVE!" Those statements, like the "dying words" written for the effigy by Lee and publicly read by him, took on a very personal meaning: they represented, in effect, a confession. At the same time, since the effigy was executed, the demonstration provided a purgation of guilt. "Gentlemen," the effigy's last words began,

> Sincerity becomes a man who is on the verge of eternity, however crafty he may have been in the former part of his life. . . . It is true that with parricidal hands I have endeavoured to fasten chains of slavery on this my native country, although, like the tenderest and best of mothers, she has long fostered and powerfully supported me. But it was the inordinate love of gold which led me astray from honour, virtue, and patriotism. . . .

[47] Lee probably provided the brief account of the Montross demonstration that appeared in the *Maryland Gazette Supplement,* October 17, 1765. Further details, apparently denied by neither Lee nor his supporters, were provided by John Mercer, the Stampman's father, who claimed to have received them from a spectator, in the *Virginia Gazette* (Purdie and Dixon), September 26, 1766.

[48] "An Enemy to Hypocrisy" in *Virginia Gazette* (Purdie and Dixon), July 18, 1766; and also account in ibid., July 25, 1766. The "Enemy to Hypocrisy" was James Mercer, the Stampman's brother: see ibid., October 3, 1766.

RICHARD HENRY LEE   *197*

To this statement Lee appended a Latin quotation from Virgil's *Aeneid* that had little meaning for the marginally literate courthouse crowd but much for him: *"Quid non mortalia pectora cogis auri sacra fames?"*—To what do you not drive man's heart, O accursed lust for gold? Then he added, in English, another allusion to slavery, the fruit of corruption: "Jove fix'd it certain that whatever day makes man a slave, takes half his worth away."

It is tempting to conclude that all the accusations of corruption hurled out by the Lees over a quarter century in politics were built upon their own guilt, and that in 1776 Richard Henry Lee simply extended to Britain the shame he had projected upon an effigy eleven years earlier. He attributed to the mother country just those traits he found most troubling in himself, above all a corrupt avarice that threatened the freedom of others, that sustained or encouraged the spread of slavery. Yet while inner conflicts founded in historical circumstances added emotional force and direction to his politics, his conversion to independence was slow and careful, not impulsive and mechanistic. Lee's views of Britain developed in response to events external to him, including news from England that often arrived through his youngest brothers, such that his espousal of independence resembled chronologically that of Old Revolutionaries elsewhere. In a curious way, devotion to family—part of Lee's dilemma—may have militated against a rapid acceptance of independence. Arthur and William Lee had, during the 1760s and 1770s, achieved prominence in English radical politics. William was particularly proud of having become the first American alderman of the City of London. Such an honor was achieved through opposition to the Crown and with the support of men who sympathized with the American cause. Still, independence effectively concluded such claims to dignity and fame, ending once and for all the common nationality upon which Americans might participate in English politics.

How then could Lee resolve the contradictions implicit in his position as a man of good family but inadequate means? The notion of virtue provided a way to sever honor from the material means it had come to imply in Virginia society, and so to ease the transition from wealth to parsimony that was or would be the fate of so many Virginians of good birth. Already as a young man Lee had been struck by the characteristics of ancient Greeks. "The love of poverty, contempt of riches, disregard of self interest, attention to publick good, desire of glory, love of their country" and above all "zeal for liberty"—these, he stressed, were principles that "cannot be repeated too often," for they had brought strength, allowing Sparta and Athens to hold off the invasions of Darius and Xerxes. By making the cause of such virtue his own in Virginia politics, and by participating in a revolutionary movement that stressed sacrifice and the priority of public over private interests, Lee came to see ever more clearly that there was an honor and contentment in poverty greater even than in wealth. "Those who sail gently down the smooth stream of prosperity," he wrote Samuel Adams in February 1776, "are very apt to lose that energetic virtue so necessary to true happiness." Wisdom and moderation, it seemed, were best learned "in the school of adversity."[49]

For the generation raised at Stratford in its golden age, the renunciation of means was difficult. Witness William Lee's lamentation of 1773: "I certainly feel that virtue is its own reward. But at the same time I cannot but be sensible, that narrowness of circumstance is a very great obstacle." The new linkage of poverty, merit, and honor would, however, serve the South and the Lees well in the darkest hours of the next century, as Robert E. Lee suggested on Christmas 1861, when he wrote his wife from Savannah, reflecting on the homestead his family had then long since lost, finding consolation in those thoughts from the miseries of the Civil War. "In the absence of a home," he wrote,

> I wish I could purchase Stratford. That is the only other place that I could go to, now accessible to us, that would inspire me with feelings of pleasure and local love. You

---

[49] Page 25 of Lee's reading notes, which probably date from the early 1760s, in "Lee Family Papers," microfilm roll 1; Lee to Samuel Adams, Chantilly, February 7, 1776, in Ballagh, ed., *Lee Letters*, I, 167–68.

and the girls could remain there in quiet. It is a poor place, but we could make enough corn and bacon for our support and the girls could weave us clothes.[50]

The values he expressed were those neither of Tidewater Virginia in the mid-eighteenth century nor of the "Cavalier" society imagined and idealized in the antebellum South, but they spoke to the human needs of the old South's first families. Only when the critical link between honor and wealth was broken, it seems, could the later Lees develop, at last, a sense of place.

And so the appeal of New England, which was important for Richard Henry Lee less as an actual location (he may never have visited the northeastern colonies) than as an ideal. New England stood for a society in which wealth and display were of little significance, where merit alone distinguished man from man. It was free of the contradictions imposed upon him as a Virginian. He knew it perhaps through reading and reputation, but above all his sense of New England was derived from its fruits, the New Englanders Lee met at the Continental Congress. In Samuel Adams particularly he found a man free of pretense, poor but unconcerned with gold, devoted to his family but unwilling to intervene for the advancement even of an only son—a man honored for his patriotism and unencumbered by contradiction. In a New England defined by such men there lay an honorable solution to a problem that confronted Lee and others like him in the eastern sections of the Northern Neck, for New England, like the ancient Greece Lee also idealized, offered even children without inherited wealth a way to rank and dignity through their virtue and ability.

In this sense, Richard Henry Lee's love of New England was a measure of the social content of his radicalism—a measure, that is, both of its limits and of its substance. He had no expectation, as did Thomas Young, that a society ordered according to merit rather than inherited status would

---

[50] William to Richard Henry Lee, Temple [London], February 14, 1773, Arthur Lee Papers, Harvard; Robert E. Lee in Hendrick, *Lees of Virginia,* p. 404.

be dramatically different from that of colonial days. Quite the opposite. Who were more likely to produce educated, capable, dedicated leaders than families such as the Lees? Virtue for him, as for some other Old Revolutionaries such as Gadsden, implied a social stability, a willingness on the part of people to remain within their allotted ranks rather than imperil the commonweal for their own interests or ambitions. The scrambling of new men (the Deanes, the Morrises) for wealth and influence in the late 1770s and the 1780s confounded his dream. It seemed to witness a debasement of morality, evidence of an alarming spread of avarice. And so he endorsed the state's continued role in supporting religion as "the guardian of morals," even as more advanced Virginians pressed for total separation of church and state.[51] Here again he resembled his beloved New Englanders, who clung to their established church longer than did their more "enlightened" compatriots in the Middle Colonies and the South.

Still, men like Lee were hardly conservative revolutionaries, dedicated only to preserving Virginia's past. Their Virginia was by nature too impermanent to afford men like Lee the "social happiness and security" they sought. The task they faced was to wrest from instability a more satisfying world. If Lee abandoned the prospect of personal migration, he could still hope to resolve his own dilemmas and those of his family not by independence alone but through a larger moral redefinition that for him and others was integral to the Revolution of 1776—by refashioning all America after his image of a sober, diligent, meritocratic Northeast. Thus it was that the ways of New England, which for Richard Henry Lee as for Samuel Adams came to represent the hope and meaning of a new American republic, had great appeal to a Virginian of good family, but poor prospects.

[51] Lee to James Madison, Trenton, November 26, 1784, in Ballagh, ed., *Lee Letters,* II, 304.

CHAPTER FIVE

———◦◦◦◦———

CHARLES CARROLL
OF CARROLLTON,
DUTIFUL SON AND
REVOLUTIONARY
POLITICIAN

THERE HANGS A PORTRAIT of Charles Carroll of Carrollton in the manuscripts division of the Maryland Historical Society in Baltimore—a copy by Michael Laty based, the inscription reads, upon an earlier painting by Robert Field. No greater contrast could exist than that between its subject and a man like Isaac Sears or his contemporary in Boston, John Scollay, who was portrayed with all his crudeness in a charcoal sketch by John Singleton Copley. Carroll looks the aristocrat to the core. His features are refined: thin lips tightly closed, eyes small but acute, gray hair combed neatly back from a high, clear brow. The fur collar of his black coat and the silken cloth at his neck are appropriate to such a face. He was clearly no man of the people but one of rank and breeding, one who kept his distance, who was cold and even uncongenial. Carroll's letters modify the portrait's impression, revealing at times a very human loneliness and melancholy, a touch of humor, even a literary playfulness more like that of polemicists in London or Dublin than those of the American Revolution. But on the whole Carroll's writings compliment rather than contradict the Laty/Field interpretation of his character. Here was a man given less to democracy than to gentility, a man of equanimity and self-discipline able to hold his position and, with one brief exception, his courage through the vicissitudes of revolution, contemplating even extreme private losses with philosophical resignation.[1]

Carroll's most revealing letters were addressed to his father, Charles Carroll of Annapolis. But how different a person emerged from the elder Carroll's pen: feisty, angry, full of a life and a passion to which the surviving portraits of that bewigged Marylander with piercing eyes and bejowled cheeks do not do justice. The elder Carroll was a character from Joyce, his son from Henry James. A tyrant of sorts, Carroll of Annapolis sent his only son to school in Europe when the boy was eleven years old and then, despite that son's intense pleas that his "banishment" or "exile" be

[1] On Carroll, see Kate Mason Rowland, *The Life of Charles Carroll of Carrollton, 1737–1832, with His Correspondence and Public Papers* (New York, 1898); Ellen Hart Smith, *Charles Carroll of Carrollton* (Cambridge, 1942), and Thomas O'Brien Hanley, *Charles Carroll of Carrollton: The Making of a Revolutionary Gentleman* (Washington, 1970), which traces Carroll's life to 1774. The most important recent addition to Carroll historiography is Ann C. Van Devanter, compiler, *"Anywhere So Long as There Be Freedom": Charles Carroll of Carrollton, His Family and His Maryland* (Baltimore, 1975). The catalogue to an exhibition at the Baltimore Museum of Art, the book reproduces a wealth of pictorial material as well as several very useful scholarly essays.

All citations listed here simply as "Mss." are from the manuscripts of the Maryland Historical Society (MdHS). Much of the MdHS's Mss. 206, sometimes called the Charles of Annapolis papers, was published as "Extracts from the Carroll Papers," in the *Maryland Historical Magazine* (*MdHM*), vols. X–XVI (1915–21). Other useful material was in Mss. 203, Carroll of Carrollton's letters to his son, Charles Carroll of Homewood; Mss. 203.1, "Letterbook of Charles Carroll of Carrollton, 1765–1768"; Mss. 203.2, Carroll's letterbook for 1770–74, which was published as "A Lost Copy-Book of Charles Carroll of Carrollton," *MdHM* XXXII (1937), 193–225; Mss. 216, Miscellaneous Carroll papers; and Mss. 220, the Carroll-McTavish papers. Some limited use has also been made of Thomas Meagher Field, ed., *Unpublished Letters of Charles Carroll of Carrollton* (New York, 1902), which is in general too inaccurate for scholarly purposes; and of the microfilm version of "The Charles Carroll Papers" edited by Thomas O'Brien Hanley and issued by Scholarly Resources, Inc., of Wilmington, Delaware, in 1972.

In the notes below, Charles Carroll of Annapolis is designated "CCA," and Charles Carroll of Carrollton "CCC."

ended, refused permission for his return until some sixteen years had passed. Carroll of Annapolis was a man who
demanded of his child—and received—at once subservience
and affection, who in later years always asked about
"Charly's" wife and children, suggesting a depth of attachment extending beyond that of Charly himself.

The elder Carroll found little of value in his political
world; he was "cast in the rebel's role" according to one
modern historian.[2] The success that marked his lifetime
(1702–82) was that of a businessman who jockeyed a hand-
some inheritance into one of the greatest of contemporary
American fortunes. Business was in that era an appropriate
vocation for a rebel. There he could act alone, aggressively,
with only a limited need to accommodate himself to other
persons. But a rebel is not a revolutionary; and with time
it became clear that the younger and less colorful Carroll
surpassed his father in strengths critical to the politics of
an age of revolution.

Charles Carroll of Carrollton (1737–1832) was different
from other Old Revolutionaries. The politics of an Adams,
a Sears, a Young, a Lee—of a Gadsden, Harnett, Thomson,
Lamb, or McDougall—were shaped within America and
under the provincial governments of the late colonial period.
But Carroll was physically absent, in France or England,
during the years in which his basic political assumptions
were formed. So late as 1760 he confessed a perfect ignorance
of Maryland's government and laws. And unlike those other
partisans of the American cause, he never led a crowd.
Carroll's political service began late—in the 1770s—and aside
from his role as a newspaper writer, he served the cause only
in the more formal extralegal institutions and then in the
constitutional governments that the Revolution created. On
any comparative scale his contribution to the independence
movement was inferior to those of Adams, Sears, Young,
and Lee. His fame is in part the product of a historical
accident, for he lived to the age of ninety-five, becoming
after the deaths of Thomas Jefferson and John Adams in
1826 the last surviving signer of the Declaration of Inde-

[2] Hanley, *Carroll,* p. 6.

pendence and so in his much-feted person a monument to that first defining act of the American nation.

Carroll was, moreover, the most prominent Roman Catholic participant in what was in 1776 a militantly Protestant revolution, one that took inspiration from the Glorious Revolution of 1688, when English Protestants overthrew James II with his Catholic wife and heir. Catholicism was associated with unconditional submission to absolute authority, Protestantism with liberty and resistance to tyranny. The American independence movement grew in part from suspicions that official British "softness" on Catholicism signaled the decay of English freedom; and George III lost his American subjects as much by endorsing the Quebec Act, and so "abandoning" the established Protestant Church and "establishing" Catholicism in Canada, as he did by closing the port of Boston or violating the Massachusetts charter. Carroll's participation in so apparently alien a political movement demands explanation.

Finally, the Carrolls, father and son, differ from other colonists in their willingness to reveal themselves. The commissioning of portraits played a part in that revelation. Thomas Young was perhaps, as a respectable New England scholar once remarked, "not the type from which a portrait at that time would be expected."[3] The same could be said of Sears. Not even verbal descriptions of those men's physical characteristics have survived. Likenesses exist of Richard Henry Lee, and Samuel Adams is known by the famous Copley portrait that John Hancock commissioned. But paintings remain of Charles Carroll of Carrollton in his twenties by Joshua Reynolds, in his sixties by Field, and several from his revered old age, including some by Charles Willson Peale and Rembrandt Peale. Portraits endure, moreover, of his parents, grandparents, cousins, children, and grandchildren, together a rare pictorial history of an early American family.

Carroll's correspondence has also survived in some quantity. More important, it is qualitatively different from that of

---

[3] George P. Anderson to Dr. Henry R. Viets, Jamaica Plain, Massachusetts, April 28, 1957, Miscellaneous Collection, Massachusetts Historical Society, Boston.

most Americans of his time. Perhaps because his letters reach back to his childhood and extend over a longer period than those of other Old Revolutionaries, perhaps because the greater part of them are personal rather than political or commercial, and possibly also because Carroll emerged from a Catholic rather than a Protestant culture they are distinctly revealing of their author. Carroll spoke of virtue, he detested corruption and valued disinterested public service. Those values shaped his politics but never defined his world or his personality to the extent they did, for example, those of Samuel Adams, whose private and public letters were so alike in hiding the man behind his cause. The younger Carroll wrote of himself, of course, in his boyish reports to his father. But even as an adult he felt no need to subordinate all private considerations to a cause, and wrote to friends abroad of his personal traits, moods, and private needs without shame or apology.

One can, then, trace Carroll's public career much as one can study the political lives of other men, noting the peculiar legal status of Catholics in Maryland, considering the influence of Carroll's Jesuit education on his political ideas, witnessing his political emergence during the revolutionary struggle. But one can go further in his case and explore the private or familial foundations of Carroll's capacity for revolutionary politics and of the commitment to America that lay behind his identity as a revolutionary.

The Carrolls were Irish in origin—not, like Thomas Young's ancestors, Protestant Dissenters who had migrated to Ireland in the seventeenth century, but Catholics, one of whom saw fit to leave that island as the Clintons and Youngs were first arriving. They claimed descent from native or Old English (Norman) "princes" who once held extensive lands in King's County, Ireland. Charles Carroll "the settler" left his native land to study at the university for English Catholics at Douai in France, then entered the Inner Temple at London in 1685. On completing his legal studies he secured a position as confidential clerk to a minister of James II. In those years Carroll also became a friend of Lord Baltimore, the proprietor of Maryland; and in 1688 he left both Ireland and England behind, setting out for the New World with a commission as Baltimore's attorney general. Maryland was a more propitious place for an ambitious Irish Catholic, for there the proprietor's famous Act of Toleration (1649) promised that "noe person or persons whatsoever . . . professing to believe in Jesus Christ, shall . . . bee any waies troubled, Molested or discountenanced for in respect to his or her religion." Accordingly "the settler" redesigned his family crest, substituting for its old motto, "Strong in Faith and War," another, "Anywhere so Long as There be Freedom." But a month after his arrival in Maryland, Englishmen overthrew James II; and the following year, 1689, the province's own Protestant revolutionaries (whom Carroll characterized as "profligate wretches and men of scandalous lives" followed by "such fooles as they have poysoned by the most absurd lyes that ever were invented") overthrew the Catholic proprietor and excluded all "Papists" from civil and military offices within the province.[4]

Carroll's insistent Catholicism, loyalty to the proprietor, and impudent behavior cost him his office and two terms in jail as well. He was, however, "a magnificent fighter because he never knew when he was beaten," and so young Carroll (he was twenty-nine in 1689) remained in Maryland, serving as the local protector of Baltimore's personal interests in the province, acquiring land (parcels of which he named after his family's Irish holdings—"Ely O'Carroll," "Litterlouna," "Doughoregan"), building the foundations of one of the greatest American eighteenth-century fortunes by serving as a shopkeeper, planter, creditor. In 1714, Lord Baltimore's son announced his conversion to the Church of England and regained title to Maryland. Carroll returned to England to plead his cause as a loyal supporter, and won from the fifth Lord Baltimore a "remarkable Commission" (1715)

[4] Rowland, *Carroll,* I, 1–8; Smith, *Carroll,* pp. 3–12, with quotations on pp. 6 (Toleration Act) and 12; DeVanter, *"Anywhere So Long as There Be Freedom,"* p. 3; Francis X. Curran, *Catholics in Colonial Law* (Chicago, 1963), p. 65.

that shocked the province's governor and lower house of assembly by granting extensive public powers to a "profest Papist" who had refused to take the oaths imposed for office in the wake of the Glorious Revolution, a man who was, as the governor put it, "by Principle . . . an Enemy to the Protestant Constitution."[5]

The sensitiveness of his situation failed to make Carroll a more politic person: he used his new authority to free two persons, one his nephew, who had been jailed for "fireing the Great Gunns" at Annapolis to celebrate the Pretender's birthday, and went so far as to insult the governor while that august person was in bed, late at night, so ill that he was composing a will. In these ways the first American Carroll contributed to a rash of new anti-Catholic laws. Maryland Papists had already been disqualified from office (1689), disbarred (1692), and forced to hold their religious services in private houses (1704). In 1715 they were also effectively excluded from the provincial assembly, and that disability was made more emphatic the following year when the legislature defined new oaths for persons holding public offices or trusts that were explicitly designed to secure the "Protestant interest" in Maryland, and demanded vows of allegiance to King George, a renunciation of the Stuart Pretender (the "oath of abjuration"), and an explicit denial of the doctrine of transubstantiation. Finally in 1718 "all professed Papists" who refused to take these oaths were declared "uncapable of giving their vote in any election of a delegate or delegates within this province, either for counties, cities, or boroughs," which meant that the Catholic Carrolls would henceforth be confined to what they called the "private station."[6]

To Charles Carroll of Annapolis "the settler" left a part of his fortune (although that son soon gained control over most of the rest) and the whole of his stubborn temperament. Like his brothers, Charles Carroll of Annapolis was educated in French Jesuit schools. An older brother, Henry,

[5] Rowland, *Carroll*, I, 5–6; Smith, *Carroll*, pp. 12–21.
[6] Smith, *Carroll*, esp. pp. 16, 20; Governor John Hart's account in *Maryland Archives*, XXXIII (Baltimore, 1913), 569–71; Curran, *Catholics in Colonial Law*, pp. 65–66, 81–83, 93–94, 96–97.

had gone on to study law in London, as had his father before him. Such, too, was the plan for Charles, but Henry Carroll died at sea while returning to Maryland in 1719, and the year thereafter his father followed him to the grave. As a result eighteen-year-old Charles was called home to oversee the family estate before he could enter the Temple. "I have from the time I came from school, in the year 1720," he later noted, ". . . been a constant servant of my family." And in the tradition of that family, Carroll of Annapolis sent his own son, the future revolutionary, first to the Jesuit College of Bohemia in Maryland, and then in 1748 to France, where he studied with the Jesuits again at St. Omer's in Flanders for six years, went on to Rheims, Bourges, to the College of Louis le Grand at Paris, and finally to London, where, like his grandfather, he entered the Temple and studied English law.[7]

Charles Carroll of Carrollton's Jesuit education distinguished him from most other Americans of his generation, but the political effects were far different from what men like Thomas Young assumed. The doctrine of unconditional submission to authority was not, as Anglo-American Protestants frequently assumed, a defining ingredient of either Catholic or Jesuit teaching. Americans might well, as Paul Conkin has noted, have derived their justifications for resisting Britain from the writings of Thomas Aquinas. "Only the fashions of language and the barriers of time and religion made a Locke or a Milton much more appealing" and turned colonists toward Protestant writers rather than "an impressive group of sixteenth- and seventeenth-century Spanish Jesuits (Molina, Suarez, Mariana) who preached virtually the same message at the same time."[8]

Whatever the Jesuits taught, however, the Carrolls were clearly in accord with their Whiggish countrymen on the subjects of resistance and revolution. If the Jesuits had committed themselves to a blind obedience—as their French opponents charged in the early 1760s—both Carrolls, father

---

[7] Smith, *Carroll*, pp. 22, 28–30, 33–35; Rowland, *Carroll*, I, 17, for quotation.
[8] Paul K. Conkin, *Self-Evident Truths* (Bloomington, 1974), pp. 5–6.

and son, felt free to criticize their old teachers. It was "dangerous to the State," the younger Carroll wrote his father in 1761, for "a body of men to implicitly believe the dictates of one Superior" and to execute his orders *with a blind impetuosity of will and eargerness to obey without the least enquiry or examination."* Reason was given men "to weigh and examin wether the actions he is sollicited or commanded by others to perform, are such as can stand the scrutiny and sentence of an unerring, if unprejudiced, judge." The elder Carroll's response to the controversy was different, but fully as radical as that of his son. "The implicit obedience professed by the Jesuits cannot be meant by common Sense and Justice to extend beyond things innocent, indifferent and Just," he wrote. Where the Jesuits' constitutions included insupportable doctrines, they were harmless because of no force: doctrines "inconsistent with reason and contrary to Morality Justice and Religion . . . are in themselves void and can have no ill effect." However much such persons might dissent from the anti-Catholic measures adopted in the wake of the Glorious Revolution, they had no fundamental disagreement with that event itself. "Should a King, deaf to the repeated remonstrances of his people, forgetful of his coronation oath, and unwilling to submit to the legal limitations of his prerogative, endeavor to subvert that constitution in church and state, which . . . he swore to maintain," Carroll of Carrollton declared in 1773, "resistance would . . . not only be excusable, but praiseworthy." And James II, "by endeavouring to introduce arbitrary power, and to subvert the established church, justly deserved to be deposed and banished." In short, the revolution of 1688–89 "was both just and necessary."[9]

The Carrolls also shared with Samuel Adams, Richard Henry Lee, and others within Anglo-American radical culture a fear of corruption as the bane of freedom, and a respect for "virtue." The sources of their convictions may have been distinct. As a result of the emphasis upon classical

[9] CCC–CCA, October 22, 1761, *MdHM,* XI, 182–83; CCA–CCC, April [8, 1861], Mss. 220; CCC as "First Citizen" in Peter S. Onuf, ed., *Maryland and the Empire, 1773; The Antilon-First Citizen Letters* (Baltimore, 1974), pp. 88, 225.

languages in Jesuit education, they drew directly upon the ancients more often than upon later political writers, although Carroll of Carrollton shared the enthusiasm of many other educated colonists for the writings of Lord Bolingbroke and for Addison's "Cato." And as with Adams and Lee, the Carrolls' intellectual emphasis upon virtue correlated with a moderation and frugality, a distaste for luxury and "debauchery" that marked their sense of style. The younger Carroll disliked the pervasive card-playing at Bourges, and in London remained disinclined to participate in the amusements of gay society, where he would only expose himself to the habits of "bad company" and distract himself from his studies. His English friend William Graves noted this dislike of self-indulgence, for which Carroll of Carrollton felt no need to apologize. "I would not accept my Father's estate upon condition of consuming the annual profits, in gaudy equipages, empty pomp and show and in company more empty than these," he wrote. There was little danger in such a renunciation, however, for his father was if anything more committed to an ethic of frugality than the son. Be content, he advised Carroll of Carollton and his young wife in 1770, with "what is neat Clean and Necessary."[10]

One man's necessity is, of course, another's luxury. The younger Carroll described his lodgings in Maryland as modest ("the furniture . . . tho' decent and useful, is neither costly nor shewy," with no attempt at "grandeur . . . or magnificence"), as it may well have been in comparison with those of an English gentleman, but to most colonists the commodious homes of the Carrolls in the various seats they maintained represented a distinct form of comfort and luxury. Carroll's dedication while in Europe to learning not just the practical skills of law, accounting, and surveying, but also fencing, dancing, and "designing" or drawing, or his father's willingness to attend the London theater (which he found scandalous), would have seemed an indulgence in "superfluities" to a more Spartan New Englander. Personal virtue was, in fact, not a public but a private way of life

---

[10] CCC–Graves, September 15, 1765, Mss. 203.1; CCA–CCC, November 30, 1770, *MdHM*, XIII, 71.

for the Carrolls. On the surface they sought to avoid any implication of parsimony, to appear "genteel"—if worked ruffles were in style in France, the son must wear them, the father advised, not indulge in a strange simplicity. "I am resolved to live as becomes a gentleman," the younger Carroll wrote Graves in 1765, which meant he must "avoid every appearance of meanness" as well as of "prodigality, and ostentation." Carroll again associated simplicity with gentility in the directions he sent an Englishwoman charged with purchasing gifts for his first fiancée. "Every Lady," he wrote, "should strive to be, what the *Spectator* finely expresses, *elegantly neat:* magnificence and finery in Cloaths is neither mine nor the lady's taste: she would chuse them decent, handsom and genteel." Yet he was ordering a necklace, lace, and silks, and made it clear he would pay for elegance: "if 10 or 12 guineas more in the price of a necklace or of the Brussells lace will buy them elegant, do not stick at such a trifle." For persons like the Carrolls, frugality and gentility were in fact complementary virtues. "Grace Economy and Generosity are so far from being inconsistent," the elder Carroll explained, "that it is by economy we are enabled to be generous without hurting our circumstances."[11]

"Without hurting our circumstances." There was perhaps the most compelling consideration in turning the Carrolls from luxury. For they were as dedicated to maintaining their family fortune and passing it on unimpaired to their progeny as Samuel Adams was to continuing the political traditions of his forefathers. "Can fine furniture Cloaths etc. be put in Competition with a provision for Children," the elder Carroll once asked. "Pride and Vanity are not to be indulged at their Expence." Industry was, moreover, as important as frugality, for the younger Carroll found that an estate in Maryland demanded far more constant attention on the part of a gentleman than was true in England. The province afforded splendid examples of downward mobility: "in a commercial nation," he noted, "the glory of illustrious pro-

[11] CCC–Graves, March 17, 1772, *MdHM*, XXXII, 212, and September 15, 1765, Mss. 203.1; CCC–"Dr Madam," October 6, 1766, Mss. 203.1; CCA–CCC, August 30, 1758, *MdHM*, X, 228.

genitors will not screen their needy posterity from obscurity and want."[12]

A painstaking attention to their property took on particular importance for the Carrolls, moreover, because they had few alternative ways to win a sense of place and purpose that might bring to their lives satisfaction and meaning. Maryland had been far too unkind to Catholics for them to identify with its past, or even to find there an altogether congenial home; and public service was of course foreclosed to them. There were also private consolations in money beyond what it could buy. It offered personal liberty, a freedom from the control of others critical to notions of gentility in the Chesapeake and to the proud temper above all of Carroll of Annapolis. One would not expect to find in such men the glorification of poverty that Adams or Young or Lee derived from the cult of virtue. Daniel of St. Thomas Jenifer once tried to console the elder Carroll for the threat to his fortune revolution had brought. "Money is far from being a soverign good," Jenifer noted, "nay frequently it is quite the reverse for to acquire and keep it together, requires more pains and trouble than it is worth." But Carroll of Annapolis would not be patronized, and his then seventy-six years only hardened his trenchancy. "Your philosophical opinion about money may be clearly refuted," he shot back. "The world with me likes it and an universall oppinion is seldom a wrong one. But above all reasons I like it, because it makes one independent."[13]

[12] CCA–CCC, November 30, 1770, *MdHM*, XIII, 71; CCC–Graves, September 15, 1765, Mss. 203.1, on the character of American estates; to the Countess of Auzoüer, September 20, 1771, *MdHM*, XXXII, 204.

[13] Jenifer–CCA, May 30, 1778; and CCA–Jenifer, June 7, 1778, Mss. 206. See also CCC–Countess of Auzoüer, September 20, 1771, *MdHM*, XXXII, 206–07: "When my Father came to the estate, which was nearly divided between him and his brother Daniel, he was but 18 years of age. The experience of his relation James Carroll, by whose advice he suffered himself to be guided, was of singular service at that critical time of life— his guardian strongly urged the sweets of independence, and as a necessary means of attaining it, a well regulated economy. My father was convinced of the justness of this reasoning, and loving independence practised economy to be independent. A prudent management during a long life has made him the richest individual in this Province, without the favor of Government, even in opposition to it, and in spight of many injustices suffered thro' the envy of public and private persons."

Like other Americans, the Carrolls understood the Anglo-American conflict in terms of a larger war between virtue and corruption, freedom and slavery. Their disillusionment with Britain was not so tied to the failure of John Wilkes as was that of other colonial radicals in part because they saw that "patriot" less as a virtuous savior than as part of a blight of corruption that had overrun English life. "If the welfare of England and the liberty of the subject were the true motives of Mr. Wilkes' conduct I should wish him well," Carroll of Carrollton noted; but instead Wilkes was of a piece with all other English opposition movements over the previous sixty years, grasping for power and place while talking of principle.[14] Nor did the Carrolls form their judgments through information provided by intermediaries such as Arthur and William Lee. Their data came directly from the London press—from the pamphlets and periodicals the younger Carroll sifted, sending the most interesting on to his father, who also received the *London Evening Post*. On the basis of these sources Carroll of Annapolis concluded as early as 1761 that corruption had become so prevalent in England that it threatened the British constitution: "Virtue has abandoned us," he wrote, "and liberty is gone with it." Later he traced the pervasiveness of corruption back to the early years of the eighteenth century and credited Sir Robert Walpole with having "Reduced Corruption into a Regular Sistem" which from then to the present was "improved and founded on so Broad and solid a Basis as to threaten the Constitution with immediate Ruine" and leave "little more than the Appearance of Liberty." His son placed the seeds of destruction even further in the past, suggesting once that the patriotism of Englishmen had been bought away by places and patronage to an increasing extent "since the Revolution."[15]

When Charles Carroll of Carrollton finally returned to Maryland on February 12, 1765, he was, then, hardly apolitical. He knew nothing of the laws and constitution of

[14] CCC–CCA, June 14, 1763, *MdHM*, XI, 336–37; CCC–Edmund Jennings, August 9, 1771, *MdHM*, XXXII, 198.

[15] CCA–CCC, April [8, 1761], Mss. 220; CCA–Graves, December 23, 1768, *MdHM*, XII, 185; CCC–Edmund Jennings, December 18, 1770, ibid., 195.

Maryland but what his father had told him, but he had read English law and constitutional history and had formed distinct impressions of the contemporary British political system. His first inclination, judging from letters to friends in England, was toward seclusion. "So little is my ambition," he wrote William Graves in September 1765, "or my bent to retirement so strong," that he was determined to abandon "all ambitious pursuits" and commit himself to the "improvement . . . of my paternal acres: may I not enjoy as much happiness in this humble as in a more exalted station? who so happy as an independent Man, and who more independent than a private gentleman?" But as the Stamp Act controversy broke around him, his convictions were decidedly on the American side. The colonists' claim to exemption from parliamentary taxation seemed to him unexceptionable: if their "essential right of internal taxation" were denied, the Americans' property would be "at the mercy of every rapacious minister." The maxim that taxation required consent seemed to him one of the "known fundamental laws essential to and interwoven with the English constitution which even a Parliament itself cannot abrogate." Britain's effort to violate that rule to gain an unlimited access to American wealth seemed to him but another symptom of "general decay" in the mother country, suggesting in turn that English liberty was "already lost, or near expiring," and that the English constitution was "hastening to its final period of dissolution."[16]

Carroll had no need of John Dickinson's "Letters from a Farmer in Pennsylvania" to awaken his opposition to the Townshend duties of 1767. Indeed, that revenue measure inspired him to compose his own "modest proposal," one that surpassed Dickinson's composition not in effect (for it remains unpublished) but in cleverness. In the manner of Jonathan Swift, whom he was currently reading, Carroll noted that by raising the cost of British imports to colonists the Townshend duties would drive the Americans to manufacture for themselves. In response, the British would

---

[16] CCC–Graves, September 15, 1765; CCC–Jennings, November 23, 1765; and CCC–Bradshaw, November 21, 1765, Mss. 203.1.

undoubtedly outlaw American manufacturing altogether and so oblige colonists to buy English products at whatever price English shopkeepers chose to ask. In effect, Americans would be told to pay or go naked—which could have good effects. For one thing, English workers, then obliged to labor six days out of seven, could earn the same profit in three and so devote the extra time to "jumping, restling, heaving the bar, boxing," all sports that would "invigorate their bodies, . . . now perhaps somewhat enfeebled by a sedentary life," and fit them better for the "toils of war." Better yet, if the greater part of the Americans were forced to go unclothed, that constraint would "put a stop to population: the severity of the weather would pinch to death thousands of poor naked americans who had hithertofore been used to cloathing," such that England would have "nothing to fear from our numbers" in the rebellion she seemed intent upon provoking. But whether depopulation would "answer the end of colonization," Carroll concluded, "I submit to the wisdom of higher powers." No other American but Benjamin Franklin could have composed such a passage; and when Carroll met Franklin in 1776 he predictably found him a "most engaging and entertaining companion," a man of extensive political, literary, and philosophical knowledge who better yet was "full of facetious stories" which he "applied with judgment and introduced apropos."[17]

There is no evidence that Carroll actively participated in the organized forms of resistance to Britain during these early years of the Anglo-American conflict. He told his English correspondents the story of American opposition to the Stamp Act with obvious relish as stamp distributors were "obliged to throw up their dirty employments" and the people remained so enraged that it was thought they would "proceed to the greatest lengths, even to the burning of the stamps." In 1766 Carroll provided Daniel Barrington with a careful account of a recent transaction by the Sons of Liberty in Annapolis and Baltimore, one that suggested

[17] CCC–Graves, August 27, 1767, Mss. 203.1; CCC–CCA, New York, March 29, 1776, Mss. 206.

strongly he was an interested observer but not a participant. Both Carrolls favored economic coercion as the most effective response to British taxation: "We have nothing to do but hold our tongues, be frugal, industrious, and cloath ourselves," the younger Carroll wrote in 1766, and the resulting pressure on the pockets of Englishmen, who received so much profit and employment from the colonial trade, would be far more effective than any appeal to their understandings. Yet neither he nor his father joined Maryland's Nonimportation Association of 1769. As Catholics subject to civil disabilities, the Charles Carrolls of Annapolis and Carrollton lacked the habit of politics; they were not already bound up in the "country party" of provincial Maryland's lower house of assembly, from which the Nonimportation Association emerged, nor did they have established constituencies (like those of Adams or Lee) that they might engage in the politics of resistance. The Carroll who did sign the Association of 1769 was, appropriately enough, a Protestant cousin, Charles Carroll "barrister."[18]

The continued effort of the Crown to win new revenues and so, as the Townshend Revenue Act made clear, to gain greater control over appointive positions deepened the Catholic Carrolls' disillusionment with Britain. By 1771 the younger Carroll wrote that "the vast influence of the Crown, the luxury of the Great and the depravity of the common People" were such that he "despaired" for the English constitution. But their conviction of a spreading venality which was, as the father long ago had observed, incompatible with freedom led them at first to exult in their incapacities rather than to throw them off. In a political world so dominated by the struggle for patronage and place, where "posts of dignity and profit are almost incompatible with virtue," their exclusion from office made it easier, the younger

<hr />

[18] CCC–Christopher Bird, September 23, 1765; and to unnamed correspondent, October 5, 1765, Mss. 203.1; CCC–Barrington, March 17, 1766, in Field, *Unpublished Letters,* pp. 109–12. (I have not located the manuscript of the last-cited letter, and believe Field's version should be treated with some suspicion.) On the Maryland Association, see *MdHM,* III (Baltimore, 1908), 144–49; and Charles A. Barker, *The Background of the Revolution in Maryland* (New Haven, 1940), esp. pp. 319–23.

Carroll noted, to remain "honourable, honest, independent." Where vice prevailed, the post of honor, as Addison's "Cato" had taught, was a private station.[19]

But they protested too much, and soon the younger Carroll seized an opportunity to shake off his political isolation and enter the public sphere. In 1770 the Maryland assembly refused to renew a law that had established the fees public officials could collect for their services at what assemblymen considered an excessively high level. It proposed a new law with a reduced table of fees, but the measure was blocked in the province's upper house, where opposition was led by Daniel and Walter Dulany, both of whom held public positions affected by the fee scale. In the ensuing deadlock, Governor Robert Eden prorogued the assembly and reinstated the original higher fees by executive proclamation, thereby awakening intense controversy. Were fees not a form of taxation, which required legislative consent? And were not the governor's advisers, particularly the Dulanys, "corrupt" in that they had compromised the rights of the people for their own private advantage? "I think our politicks are as contemptible, and more pernicious than those of England," Carroll of Carrollton wrote a cousin in December 1771. "Could you imagine the right of fixing officers' fees by proclamation would be claimed at this time of day? . . . War is now declared between the Government and the People, or rather between a few placemen, the real enemies to Government and all the inhabitants of this Province."[20]

The main spokesman for the other side was Daniel Dulany, who defended the governor's proclamation in an unsigned dialogue between "First Citizen" and "Second Citizen" that the *Maryland Gazette* published in January 1773. A month later, to Dulany's surprise, a response appeared signed "First Citizen" and written by Charles Carroll of Carrollton. So began a series of exchanges between "Antillon," the name Dulany assumed, and "First Citizen" that

[19] CCC–Jennings, August 9, 1771, *MdHM*, XXXII, 197; CCA–CCC, September 3, 1763, in Field, *Unpublished Letters*, p. 78; CCC–CCA, June 14, 1763, *MdHM*, XI, 337. See also CCA–Graves, February 10, 1775, Mss. 206.
[20] Smith, *Carroll*, pp. 99–100; CCC–Charles Carroll "barrister," December 3, 1771, *MdHM*, XXXII, 209–10.

extended into July. The antagonists laced their essays with Latin as they displayed their erudition in the classics, law, and history; but they also traded scurrilous accusations of a personal nature, which accounts in part for the interest they attracted. Carroll became a local hero (whenever he appeared in public "the Whisper immediately Ran there is the 1st Citizen"); his arguments contributed to the victory of the country or "popular party" in the provincial elections of May 1773 and solidified Carroll's association with Samuel Chase, William Paca, Thomas Johnson, and others who had in the past opposed both Governor Eden's and Parliament's efforts to tax Marylanders without their consent; and he emerged from the controversy as a recognized patriot whose role as a "distinguished advocate" of the rights of his country had been publicly praised by Annapolis's delegates to the legislature, and who had received the singular honor of a visit from the lower house of assembly, whose members marched *en masse* to his home on July 2, 1773, to thank him for his efforts.[21]

Carroll's days of closet patriotism were over. In May 1774 a public meeting in Annapolis appointed him to its committee of correspondence, the first of several positions he assumed in the extralegal institutions of the mid-1770s. He was also elected to the Maryland convention and served on several provincial committees including the committees of safety, observation, and correspondence. He was chosen by the voters of Annapolis and Anne Arundel County as a member of the local committee to enforce the Continental Association, and attended the Continental Congress as an unofficial member of the Maryland delegation. In the spring of 1776 Congress appointed him part of a special mission to solicit Canadian support for the American cause. Carroll's presence on that delegation, like that of his cousin John Carroll, who would become the first American Catholic bishop, was meant to counteract French Canadian fears of American anti-Catholicism; but the mission was doomed

---

[21] CCA–CCC, March 17, 1773, *MdHM*, XIV, 368, for quotation. Also Smith, *Carroll*, pp. 99–117; Hanley, *Carroll*, pp. 223–60; Onuf, ed., *Maryland and Empire*.

by the failure of the American army in Canada. On his return to the United States, Carroll visited Congress, noted the increased support for independence there, and was instrumental in convincing the Maryland convention to rescind instructions to its Congressional delegates that had forbidden their consent to independence. Finally Carroll was elected an official delegate to Congress, where, on August 2, 1776, he signed the Declaration of Independence. ("There go a few millions," a bystander is said to have quipped, referring to the confiscation of property that convicted traitors faced under British law.) In the new republican constitutional order the Revolution brought to Maryland, and which Carroll helped design, Catholics were freed of civil disabilities. He was, therefore, able to continue a life in politics, serving as state senator from 1777 until he was defeated in the Jeffersonian triumph of 1800, and as a member of the United States Senate from its first meeting in 1789 until 1792, when he was required by law to choose between his state and national senate seats.[22] It was, however, for his contribution to American independence that Carroll of Carrollton is appropriately remembered, for it was during the 1770s that his personal and political powers were most severely tested, and it was then that he performed his most distinguished public service.

⤛∞⤜

Few embraced independence with greater fears or less passion than Carroll of Carrollton. For him, as for his father, separation from Britain was inevitable: in a letter of 1763 he casually remarked that America was a growing country which "in time . . . will and must be independent." What was ultimately inescapable was not, however, necessarily desirable at present. Independence might yet be deferred, he hoped in September 1774. The colonists, led by men of "strong

[22] Biographical sources cited in note 1. For the quip, see Rowland, *Carroll,* I, 181.

sense" in their Continental Congress, should steer a "proper course" between "Independency and Subjection"; they should eschew violence and appeal through political and economic measures to the reason and interest of Britain. In war, he wrote from Philadelphia, both Britain and America had "as much to fear from victory as defeat." The mother country could win at best "a depopulated and impoverished country, uneasy, dispirited, impatient of subjection." Triumph would leave the Americans with "a heavy debt, unsettled governments, and jarring factions." When the British examined the cost of the enterprise and balanced the "probability of success against the consequences of defeat," they would, he hoped as late as August 1775, "readily seize the occasion . . . of making peace with us." But those were "critical times" in which, as he noted, "a few weeks, nay a few days makes a great alteration in the political Barometer."[23]

Scenes he witnessed along the way to Canada in the spring of 1776 allayed for the moment his fears for national unity. Citizens of all ranks were working on the fortifications at New York, he wrote his father in late March. Some gentlemen unused to laboring with a spade worked so long "to set an example" that "the blood rushed out of their fingers— while this spirit continues, the Americans will ever remain unconquerable." Nor did Britain seem amenable to reason. "The Difficulties and objections to reconciliation and dependence are every day encreasing," he reported that month. "The restraining bill, or rather the bill for confiscating american property, breaths such a spirit of depredation and revenge, that I am satisfied, peace with GB is at a great distance, and Dependence out of the question. These Colonies will never again be dependent on GB," nor would they have peace except such as they could obtain "at the point of the sword." In those circumstances, his course was clear, for there was not and ought not to be, in his view, an option of neutrality in civil war. "I will either endeavour to defend the liberties

   [23] Inevitability: CCC–CCA, November 12, 1763, *MdHM,* XII, 21; and see also CCA–Graves, December 23, 1768, ibid., 183. CCC–CCA, September 9, 1774, August 18, 1775, May 5, 1776 (from Montreal), all Mss. 206.

of my country, or die with them: this I am convinced is the Sentiment of every true and generous American."[24]

His confidence in the future was far from deep-rooted, however, and in late 1776 Carroll suffered a real if temporary crisis of faith. "Our army is badly provided, exposed to the inclemancy of the weather, inferior in numbers to the enemy, etc. etc.," he wrote his father—but that was not the greatest difficulty his country faced. "We are miserably divided not only Colony against Colony, but in each Colony there begins to appear such a spirit of disunion and discord" that even if Britain were defeated he feared "we shall be rent to pieces by civil wars and factions." Above all he execrated those "men of desperate schemes or of desperate and wicked designs" who were endeavoring "under cloak of procuring great privileges for the People to introduce a levelling scheme," by which those evil men were sure to profit; and he feared "the horrors of an ungovernable and revengeful Democracy." "If safe and honorable terms can be had," he decided in early October, "we had better return to our old connections and forms of Govt . . . than hazard civil wars among ourselves and the erection of a despotism as a sure consequence." Nothing but peace with Britain could avert destruction.[25]

Carroll's despondency reflected the genuinely desperate circumstances of the American army in late 1776. And while Washington suffered his defeats in New York and retreated across the Delaware, the state of Maryland became enmeshed in civil war. Radicals in Baltimore adopted ever more violent measures against persons cool to the American cause; Loyalists on the Eastern Shore, often supported by blacks, staged a full-scale insurrection; and even the militia became restive, more a cause than a remedy for disorder.[26] Well might Carroll recall that popular governments were known through history to dissolve in anarchy, leaving new-formed despotisms in their places.

[24] CCC–CCA, March 29, 1776 (from New York), March 18, 1776, and September 7, 1774 (from Philadelphia), Mss. 206.
[25] CCC–CCA, October 4, August 23, and August 20, 1776, Mss. 206.
[26] See Ronald Hoffman, *A Spirit of Dissension: Economics, Politics, and the Revolution in Maryland* (Baltimore, 1973), pp. 184–95.

Carroll of Carrollton's distaste for an "ungovernable and resentful Democracy" built, too, upon suspicions of popular rule that predated the chaos of 1776. Both he and his father knew at the outset of the Anglo-American conflict what many of their countrymen would learn in the course of the American Revolution: that threats to freedom could come from the people as well as from kings. Maryland's colonial assembly, the agency of government closest to the people, had long posed the greatest challenge to the liberties of Catholics. Its efforts to impose upon them ever more severe disabilities had been checked from above—by the colony's governor, its upper house, and even, on one occasion, by the British monarch. Where Catholics escaped the assembly's oppression, moreover, they had still to contend with the hostilities and prejudices of juries, which the Carrolls trusted no more than they did the people who composed them. The mass of Marylanders were for the younger Carroll "an uncultivated insolent rabble," a "despicable vile mob" whose "tyrannical proceedings" and "arbitrary laws" demanded checks by "lawful power." His father found Maryand's people the one major drawback to living in that province. They were, he said, "in fact and in general . . . ignorant mean and malicious." If the province's "house of Commons" could have its way, he claimed in 1760, "such is their Malice that they would not only deprive us of our prosperity but our Lives."[27]

The problem was, however, hardly confined to that province. In England Catholics were left "quiet and unmolested," Carroll of Carrollton believed, only because the King did not share popular prejudices against them. Tyrannical laws remained on the books and could be put into execution "whenever it shall please the King for the parliament wou'd allways readily comply with such a demand." The prosecution of Jesuits by local French parliaments also proved to the younger Carroll that "the decisions and proceedings of most assemblies, when once Passion or interests prevails, are

[27] CCC–CCA, August 14, 1759, and April 10, 1760, *MdHM*, X, 239, 255; CCA–CCC, July 14, 1760, Mss. 220. On the intervention of Queen Anne in Council to suspend a Maryland act of 1704 "to Prevent the Growth of Popery," see Curran, *Catholics in Colonial Law*, p. 82.

more tyranical and oppressive than the sportive cruelty of a Lawless Tyrant." Nor, it seemed, were Catholics the only victims of popular malice. In 1765 Carroll described the ungenerous tendencies of a democratic society much as Alexis de Tocqueville would describe them over six decades later. "There is a mean low dirty envy which creeps thro' all ranks and cannot suffer a superior of fortune and merit or understanding in a fellow citizen," he wrote. "Either of these are such to entail a generall ill will and dislike upon the owner," one that would fall upon him by reason of his wealth even if he were to escape popular displeasure by reason of his religious faith.[28]

These experiences and observations inured the Carrolls to the popular utopianism of the mid-1770s. They who had known the reality of majoritarian tyranny could hardly believe with Thomas Paine and the enthusiasts of *Common Sense* that America would show the world a new birth of peace and freedom once it left behind the corrupting hand of hereditary rule and invested power in the people alone. Carroll of Carrollton was a more conservative member of the generation of 1776; and his conservativism lay most clearly and consistently in a firm conviction that freedom demanded constitutional checks upon the people and the assemblies they controlled. The most reliable of such checks, he thought, were in independent senates composed of those men of means in whom he, like Richard Henry Lee, rested his greatest trust. Not that the wealthy were always less self-serving, less corrupt, than the people at large. Carroll admitted in his "First Citizen" letters that riches failed to guarantee virtue, but he also no doubt agreed with his father that if "independence is not allways a concomitant of wealth, yet among the wealthy it is looked for and there it is most commonly found."[29] Carroll of Carrollton designed the electoral college by which senators were chosen under the Maryland

[28] CCC–CCA, December 10, 1759, Mss. 206, and February 5, 1763, *MdHM*, XI, 327; CCC–Jennings, November 23, 1765, Mss. 203.1.

[29] On popular utopianism of the Revolution's "Golden Age," see Gordon S. Wood, *The Creation of the American Republic 1776–1787* (Chapel Hill, 1969). CCC in Onuf, ed., *Maryland and Empire,* pp. 57–58; CCA–Jenifer, June 14, 1778, Mss. 206.

constitution of 1776, and which served to remove yet further from the people an upper house whose members were drawn due to property qualifications from only 7.4 percent of the state's population. For him the essence of republicanism lay in equal protection of the laws, not equal participation in their formation: faced with the constitutional problems of the late 1780s, he suggested that a reformation of state governments precede that of the Articles of Confederation. The powerful popular assemblies born in the first bursts of revolutionary enthusiasm should everywhere be checked by upper houses, and the annual elections which welded legislatures to the popular will should be ended. Members of lower houses should serve for three-year terms, those of the upper for seven. Most important, suffrage should be limited "to such citizens as will be most likely to exercise this important right most wisely." In Maryland, he suggested, the franchise should (except in trading towns) be confined to men with 150 acres of land in fee simple, a dramatic restriction of popular influence in a state already characterized by the elitist character of its governing institutions.[30]

Carroll's suspicions of the people severely limited the revolutionary content of his politics. He embraced independence with misgivings, and welcomed the internal transformations that republicanism demanded only as long as they remained within defined bounds. Carroll of course favored the expansion of religious freedom in the wake of independence, and expressed a hope in July 1776 that the rejection of Britain would open the way to a "more equal representation"— but not, it would seem, until "more settled times." In the first federal Congress he was for a time a close associate of that strong-minded democrat William Maclay, with whom he shared a dislike of titles and ceremonies, a penchant for republican simplicity that was fully in accord with the Carrolls' long-time familial style. The two men parted ways, not surprisingly, when Carroll revealed himself as a far readier

---

[30] On Maryland senate, see Rowland, *Carroll*, I, 190–91; and, for the number of men who qualified for membership, Hoffman, *Spirit of Dissension*, p. 180. Copy of CCC letter, Doughoregan, July 23, 1787, apparently to Daniel Carroll, under date of November 22, 1828, Mss. 206.

supporter of presidential power. Carroll also approved of the French Revolution in its opening stages. Its success, he claimed in 1791, was critical to the happiness not only of France but of the rest of Europe, and perhaps of the United States as well. His enthusiasm died, however, with the rise of the Jacobins and the execution of the King. He criticized French revolutionary government above all for its lack of checks on popular power. "A democratical Assembly consisting of seven or eight hundred members, without any *control,* and without the most vigorous executive, must produce a worst despotism than that of Turkey," he wrote in 1792.[31]

Carroll became of course no partisan of Jefferson, but a Hamiltonian Federalist who expressed fear in 1800 that he might be driven into exile "by the prevalence of an execrable faction." The "approaching revolution," he wrote on the eve of that year's election, would subvert the social order and the rights of property. Yet his political development was different from that of Hamilton, who had harbored few fears of the people in the mid-1770s, but became disillusioned later as new-modeled democratic legislatures interfered with the rights of creditors and Loyalists. In a way Carroll resembled more closely those Loyalists who disagreed with British imperial policy in the 1760s and 1770s, but who saw the beginnings of popular tyranny in the demands of revolutionary committees, and rejected independence rather than endorse a republican future. For a man who believed so early in the necessity of checks on popular power, independence involved real risks and sacrifices: in Maryland, for example, it brought to an end the power of the proprietor, whose appointed governor and council had protected the Catholic minority from the extremes of majoritarian intolerance. And so Carroll's misgivings about popular rule, like the Catholicism with which those fears were historically linked, make

---

[31] CCC–CCA, July 2, 1776, Mss. 206, on representation. *The Journal of William Maclay, United States Senator from Pennsylvania, 1789–1791* (New York, 1927), *passim;* or the summary in Rowland, *Carroll,* II, 118–66. On the French Revolution: ibid., 148, 171–72, 201–02, 216–18, and, for final quotation, 195.

his commitment to the American cause far less obvious for posterity than it seems to have been for him.[32]

For the Carrolls, the crisis of the Revolution was less in 1776 than in 1777, when their worst fears seemed to be realized. In that year the Maryland legislature passed a Legal Tender Law which required the acceptance of paper money in retiring all debts, including those contracted in sterling before independence. The act was announced as an effort to support the value of paper money, which had already begun to depreciate, but its effect was to ease the burden of debtors at the cost of creditors. The Carrolls agreed on the injustice of the act, but not on how to respond. Their tactical differences were, moreover, closely tied to their temperaments, and reveal much of the paradoxical qualities requisite to a successful revolutionary.

"Should a Law pass to make the Continental and Our Currencies a legal Tender in all cases," Carroll of Annapolis wrote his son on March 13, 1777, "it will Surpass in Inequity all the Acts of the British Parliament against America." Parliament asserted its right to seize the property of Americans but in fact imposed only "trifling" taxes, while the Tender Act would take away "a Reall and Universal Medium of Commerce by Substituting a Medium which Eventually may be of no Value." Laws should give debtors "all reasonable indulgence" against rigorous creditors, but how could it be "consistent with Justice to Bestow the Property of Creditors on Debtors . . . I shall look on every Man who Assents to such a Law as Infamous," the father declared, "and I would as soon Associate with Highwaymen and Pickpockets as with them." Compose a "Strong and Nervous Protest" against the proposed law, he advised his son; and if it became law nonetheless, Charly should resign from the

---

[32] CCC–Charles Carroll of Homewood, November 2 and October 23, 1800, Mss. 203. On Hamilton's course, see John C. Miller, *Alexander Hamilton and the Growth of the New Nation* (New York, 1959); and on disillusionment in general, Wood, *Creation of the American Republic, passim.*

state senate—"quit a Station which You cannot keep with Honor."[33]

From the beginning Carroll of Carrollton saw his parent's righteousness as folly. Withdraw? "Where shall I withdraw?" he asked. "The person who now withdraws from his country's service will be deemed its enemy." Persons obnoxious to the cause could expect to be heavily assessed, and that to no purpose, for withdrawal from the senate would not prevent the measure from going into effect. He did draw up a protest against the Tender Act (which his father found "too temperate") and was the only senator to vote against that measure, but when the elder Carroll asked that his letters on the subject be shown to Chase and Paca the son refused because those writings "discovered too much warmth." A man who wants to succeed in any public measure "must be cool and dispassionate," he argued, "or his opposition will surely be imputed to interest and consequently his arguments have less force on others." He who breathes "a spirit of resentment . . . will only be laughed at," he counseled; "these are times in which men do not stick at trifles." Passion was a weakness. It interferred with reason and undercut the wisdom of experience.[34] The Tender Act was certainly unjust, but having "long forseen the consequences of this evil war" the younger Carroll had tempered his mind to bear adversity with firmness and even with a considered resignation. "It cannot be expected," he told his father, "that such great revolutions should happen without much partial injustice and sufferings." If injustice was done to individuals, yet "my country on the whole is in the right"; the public cause was just. The Carrolls could hardly expect to hold their fortune intact through the revolutionary crisis. If the Americans lost the war, their estates would be confiscated. If they won, much of it would be taxed away to support their share of the financial burden. "In short," he concluded, "I have long considered our personal estate, I mean the monied part of it,

[33] CCA–CCC, March 13 and 18, 1777, Mss. 206.

[34] CCC–CCA, March 15 and March 28, 1777; protest of April 11, 1777; CCA–CCC, April 13, 1777; CCC–CCA, April 11 and June 16, 1777, all Mss. 206.

to be in jeopardy. If we can save a third of that, and all our lands and negroes I shall think ourselves well off."[35]

Carroll of Annapolis remained unconvinced: were he at Annapolis, he wrote, the threat of neither prison nor death would deter him from publicly declaring what he had said in his original letters "and more," for "wicked men may be awed by shame and being publickly exposed, when reason and injustice has no weight with them." He wrote Governor Thomas Johnson politely, then addressed Chase with a "coarseness of expression," as that recipient characterized it, "applicable only to the basest and vilest of mankind." He asked Thomas Jennings to bring into the senate a petition demanding repeal of that "infamous" law by which, he claimed, he was robbed of the greatest part of his property; and he petitioned the house of delegates, only to have his language censured as "highly indecent and justly exceptionable." Not even censure could quiet him. In March 1779 he submitted another petition and remonstrance against the Tender Act, which was again condemned as "in several parts scurrilous and abusive." Yet again he responded. What were those offensive parts? he asked. He would delete them so the house could consider only "the certain facts and unanswerable reasons" he had set forth and so judge the matter "according to reason and justice." "You will not let the Tender Law sleep," Daniel of St. Thomas Jenifer correctly observed.[36]

Nor could he appreciate his son's patience and resignation. "I wish you had a great deal more warmth and ernestness in your temper," he wrote; "men seldom if ever act with spirit who despair of success." The likelihood of failure was no reason not to try, and try again: if his son did not do all in his power for repeal of the Tender Act "you ought not to complain of being robbed, nor do you deserve any property,"

---

[35] CCC–CCA, March 15, March 28, and April 4, 1777, Mss. 206.

[36] CCA–CCC, March 23, 1777; CCA–Johnson, April 13, 1777; CCA–Chase, June 5, 1777, and Chase's reply of June 6, 1777; CCA–Jennings, June 7, 1778; and the summary of CCA's record with the legislature in CCA–Hon. Col. William Fitzhugh, Speaker of the House of Delegates [July 1779?], Mss. 206. See also *Votes and Proceedings of the House of Delegates of the State of Maryland. October Session, 1778* (Annapolis, 1779), p. 17. Jenifer–CCA, July 25, 1779, Mss. 206.

he scolded. "To treat barefaced villains mildly and with moderation, indicates pusillanimity or folly." If love of justice could not raise a man's warmth, what could? "In this instance, moderation is criminal," he insisted. Prudence was "idle and out of Season," temperance "weak and dishonourable." Were they to be robbed and not point out the thieves? "Believe me your prudence and caution is ill judged, a tame submission is more likely to draw on fresh oppressions." As late as December 1780, while the Tender Act was in the course of being repealed, Carroll of Annapolis urged his son to refuse a position in the Continental Congress if it were offered to him unless the repeal was complete and satisfactory, for the nation had forfeited his service by "the most shamefull injustice."[37]

In his righteousness, the elder Carroll might seem the quintessential revolutionary. Like him, or so the Loyalists would have it, his country had stood before the King and Parliament of Britain, unbending in its insistence upon its rights, impolitic in its unwillingness to modify language for the ears of men used to diffidence, used to a servility which, Thomas Jefferson once said, was not the way of an American.[38] Their demands denied, the colonists quit the Empire. But here the Revolution was Janus-faced. Intransigence toward Britain was matched among revolutionary leaders by a patience in righteousness at home, a discerning flexibility, a readiness to wait for others. Successful revolutionaries are marked by the consistency of their vision for a better world and the persistence with which they seek it, by their triumphant sense of when to yield and when to hold firm. They are in this sense consummate politicians, distinct from the rank and file of such men over time only through the profundity of their cause, the strength of their skills, and the accident of time. Samuel Adams had absorbed the necessary qualities into his being. Thomas Young tried to learn them; but his achievement was imperfect, and he earned Congress's

[37] CCA–CCC, November 9 and 4, 1779, March 27 and April 16, 1777, Mss. 206.

[38] Jefferson's comment in *A Summary View of the Rights of British America* (Williamsburg, 1774), p. 21: "Let those flatter who fear; it is not an American art."

censure for the incompleteness of an effort Charles Carroll of Annapolis saw no need to make.

It was in the end not the intransigent father, but the less colorful son who proved more suited to the work of revolution. Not that his achievement was great (Carroll of Carrollton himself understood in his declining years that his greatness was often exaggerated), nor that his overall capacities were of a heroic order. His abilities, he admitted in 1776, were "not above the common level." But he had "integrity, a sincere love of my country, a detestation of Tyranny," and beyond that perseverance and the "habit of business." By these traits he left his mark upon the Revolution. Refusing to alienate persons unnecessarily or to leave the field, he was better able to offset those leveling tendencies he feared, winning a constitution that offered substantial protection for the rights of property, holding out for a time against the confiscation of Loyalist property, helping defeat a scheme for new emissions of paper money that was supported by his old allies, Chase and Paca, some five years after the original Tender Act had been repealed.[39] Of more enduring importance, he proved by his persistent service that even a Roman Catholic could be a good American, making the way easier for the acceptance of his co-religionists in a new nation born of Protestant parentage, bringing to an end the civil disabilities upon Maryand Catholics that the belligerence of his grandfather (so like that of his father) had helped provoke.

Why was the son so different from his father and grandfather before him? Genetics play tricks, as Paine noted fully in his arguments against hereditary rule; and children are, in any case, the products of their mothers as well as their fathers. But as Carroll of Carrollton understood, his equanimity was less the result of his nature than of conscious private effort. What he probably did not understand, but what is clear to the historian looking back through his life, is how much the political skills he brought to the revolution as well as the insights that lay behind his commitment to the American cause had been learned in the thirty-six years of life

---

[39] CCC–CCA, Montreal, May 5, 1776, Mss. 206; Hoffman, *Spirit of Dissension,* esp. pp. 257–68.

that preceded his entry into the public sphere, and how much the qualities that distinguished son from father had developed ironically from the father's role both in defining the circumstances of the son's existence and in directing his upbringing.

Revolution is a crisis of legitimacy. For many people such periods of time in a legal limbo, where the lawful order that defines their world is in disarray and their own status (heroes or traitors?) is open to dispute, are characterized by tension and fear. But for Charles Carroll of Carrollton, such a situation was less out of the ordinary than it was for others. From birth he had lived in the shadow of illegitimacy by virtue of his birth to unmarried parents, and by virtue of his religion.

Details of Carroll's family situation are swathed in some mystery, but the basic facts are certain. Documentary proof of his parents' marriage is preserved at the Maryland Historical Society: "I Mathias Maners a Priest of the Society of Jesus do hereby certify that I did on the 15th day of February in the year of our Lord 1757 marry Charles Carroll Esq: and Elizabeth Brooke Daughter of Clement Brooke esq. late of Prince Georges county deceased."[40] Their son was in his twentieth year, having been born on September 8, 1737. The reason why his parents' wedding was so delayed is unknown. Sally Mason, who in 1976 became the first historian to note in print the fact of Carroll of Carrollton's illegitimate birth, speculated that the elder Carroll sought to protect the family fortune from threats posed by the right of dower, which in Maryland law allowed a widow one third of her husband's estate, and the guardianship right, by which a widow would supervise the rest of the estate on behalf of minor children. His concern that his property not be carried to another "strange" family by a widow rendered so financially attractive by her husband's death was real, as can be seen in his

[40] Mss. 220.

insistence that his son negotiate a marriage agreement before he married. Previous to their marriage, Carroll of Annapolis and Elizabeth Brooke negotiated just such a contract, under which Brooke renounced "all Right Title Claim and Demand to any Dower of the Reall or Personall Estate of the said Charles Carroll" should she survive him except for a yearly sum of £100 sterling (November 7, 1756). That agreement could, however, have been negotiated twenty years earlier, particularly since Brooke was twenty-eight years old when her son was born, and so not a minor. Carroll of Annapolis undercut the threat of guardianship by waiting until his son was almost of age before marrying the boy's mother. But by delaying his marriage so long, he perhaps incurred a yet greater danger.[41]

One of the greatest mysteries surrounding Carroll of Annapolis is why a man so dedicated to the creation and continuance of a great family fortune, a man wholly given to the imperative of constant effort in matters of importance, left but one heir, who was at that a sickly boy of "puny" constitution whose survival over nine decades was hardly predictable in his youth. Charles "the settler" had fathered eleven children, of whom only three survived him. Indeed, Carroll of Annapolis, who became his father's heir, was the fifth of that parent's seven sons. There is some reason to suspect that Carroll of Annapolis had no more children because, in short, he took Brooke into his house but not into his bed. Throughout the long years of family correspondence between Charly and his parents there is no mention of any pregnancy real or suspected until after his parents' marriage. Then, on April 10, 1760, the son expressed great uneasiness over his "Mama's indisposition," for he had been "informed

---

[41] Mason, "Charles Carroll of Carrollton and His Family 1688–1832," in Devanter, *"Anywhere So Long as There Be Freedom,"* pp. 17–18; CCA–CCC, September 1, 1762, *MdHM,* XI, 274. Carroll-Brook marriage agreement in Mss. 2018. Mason's emphasis upon a "guardianship right" is also questionable. Maryland law was not so explicit upon the "right" of widows to serve as guardians over their children as it was on the right of dower. It provided for children naming their own guardians, or for county courts appointing them in some circumstances. The relevant laws, with a convenient index to measures on guardians, are available in Thomas Bacon, *Laws of Maryland at Large, with Proper Indexes* . . . (Annapolis, 1765).

that she was with child." Later his father confirmed that since February 1759 Elizabeth Brooke Carroll had experienced a "swelling" and erroneously "thought herself with child." Both the rumor and Mrs. Carroll's suspicions may have reflected an altered domestic arrangement. In the ordinary course of affairs a pregnancy, though not impossible, would hardly have been expected. In 1759 Mrs. Carroll was in her fiftieth year.[42]

Carroll of Annapolis's stubborn personality, his constant striving for "independence," for freedom from the control of others, were likely components of his decision not to marry in the 1730s. Did he resent the circumstances in which he found himself prior to his son's birth? Did he feel maneuvered toward a marriage he had not freely chosen? As young Charly came of age, his father was ready with advice on how to conduct himself with what the son came to call the "deceitfull sex": the younger Carroll should "avoid any intimacy or familiarity with the fair sex especially Visits or Conversations without witnesses."[43] On the other hand, the father harbored no deep hatred of females. "I should chuse that Women should all most always make part of your Company," he went on, for "they will contribute to soften and polish your manners." When his son claimed a disinterest in women and marriage, Charles of Annapolis was quick to call him on his silliness. "Many Men talk as you do," he wrote, "untill they are far Advanced in years some untill they are Past their Grand Climacterick and then become fond Doting Husbands." A man should choose a wife with full consideration of the genetic consequences for the family, which he considered far more important than her fortune. "It is of Importance to the Offspring, that a man and women should be of good Size well Proportioned, and free from the naturall defects of Lameness, Deafness, Squinting, Stammering, Stuttering, from Hereditary disorders such as the Gout, Gravell, Consumption, etc." Madness, he added,

---

[42] Information on Carroll "the settler's" family in Devanter, *"Anywhere So Long as There Be Freedom,"* charts following p. xvi. CCC–CCA, April 10, 1760, Mss. 206; CCC–CCA, January [9?], 1760, Mss. 220.

[43] CCC–CCA, January 29, 1760, Mss. 206; CCA–CCC, August 30, 1758, Mss. 206 and Mss. 220.

also "runs in the Blood." Would a nobleman who "would not suffer an undersized Pyebald watrayed spavined mare in his stud . . . urge his son to Marry a Humpbacked Puny women with a great fortune?" Would he prefer his beast to his family? The elder Carroll's preferences in women were traditional and appropriate to a man who wanted to be obeyed, not challenged: a wife should be "virtuous, sensible, good natured, complaisant, Complying and of a Chearfull Disposition," he wrote his Charly, or else "you will not find a Marryed State a Happy one." Not one female in 10,000 fit that description, the son answered; but even that charge seemed to the father an unfair criticism of womankind. "Pray," he countered, "How many Chearfull sensible virtuous good natured men do you Reckon in a like number. To do the Sex Justice I believe they would out number us in good Qualities."[44]

But if any woman qualified as such "a Prodigy, a miracle, a deviation from the general and fixed laws," it may well have been Elizabeth Brooke. Her surviving letters, written to her son when he was in school abroad, are warm and human, familiar in their domesticity, touching in their diffidence. "You wer always an affectionate tender good Child," she wrote, "and I find you are still the same that you have the same concern and care for me as useual which is no small Comfort to me." She yearned like all loving mothers for letters from her distant son, and for paintings that she might know how he looked. When she heard Charly was learning to draw, she asked for some pieces of his work not just for herself but also for his Aunt Jenny, who wanted "some Comical little fancy of your own in design." In return she sent him news of his relatives and friends—of the progress of Jenny's cancer, of his Grandmother Brooke, who lived with the Carrolls in her final years, of his old friend Watty Hoxton, who was really too young to marry, she volunteered in 1760, and who had refused to inform Charly of his marriage because it would "scare" him. She told him of

[44] CCA–CCC, August 30, 1758, Mss. 206 and Mss. 220. CCA–CCC, June 22, 1763, and September 1, 1762; CCC–CCA, February 19, 1763; and CCA–CCC, June 2, 1763, *MdHM*, XI, 340, 272–73, 328, 339.

his old home, which was "greatly improved," she wrote in 1756, when it had "a fine flourishing young Orchard with variety of choice Fruit, the Garden inlarged and a Stone Wall round it, 2 fine large Meadows several Houses Built, all this done since you left it." Occasionally she revealed fear that she had lost this very beloved only son, whom she had not seen since he first left for France in 1748: "It is really a pretty Place," she said of the plantation, "but I suppose it wou'd seem insipid to you after being at Paris and seeing le beau Monde." She once asked her son for a personal gift, a snuffbox from Paris, and took special pride in it as his choice for her. "You are always at heart my dear Charly," she wrote in the late 1750s, after her husband had returned from an extended visit with their son, "and I am never tired asking your Papa questions about you. Sometimes to tease, he answers me that you are a good for nothing Ugly little fellow, but when he speaks his real sentiments of you there is not any thing can give me greater Comfort." She loved Maryland (never having been anywhere else, as her son noted), and dreamed that "after a little more time we shall all Live together in it happily, and peaceably."[45]

There is no suggestion anywhere that Charles Carroll of Annapolis then harbored anything but love for this woman with whom he lived so many years before making her his wife. Her account of the teasing they exchanged over their son suggests a warm domestic relationship; and in a letter to Charly of September 8, 1756, Brooke pronounced in a straightforward way her confidence in the feelings of Carroll of Annapolis. "I hope the next letter I send you will be more Satisfactory to you then any you have yet had from me," she began, referring most likely to her forthcoming wedding, "for what may I not expect from your Papas tenderness and affection which I have hitherto been happy Enough to pre-

---

[45] CCC–CCA, February 19, 1763, ibid., 328; Elizabeth Brooke–CCC, September 8, 1756, *MdHM*, X, 147–49, and Mss. 206. It is noteworthy that the printed version of this letter added the name "Carroll" to Elizabeth Brooke's signature, such that in this important detail the *MdHM* differs from the original manuscript. Elizabeth Carroll–CCC, September 19, 1759, and another letter dated on its folder as 1760 but probably 1759, Mss. 220. This paragraph draws upon a range of letters to Carroll from his mother, most of which are available in Mss. 220.

serve." Her death in 1761 caused a torrent of agony in husband as well as son. She had been, the elder Carroll said in writing Charly of her passing, "to me the best of Wives being a Charming Woman in every sense, remarkable for her good Sense evenness and Sweetness of temper." Clearly he had done all a man of wealth might do to preserve her: "If 4 Physicians could have saved her I should still be blessed with her." His grief was greater than these words convey, or than that strong man could manage except by avoiding the topic wherever possible. Six months later he answered his son's additional inquiries about his mother's last days. "I could not say less as you desired to be informed as to these particulars," he noted, and "I cannot say more the Subject being too moving." He mentioned that "from a tenderness for each other" husband and wife had come to avoid the subject of their son, whose continued absence had become a cause of great pain. If she was speaking of that child in the presence of another member of the household, the father reported, "upon my coming into the Room she was Silent. In the future let us mention her as seldom as possible," he asked, though "we can never cease to think of her and pray for her."[46]

But if Elizabeth Brooke succeeded by her complaisance in winning or preserving the elder Carroll's affection, she had few if any attractive alternatives. She could not, for example, easily have become one of those "fond mothers" whose unwillingness to part with their young sons meant that they entered St. Omer's a year or two later than did Charly. Though she came from a good family (one with which the Carrolls felt comfortable intermarrying generation after generation) and her father, Clement Brooke, held a sizable estate, she had no assets of her own. In a will proved in June 1737, three months before her son was born, her father made no mention of her.[47] Again the reasons are unknown, though he may well have been angered by his daughter's pregnancy. The result is, however, certain. Elizabeth Brooke was totally

[46] Brooke–CCC, September 8, 1756, *MdHM,* X, 148, and Mss. 206; CCA–CCC, May 22, 1761, Mss. 206, and November 10, 1761, *MdHM,* X, 184.

[47] Anthony Carroll–CCA, February 29, 1751, Mss. 206; Mason, "Carroll," p. 18.

dependent upon the goodwill of the man with whom she lived. Had she incurred his displeasure she risked losing not only her own comfort and maintenance, but also her son, the paternity of whom Carroll of Annapolis fully acknowledged (giving the boy not only the name Carroll, but the forename Charles, after his father and grandfather), and for whom she could wish no more than what Carroll of Annapolis could give. By politic, if traditionally female, virtues, she eventually won the lawful commitment that was at first denied her, and by her example taught her son the importance of patience and submission in the pursuit of greater aims. The skills of revolution were, in this sense, womanly skills.

What difference did his illegitimate birth make to Carroll of Carrollton? The fact that his parents were unmarried was certainly known to him. His mother made no secret of her situation, and signed letters to her son "Elizabeth Brooke" until after her marriage, when she changed to "Elizabeth Carroll." Her suggestion in a letter of September 1756 that good news was coming, along with the fact that the marriage articles preserved in the Maryland Historical Society were endorsed "To Be Delivered to my Son" (perhaps by the father during his visit of 1757), also reveal that the son understood the nature of his parents' relationship. Nor, it seems, was their state unknown to friends and neighbors. "I am glad that Miss Brook that was, is now Mrs. Carroll," wrote Onorio Razolini, a one-time Marylander then living in Italy, to his old friend Carroll of Annapolis on receiving the news in October 1757.[48]

The marriage itself made no difference to the legal status of the couple's child. As Blackstone emphasized in his *Commentaries on the Laws of England,* all children born of unwed parents were bastards under the common law. Civil and canon law provided that the subsequent marriage of parents could legitimize any earlier children, provided that the husband acknowledged paternity, but in that regard they differed from the English practice, whereby only an act of

[48] Brooke–CCC, September 8, 1756, Mss. 206. See notation on printed version of this letter and other references above note 45. Marriage articles in Mss. 206. Razolini–CCA, October 17, 1757, Mss. 206.

Parliament could legitimize a bastard (as was sometimes done for noble families). In 1786 Maryland adopted the civil- and canon-law provisions in a revolutionary statute whose preface declared that the inherited law of descents had "originated with the feudal system and military tenures," was "contrary to justice, and ought to be abolished." Before that time, however, Maryland's testamentary statutes failed to interfere with the common-law practice. The disabilities imposed upon bastards in English law did not, however, reach beyond the conveyance of property, as Blackstone emphasized: the children were, after all, innocent of their parents' wrongdoing. In law a child born outside wedlock was "filius nullius," the son of no one, and so could not inherit, nor could he have heirs except those born of his body.[49] These provisions applied only to cases in which a parent died intestate. In the case of Carroll of Carrollton, an only child whose father clearly acknowledged paternity and accepted responsibility for the child's support, and whose father's fortune and compulsion for personal control made it highly unlikely he would die without a will, bastardy had but one major effect: to put a child more completely under the control of his father. He had no claim in law to his father's fortune. His fate, like that of his mother, depended upon his capacity to please his father, who in his will could leave him everything or nothing.

Bastardy, in this sense, served to augment the dependency natural to the lot of all young children, and helps explain the exaggerated servility that characterized Charly's letters home from age eleven, when he was first sent to France, through early manhood. The earliest of his surviving letters was addressed to "Papa and Mama": "I cannot be better satisfied with a Place than this where I hope to accomplish my studies to your greatest satisfaction," he wrote them on September 4, 1749. His father dominated his attention: address letters to both Mama and Papa, the elder Carroll told his son, but that perhaps alone of his suggestions went most often un-

---

[49] Blackstone, *Commentaries on the Laws of England* (London, 1787), I, 454–59, and also II, 248–49; *The Laws of Maryland* (Baltimore, 1811), pp. 16, 18, and, for comparison with earlier laws, see Bacon, *Laws of Maryland at Large*.

heeded. "I am extream glad to hear that you are pleased with me," Charly wrote Papa from France in March 1750, "and I assure you I will do all my endeavours that you may continue in the same sentiment. I can easily see the great affection you have for Me by sending me hear to a College, where I may not only be a learned man, but also be advanced in piety and devotion"; or again, in September, "I am extremely anxious to hear from you and am much desirous to obey your commands . . . Dear Papa I am your most dutiful son. Charles Carroll." Separation from the immediate surveillance of so demanding a father may have been a liberation for Charly. It might also have served to lessen the father's importance, except that the new figures of authority in the young boy's life, such as his older cousin Anthony Carroll, whom Carroll of Annapolis sent to accompany his son in France, served so consciously *in loco parentis*. Thus the one refreshing sign of impatience ended, once again, in formal submission: "Cousin Antony forced me to write to you. I have very little to tell you onely that I am very wel. I am your most dutiful and obedient son."[50]

Fear of incurring his father's displeasure seemed to run through the boy's life: "I hope you will not blame me for spelling ill for My Cousin Antony blames me very much for it" (March 3, 1750); or again, "I hope you wont be angry with me for not writing to you oftener than I do. You desir'd I should write to you at least twice a year. I assure you I shall obey your orders very punctually. This is the third letter. So I have done pretty well, for I think I have not been much above eighteen months out of Maryland" (March 22, 1750). Did Carroll of Annapolis criticize his son's penmanship? "I am sorry that you don't like my writing but that letter was not my best, because I was in grate haste," and his script became egregiously clear, with generous spaces between the lines, though later his zeal would wane, and his father would find reason to complain again of letters "very much interlined and Blotted."[51]

[50] CCC–parents, September 4, 1759, Mss. 206. Father's instructions on addressing both parents in CCA–CCC, September 30, 1754, Mss. 220. CCC–CCA, March 3 and September 24, 1750, and March 23, 1751, Mss. 206.

[51] CCC letters of March and May 1750, Mss. 206; CCA–CCC, October 9, 1752, Mss. 220.

As time went on, the elder Carroll made ever greater efforts to direct his son's life and education through letters. Study poetry, he wrote in 1754; find a fencing and dancing master, as both exercises "contribute greatly to a graceful Carriage. A Gentleman should know how to appear in an Assembly [in] Public to Advantage, and to defend himself if attacked." You had good hair as a child; wear it rather than a wig for it would become you more and be in greater fashion. Take care of your teeth. Do not neglect geography and arithmetic: "Would it not be very odd for a man to know Greek and Latin and not be able to describe the Position of any noted place or Kingdom, or to Add, Multiply, or Divide Sum[s]"? Keep the letters from me together, and review them periodically, the father asked. On his part, Charles Carroll of Annapolis entered all letters to or about his son in a book "so that in case you should be so unfortunate [as to] return not improvd in proportion to the Money Time and Cair laid out on you [it] will at least be undeniable Testimonies of my Attention to your Welfare and a cons[tant] Reproach to you for not corresponding on your part to that attention." But in truth the accounts he'd received of the boy suggested he "should have no reason to apprehend your doing otherwise than Well," so he asked only that Charly make it his "Constant Study and Endeavour" to deserve the continuance of his teachers' and his father's approbation.[52]

As the son grew older, letters from home were keyed to his evolving needs. They noted the increased freedom he would have at Rheims compared to St. Omer's, and later the particular dangers of London. They discussed style ("I would not have you appear mean in anything, but I would have you act with Oeconomy"), suggested he take up horseback riding to improve his posture, that he learn surveying and bookkeeping; they insisted that he not neglect his prayers, his religion, or his God. Always it was clear the boy was not just the object of his father's affection, but an investment. Thus the advice to avoid "the Women of the Town" in London "as you would a Rattle snake," for "some young men

[52] CCA–CCC, September 30, 1754, and October 9, 1752, Mss. 220.

after as much time and Money spent on their Education as has been on yours" had been "snatched from their Expecting parents by the Poison received from Prostitutes." The son understood. "I own I cost you a deal of money, more than ever I shall be worth," he volunteered in February 1759. And he responded to his father's directives with a litany of submissions. As for learning to ride, "certainly nothing can contribute more to form a genteel and easy carriage, of which I stand in great need"; "I shall endeavor to be as great an economist as decency will permit"; "I observe my religious duties" and "trust in the mercy of God"; and "I thank you kindly and sincerely for the good advice contained in your last letter." "For my own part I had rather be disinherited than obliged to marry against my inclination," he bravely wrote in February 1763, after his father had already assured him of his autonomy in choosing a wife. And then the letter closed, "I here solemnly promise . . . never to marry without your full and free consent and approbation. I am Dear Papa Your most dutiful and affectionate Son. . . ."[53]

The bonds of affection between parent and child did not cool, as one might expect as a child approaches adulthood. Instead they deepened. Charly's early years at St. Omer's were less traumatic than they might have been were it not for the presence of familiar persons who tied his life in France to that of his earlier childhood. Cousin Anthony was there, and Charly could write his father news of cousins John ("Jacky") Carroll and Watty Hoxton, of Bobby Darnall and other Marylanders who, he said, did very well at school. But as those boys returned home or went their separate ways, young Carroll was left increasingly alone. The year 1757, when he finished his "universal philosophy," marked a critical divide. Thereafter Anthony returned to Maryland, and Carroll began to study civil law at Bourges accompanied only by a servant. More important, that year the young man of nineteen saw his father for the first time in eight years. He had awaited his parent's arrival during the summer of 1757 with the "greatest impatience," and after

[53] CCA–CCC, August 30, 1758, Mss. 206, and October 5, 1758, Mss. 220; CCC–CCA, February 17 and July 17, 1759, and February 19, 1763, *MdHM*, X, 234, 229–32; XI, 328.

they parted, and he began residence at Bourges, a profound loneliness replaced the closeness of their weeks together, a grief he felt confident his father shared. "I think of you very often in the day and [of] the agreable time we spent to-geather in Paris," he wrote, and that alone seemed to relieve a life he characterized as "a true solitude." Memory of their days together—when they visited the Tuileries, the Louvre, the Palais Royal; when they made little excursions outside Paris—were alive to him still on August 10, 1758, the anni-versary, he noted, of the day he and his father had been re-united. Nor could he recall them without crying, a weakness he hoped his father would love, for the tears were shed for him.[54]

Evidence suggests young Carroll had long been warm and affectionate toward his mother (though many of his letters to her from the mid-1750s have apparently been lost), but now she, too, seemed to share in a new effusiveness of feel-ing. His parents' marriage, which immediately preceded the elder Carroll's departure for Europe, identified her more completely with the father. The family was defined as it had never been before; Charly was part of it—"our greatest hap-piness, your Papas and mine," his mother had written, ". . . depends upon your welfare. Take this for granted that Our hearts is quite fixed on you"—and he felt his absence the more keenly.[55]

Among the differences between lovers and friends, he later noted to a correspondent, Swift had pointed out one, that lovers were "constantly scribbling" to each other, while friends found it hard to write two or three times a year. Once friends, parents and son exchanged letters like lovers (indeed Charly likened the love of parents for their children with that of lovers for each other).[56] Where once Carroll of An-napolis had demanded two letters a year, six was the new minimum, and Mrs. Carroll expressed a wish her son might

[54] CCC–CCA, March 3 and 22, 1750, July 26, 1757, January 1 and August 10, 1758, Mss. 206.

[55] Elizabeth Carroll–CCC, September 8, 1756, Mss. 206.

[56] CCC–Jennings, April 14, 1768, Mss. 203.1; CCC–CCA, December 26, 1759, *MdHM*, X, 247–48 ("Parents like Lovers are apt to be so much blinded as not to discover the faults of their Children, unless strongly pointed out, or perhaps to think those very faults good qualities").

write twice that number. I will write you often, Charly promised his father in January 1758, and would have him do the same, "yet I need not desire it, because I am certain your inclination and love for me are sufficient motives for your writing: pray let me know how my Mama does. . . ." Then again in February: write me when you set sail for Maryland and again immediately on your arrival. "Embrace my Mama at your meeting a thousand times for me, assure her of my love and affection et n'oublier pas dans un moment si doux un fils qui vous aime tout deux de tout son Ceur et qui vous aimora toujours (don't forget in a moment so sweet a son who loves you both with all his heart and who will love you always)." He wrote longer and more labored accounts of his experiences, often in French, addressed his letters more often to both parents, and asked for longer letters from his mother, who would no doubt have many questions about Charly to ask her husband on his return. "I wish I cou'd satisfy them myself by my presence. I long to see you both with all my heart."[57]

Why suffer so protracted a separation? The law was never Charly's subject. At Bourges he found the civil law dry and tedious. He applied himself nonetheless, and as he advanced found the task more agreeable, although he preferred reading Horace, Racine, Virgil, or history, by which, he said, "I learn to be wise at the expense of others." His complaints became more insistent after September 1759, when he arrived in London and advanced from the civil to the common law. The difficulty with that subject came, he volunteered, from "its want of a certain method and order." It was "a mere chaos . . . which added to the natural dryness of this study, renders it almost insupportable to every beginner." Still he was "convinced of its utility and therefore . . . resolved at all hazards to plunge into this Chaos" though he expected "to meet no smaler difficulties than attended Satan on his voyage thro' the primeval one." The difficulty did not this time recede with effort. Fifteen months after his arrival in England Carroll found he had made "little or no ad-

[57] CCA–CCC, September 22, 1759; and Elizabeth Carroll–CCC, March 4, 1759, Mss. 220; CCC–CCA, January 1, 1758, Mss. 206, and February 4, 1758, *MdHM* X, 159; CCC–both parents, June 14, 1758, Mss. 206.

vance" on the subject despite "a pretty serious application," a failure he explained by personal incapacity, the intrinsic difficulty of the subject, and a lack of adequate instruction. Reading law and attending courts was insufficient; the student needed contact with skilled lawyers to help him through the "many intricate passages, obscure reasons of Law" that "frighten the student, almost cast him into despair and create an antipathy even to what he is most desirous of knowing." And law books were so dry. "Why cannot good sense and knowledge be delivered in good language," he asked. "Law must be wrote in an unintelligible Jargon." He preferred the mathematical work he undertook as part of his course in surveying. Geometry was "much more entertaining than the Law; the mind is convinced, strengthened, and instructed by the strict reasoning of the former, puzled, perplexed, and dismayed by the uncertainty, and obscurity of the latter science, founded upon, and still subsisting by villany."[58]

How long must he remain abroad to study such a subject? "Three years in my opinion with all due defferance to yours, will be sufficient to acquire a competent knowledge of the law, so far as will be necessary and useful to me," he suggested. If his father wanted him to become "another Lord Mansfield," a serious application over twenty years aided by a bright capacity would prove insufficient. He needed only a "tincture" of law "so as to be able to study it, without being obliged to attend the courts of judicature or the assistance of others," and that, he argued, he might do as well in Maryland as in the Temple, and "perhaps better." To enter the Temple was costly, he claimed, and to no good purpose since his Catholicism was an "invincible obstacle" to his being called to the bar, which was the whole purpose of entering the Temple. And so in early 1761 he decided to be "so bold for once" as to disobey his father's directions there. But if the elder Carroll persisted in his resolution that his son enter the

[58] CCC–CCA, December 28, 1757, February 4 and June 14, 1758; December 26, 1759, and January 1, 1761, *MdHM*, X, 156, 157, 221, 250, 332–33; CCC–CCA, May 14, 1761, Mss. 206, and April 29, 1763, *MdHM*, XI, 331.

Temple, he added, "let me know it, and I will tho' unwillingly obey."[59]

After his mother's death in May 1761, the young man's desire to return home became overwhelming. "I loved my Mama most tenderly," he wrote his father on hearing the news; "how affectionate, how tender, how loving a mother was she to me! what fond delusive hopes have I entertained of seeing her again! I was too credulous: all my imaginary Joys are vanished in an instant: they are succeeded by the bitter cruel thought of never seeing more my loved lost Mother." The greatest blessing he sought in this life was "to see to enjoy my Parents after so long a separation to comfort to support them in advanced age: one is forever snatched from me!" Remember, "you are now my only consolation in this world . . . I wish you wou'd permit me to return to Maryland in the next fleet!" As for the law, "I am only doing here what I cou'd do as well at home. I am persuaded I can apply as closely to the Law in your house as in the temple: what more distractions shall I meet with in Annapolis than in London?" As it was, he lived in isolation. "I am intimate with nobody." Perhaps because he was "naturally timied and bashful" he disliked going out in company, and his forbearance confirmed a tendency toward "silence and retirement." The laws of his country excluded him from a public career, but he lacked the necessary "openness and affability" for such a course anyway. I am, he said, "too stiff and reserved" and could "only be free and open with an intimate friend." And so his sphere would be a private one —"rural amusements such as farming and other country occupations united to Philosophy (its best allies) form that plan of life which to me appears of all others the most eligible." Yet he was "utterly unacquainted with business." And who could teach him the management of his affairs so well as his father? "If I should lose you too . . . who is there to help me? what experience have I? none . . . I ardently long to be with you. Please write to me by every op-

[59] CCC–CCA, February 30 and April 10, 1760, and March 28, 1761, *MdHM,* X, 253, 256, 338.

portunity: you cannot conceive what pleasure it gives me once to hear from you."[60]

The father held firm. Read only law and what is essential for amusement and relaxation, he advised. What a shame it would be for a gentleman to be ignorant of the laws of his country and so "dependent on ev'ry dirty Petty fogger whose Interest it may be to lead him by such a dependence into endless difficulties"; how commendable for a man of independent fortune to be free of such mercenary advisers and able to advise and assist friends, relatives, neighbors. And suppose Charly should be called to act in a "Publick Character": what an "awkward figure would you make without the knowledge of the Law either as a Legislator or Judge or even an Arbitrator." Law in England was a road to riches and to the highest honors. "It is true," he agreed, "as things now stand you are shut out of the bar." But could he not act as a counselor, in which role "many great fortunes have been made"? Even if he did not want to make law his profession, "yet . . . the knowledge of it is absolutely necessary to ev'ry private Gentleman of fortune who has the least Idea of [being] Independant. I do not send you to the Temple to spend . . . 4 or 5 years to no purpose. I send you to Struggle and Labour . . . as if your whole and sole Dependances was to be on the knowledge of the Law." Charly should enter the Temple and devote himself to English law a full four years. "You vainly at present fancy you might study here," but the "distractions and various occupations" of a man entered into the world made such a scheme almost chimerical. "A long series of years, Reason and experience" had proved it was "necessary to have particular places appointed for the Study of the Law." Carroll of Annapolis had himself wanted to enter the Temple, but on his father's death had returned to Maryland hoping to study law there. He had tried, but to no purpose, and would not have his son make the same error. "A sincere love guided by Reason prompts me to make the rest of your life happy, easy and Ornamental," he assured the young man, "by giving you the best Education in my power and in particular by giving you an Opportunity of acquiring

[60] CCC–CCA, June 10 and July 15, 1761, Mss. 206.

a perfect knowledge of the Law without which I may say a Gentleman is unfinished."[61]

As the son pressed, Carroll of Annapolis suggested that the law might have a more specific utility in the young man's future life. Charly's mastery of the law was "Essential . . . as I shall leave you to dispute many things of Consequence which the present Injustice of the times will not permit me in prudence to contest." Could he not be informed of the nature of these disputes, Charly asked, "of our right and title," of the "pleas of our adversaries? and by whom can I be informed and instructed in all this but by yourself?" The answer was no more direct. "Your estate for this part of the World will be a Considerable one," the father noted, "and of Course lyable to many disputes, especially as a Roman Catholick stands but a Poor Chance for Justice with our Juries in Particular."[62] He turned instead to reinforce his arguments with more emotional appeals. "Isn't it of some satisfaction to you to see by the certificate I sent you that your grandfather was entered of the temple?" Since law was a liberal profession and "being entered of the Temple is a proof of gentility," would not his grandson be equally pleased "to see that you was of the Temple as you are to know your grandfather belonged to that Society?" The costs were a trifle, and perhaps a "gratuity properly placed or some other expedient" could make it possible to enter the bar without taking the required oaths. If Charly was lonely, so was his father. "In you my whole Satisfaction is centered," he had written after his wife's death; "you are the Object of all my Cares." And again, "I love you entirely and my present lonesome condition added to that love might (if any thing could) incline me to call you home, But no Consideration . . . can influence me to call you from the study of the Law: Hence judge how necessary I think the knowledge of it is to you, and let me not suffer so cruel an Absence without answering the end for which alone I submit to it." Still Charly pleaded to return until, on July 24, 1762, Carroll of

[61] CCA–CCC, February 9 and October 5, 1759, and July 14, 1760, Mss. 220.

[62] CCA–CCC, January [9?], 1760, and September 9, 1761, Mss. 220; CCC–CCA, April 10, 1760, Mss. 206.

Annapolis wrote a final letter on the subject in his own hand "because I do not Care my Clerk should know that you still persist after what I have said to you." Was a year more or less to be "Higgled for by a man of your sense and Age?" The son had spent two years studying civil law in preparation for his study of the laws of England. Were six years of his life to be thrown away? "If that should be the Case I have done my duty, you will too late Repent your not Corresponding with my will and intention."[63]

The son politely refused the suggestion that a gratuity might allow him to enter the bar without taking the required oaths (he could not act as a counselor, he said, in so "double and ignominious a character"), but otherwise gave in. "Forced" by his father's "reasons," as he wrote in September 1760, he entered the Temple, and left England in September 1764, a full five years after his arrival. His submission was in fact far more to his parent's will than to his reason, as the elder Carroll recognized, and it took the form at times of a religious surrender. His words resembled those of Christ at Gethsemane (". . . must I live all my life time separated from you? what crime have I done to deserve perpetual banishment? but if it is your will and pleasure that I remain 4 years in London I readily submit"), or of a Catholic in confession. "I must confess you have some little reason of complaint," he once wrote; "I acknowledge my fault, am sorry, and will atone for it. . . ."[64]

In such a compliance there was no doubt great anger, such that the egregious solicitude of young Carroll masked feelings of an opposite character. Where resentment was most natural, as when he heard of his mother's death, he responded instead with extreme concern for the health of that man who had imposed his "banishment" and so denied him access to his mother through the final thirteen years of her life. "Were you to leave me too," he wrote his Papa, "oh then I shou'd be compleatly miserable indeed: death wou'd then be the only comforter of a sad, distressed, unhappy son."

[63] CCA–CCC, letter dated July 1761 on folder; also May 21 and April 16, 1761, Mss. 220; July 24, 1762, *MdHM*, XI, 271.

[64] CCC–CCA, October 13 and 21, 1761, September 16 and April 10, 1760, Mss. 206; also March 29, 1761, *MdHM*, X, 340.

Open hostility was impossible, for at age twenty-three Carroll remained utterly dependent upon his father for material support, present and future, and for affection. There was truth in his appeal of July 23, 1761: "Pray do not talk of leaving me: there is nothing after your displeasure, I so much dread as your death: you are my only support my almost only friend in Maryland."[65]

Anger was contained, moreover, since neither the son nor contemporary society offered any opposition to the conditions of the younger Carroll's subjection. The extent of his dependence upon his father's will in inheriting the family fortune was but a more extreme case of the normal situation of children. Power over the conveyance of property was used by Carroll of Annapolis, as by the seventeenth-century founders of Andover, Massachusetts, or their equivalents anywhere in the contemporary western world, to reinforce patrimonial authority. Of necessity it was so, the younger Carroll thought: if his own future children had claims to his property independent of his will, he suggested in 1767, they might become ungrateful and disobedient. And he, like his father and his grandfather as well, insisted upon the power to apportion his children's inheritances according to how deserving they were.[66]

Charles of Annapolis sent his son to France at a tender age, but he never abandoned the boy. His letters were regular proofs of concern for his son's welfare and dedication to his future—material aplenty to sustain the tendency of all injured, lonely children to idealize a distant parent. In the

[65] CCC–CCA, June 10, 1761, Mss. 206, and July 23, 1761, *MdHM,* XI, 178. See also CCC–CCA, September 16, 1760, Mss. 206, in which CCC submitted to his father's will, agreed to enter the Temple, and again anticipated the sadness he would feel at his father's death while reflecting upon his own precarious health. "If I survive the remainder of my life may be easy and ornamental but not happy; your remembrance will always be accompanied with grief: how shall I ever be able to think of you without shedding tears due to the memory of the best, the dearest, tenderest Parent? but wherefore do I anticipate pains which perhaps I shall never live to feel."

[66] CCC–Graves, November 7, 1767, Mss. 203.1. For a study of the use of property to reinforce parental will, see, for example, Philip J. Greven, Jr., *Four Generations: Population, Land, and Family in Colonial Andover, Massachusetts* (Ithaca, 1970).

father's eyes Charly's years abroad were not a banishment but an investment in the future of a sort that seemed as much a part of the natural order as was the role of property in supporting the dignity and authority of the old over the young. Pain and sacrifice were the price of all great harvests.[67] His insistence that Charly study English law through a full four-year term was the most questionable of his demands. Was he not attempting to win vicariously the legal education denied to him a half century earlier, training his child in a discipline more suited to his own talents and inclinations than to those of that son?[68] Yet even there he was, as the younger Carroll understood, consistent with his own rules of family governance. Your parents will require nothing of you, the father wrote in 1756, "but what we shall be persuaded will be for your true Interest." The younger Carroll offered plentiful objections to his father's sense of his "true Interest" in their controversy over the length of his stay in London, but never doubted that Carroll of Annapolis acted for his son's benefit as he, the father, understood it, rightly or wrongly. "Nothing but a sincere love guided by reason, I am persuaded, cou'd have kept me so long from you," the younger Carroll wrote in September 1760. "The education you have given me, the care you have taken, the trouble and expence you have been at, are strong convincing proofs of this well regulated love." And in the end, when Charly had lived out his time in England, and it seemed his abortive courtship of an English girl, Louisa Baker, might delay still further his return to Maryland, it was the father who could tolerate his absence no longer and insisted that his son not postpone his departure. The child's confidence in his father's

[67] See CCA–CCC, October 10, 1753, on the microfilm of "Carroll Papers" edited by Hanley: "The Husbandsman Annually repeats the Toil of . . . Sowing for his Harvest. When you have compleated higher Studies your Toil will be over, and your Harvest will Daily and always come in."

[68] The elder Carroll remained an active amateur lawyer. He seems to have drawn up a brief for a legal dispute in which he was a party. See CCC–CCA, April 26, 1762, *MdMH*, XI, 265: "the case you have drawn may assist and save some trouble to the Lawyer but is not explicit enough to make him understand the true state of the question or enable him to give his opinion." Note, too, his brief treatise on Maryland dower law in the fragment of a letter to Graves, [1768?] Mss. 206.

affection undercut the tension he might have felt as a result of his illegitimacy. In 1761, when Carroll of Annapolis sent Charly a copy of his will, the young man found that gesture "an unnecessary step if with an intent to remove any apprehensions or disquiet I might feel on the subject. I have been all along pers[uad]ed," he claimed, "that your good sense, steady conduct, and our mutual love were a sufficient security against any disposition of your estate that might greatly prejudice me."[69]

Whatever the ingredients of that mystery which is affection, the bond between father and son remained warm after Charly returned to Maryland. The gentleman who informed you my father gave me £40,000 on my arrival was misinformed, the son wrote William Graves in September 1765, because far more had been put at his disposal, in fact the whole of his father's estate. "We are and are like to continue, on the best terms, never Father and Son were on better." Charles of Annapolis took great pleasure in his son's company and in his accomplishments. Never, however, was his pride greater than in 1773, when his son first won political prominence. He had heard how impatient the people were to read Charly's second "First Citizen" letter, he told his son in March, how crowded the news offices were as people awaited its appearance, how public houses fell silent once it was out, how strangers retired to their lodgings to study it without interruption, how the next morning "every mouth was open in praise of the 1st Citizen." And he wanted to hear more—"every little that is sayed Pro and Con. . . . I may not think things trifling when you may think so." He could not better express his approval, he said, "than by wishing that you may with good Health live to see a Son think as you do and express His thoughts with your force Elegance and Ease." Should that happen, "you will be sensible of the Pleasure I feel."[70]

---

[69] CCA–CCC, July 31, 1756, and also June 29, 1762, Mss. 220; CCA–CCC, September 16, 1760, Mss. 206. CCA–CCC, January 9, 1764, *MdHM*, XII, 28; CCC–CCA, October 13 and 21, 1761, Mss. 206.

[70] CCC–Graves, September 15, 1765, Mss. 203.1, and see also CCA–Graves, December 23, 1768, *MdHM*, XII, 179. CCA–CCC, March 17, and March 25, 1773, ibid., XIV, 368; XV, 56.

The father's satisfaction was sustained as Charles Carroll of Carrollton was entrusted with ever greater public offices. His son's appointment to the Maryland provincial convention of 1774 "shews that His Country Men Esteem him," the elder Carroll wrote Graves. "The Choice was unexpected unsolicited and therefore is a reall Honor." And the honors continued. "Every instance of Confidence in you shewed by the Publick is pleasing to me," he confessed to Charly in August 1775. Through all the intemperate letters he sent his son between 1777 and 1780, including the biting "nor do you deserve any property," pride and affection held true. Even his demand that Charly withdraw from the Maryland senate marked but Charles of Annapolis's effort to revenge himself on an unjust people in the most extreme way known to him, denying it for a time the service of that most esteemed son whom he had raised and educated with such scrupulous attention. Their correspondence was laced with expressions of concern for each other's welfare; and when it seemed his son's spirits were being weighted down by the "dominion of rogues," Charles of Annapolis called to him to let up on public business, "suffer not your spirits to be depressed . . . nothing is dearer to me than your health."[71]

In truth, the younger Carroll's subjection to his father had gone at times beyond what the father expected. He seemed to take criticisms too seriously: "I may perchance again now and then chide you," the elder Carroll once noted, "but you must know a tender parent is always more disposed to receive a Child's apologies favourably than to Censure him." "I never wrote to you as a Child," he claimed on another occasion, that is, he never spoke down to his son or subjected him to simple orders. "I endeavour to convince, I would always avoid the harshness of a command." In 1752, when fifteen-year-old Charly expressed an interest in returning to Maryland, his father depended not only upon his paternal authority but also upon the son's "good sense" to keep the boy at his desk. "I flatter myself," he wrote, ". . . that if it were in [your] power to come you would chuse to stay to

[71] CCA–Graves, December 29, 1774; CCA–CCC, August 14, 1775, and December 8, 1779, Mss. 206.

accomplish yourself as much as possible by purs[uing] your studies."[72] As the boy gave way to a man, Carroll of Annapolis loosened his reins, allowing his son ever greater discretion, as over the management of his personal finances, or the purchase of books, and he gave evidence of respecting the son as a separate and responsible adult. The younger Carroll responded quickly: he decided against showing Cecelius Calvert a letter from his father, as the father suggested, because the circumstances were wrong—and received his father's approbation for that decision; he suggested his father might yield on a dispute with relatives rather than be involved in a long, expensive, and troublesome lawsuit, exchanged letters with his father over the issue of whether or not the interest charged by Carroll of Annapolis on outstanding loans constituted illegal usury, and even guided his father on more trivial matters where he had special expertise. "Let me advise you," he wrote from Paris, "if you buy french wines always buy the best." Without the new independence allowed by his father, and without the confidence of his father's affection, the younger Carroll would not have "made bold" to refuse entering the Temple at first, nor to reopen continually the subject of his return to Maryland—and there, Carroll of Annapolis charged, his son had simply let his reasonings get the better of his good sense.[73]

The largest issue on which father and son differed, one with long-term consequences, concerned their response to Maryland's oppression of her Roman Catholics. The full English Penal Code was never in force in Maryland, although as late as the 1750s the province's lower house of assembly tried to adopt it. Nor were England's statutes against Catholics so severe as those of Ireland, where restrictions upon the purchase, lease, and inheritance of property were added to the civil disabilities imposed upon Catholics and the repression of Catholic worship and education. The Irish Catholic gentry from which the Carrolls descended

---

[72] CCA–CCC, letter in folder marked "Fragments not Readily Identified," probably between 1758 and 1761, Mss. 220; also CCA–CCC, September 30, 1754, June 29, 1762, and October 9, 1752, Mss. 220.

[73] CCC–CCA, October 11, 1763, *MdHM*, XI, 345; CCA–CCC, June 29, 1762, Mss. 220.

suffered most from these restrictions in the eighteenth century, as that family understood: "the present situation of the Isle land, will only renew the memory of past wrongs," the younger Carroll noted in explaining why he had decided not to visit his ancestral home in 1761. "How unavailing to remember what we can not revenge! how melancholy to behold, ancient, noble, and once flourishing families now reduced to beggary." Maryland Catholics were, then, better off than those in England or Ireland; yet the civil and religious disabilities imposed in the lifetime of Charles "the settler" remained to harry his son and grandson, and the hostility of the provincial legislature continued a threat. Its efforts to adopt English laws against Catholics failed; but in 1756 it succeeded in imposing a double tax on all land held by Roman Catholics so as to help finance the French and Indian War, and thereby awoke a new surge of anger and resentment in Carroll of Annapolis.[74]

Catholics could avoid the burden of Maryland's discriminatory laws by taking the required oaths and renouncing their religion. Daniel Dulany once suggested that Carroll of Carrollton awaited only his father's death to take that course, "shake off his fetters, and dazzle the world with the splendour of his talents." Carroll denied the allegation; yet devotion to his father was probably a far greater impediment to conformity than was his faith itself. He wrote a little on the subject of religion, and what he did write suggests that his Catholicism, like that of Alexander Pope (his favorite poet) and other English Catholics, was suffused by the rationalism of the Enlightenment. Granted for purposes of argument that his religion was absurd, he wrote Graves in 1774, "What,

---

[74] *Maryland Archives,* LII (Baltimore, 1935), xviii-xix; CCA–CCC, July 26, 1756, Mss. 220 ("Tho we are threatened with the introduction of the English Penal Laws into this Province, they are not yet introduced. But last May a Law pass'd here to double Tax the Lands of all the Roman Catholics"). On the last measure, see also Curran, *Catholics in Colonial Law,* pp. 104–05. For English hostility to Catholics, see Mary Peter Carthy, *English Influences on Early American Catholicism* (Washington, 1959), pp. 1–12. Brief summaries of Irish and English legislation are provided in J. C. Beckett, *The Making of Modern Ireland, 1603–1923* (New York, 1966), pp. 151–52, 157–59; and Basil Williams, *The Whig Supremacy, 1714–1760* (Oxford, 1962), pp. 68–75. CCC–CCA, March 28, 1761, Mss. 206.

then, do you advise me to quit a false religion and adopt one equally false, and this merely to humour the prejudices of fools, or to be on a footing with knaves? I have too much sincerity and too much pride to do either," he added, "even if my filial love did not restrain me." If his countrymen considered him incapable of serving in public office "for believing the moon to be made of green cheese, in this respect their conduct, if not wicked, is not less absurd than my belief," he wrote, and rather than comply he would serve his country from the private sphere. Carroll did not leave the church after his father's death in 1782. By then Catholicism was far more than a creed to him. It was a tradition that distinguished his from other branches of the family and from the mass of his countrymen, for he, his father, and his grandfather had held true to their faith despite laws that the Revolution confirmed to have been unjust and oppressive. By then, too, the Carrolls could remain Catholic with pride but without cost, for Maryland's discriminatory statutes had become but part of the colonial past.[75]

During the earlier years of the eighteenth century, if the Carrolls chose to avoid the burden of their province's anti-Catholic laws and yet to remain within their preferred religion, they had but one choice—to leave Maryland. And in the wake of the assembly's double tax, Carroll of Annapolis seriously considered the possibility of migration. He was determined to quit his plantation and all his other possessions, he wrote his son on July 26, 1756, "if I can meet with the success I expect from my scheme," which may have included resettling in the Louisiana Territory. He predicted that the sale of his settled and improved estate would entail a loss of at least £10,000 sterling, "but to procure Ease to myself by flying from the pursuits of Envy and Malice, and to procure a good establishment for you, I am willing to undergo and struggle with all the difficulties and inconveniences attending on a new Settlement in a new Climate." One purpose of his trip abroad in 1757 may have been to win a grant of land near the Arkansas River in Louisiana. If so, it was unsuccess-

[75] Dulany and Carroll in Onuf, *Maryland and Empire*, pp. 74, 79; CCC–Graves, August 15, 1774, *MdHM*, XXXII, 222–23.

ful. Still he continued to sell his Maryland properties. Since his return he had sold £2,000 sterling worth of his possessions, he wrote Charly on February 9, 1759, and he hoped that with the peace they would sell more quickly and at a better price. "The Disposition of our Lower House of Assembly is as inveterate as ever," he reported. Even if its efforts further to distress Catholics met failure, who would willingly consent to live among such men? It would be, he thought, to his son's "Advantage Comfort and Satisfaction" if he sold his estate; yet he would retain his properties in and near Annapolis, two seats of land each containing about 13,000 acres, his slaves, and his share in the Baltimore Iron Works to the very last so Charly would be able to choose for himself whether or not to remain in Maryland.[76]

At first the younger Carroll supported his father's course. "Pray have you as yet met with an offer for selling your lands?" he asked in June 1758, "or do you remain still determined to sell them: does our ennimies still continue to persecute us? Their injustice and ungratefulness quite surprises me. . . . Their complaints as well as their reasons . . . are entirely groundless." Within five months he had swung to the negative: "Were I to counsel you I would say do nothing, or at least wait until affairs are clarified, until European troubles have subsided." But he remained uncertain, ready to consider the arguments for his father's position. Elizabeth Carroll preferred Maryland to all other countries, he noted, but she had seen no other, knew no other, had no friends elsewhere. "Perhaps had she been as long absent from it, as I have been, that love so undeservedly bestowed on an ungratefull Country, would be greatly diminished. I cant conceive how any Roman Catholic especially an Irish Roman Catholic can consent to live in England or any of the British dominions," he wrote in December 1759, "if he is able to do otherwise." True, Catholics were at present unmolested, but the penal laws remained legal and could be put into execution at any time. This dependency upon the forbearance of the powerful was offensive to a "man of spirit," and the younger Carroll confessed a "natural aver-

[76] CCA–CCC, July 26, 1756, and February 9 and April 16, 1759, Mss. 220.

sion to all such oppressions, and to an humble, silent, groveling submission." Yet he could bear that humiliation in Maryland, he decided, "rather . . . than be deprived of the pleasure and comfort of living happily togeather" with his family.[77] The decision was critical. Maryland was home, the only one he had ever had, the only place he might be easily and speedily reunited with his parents. These were the years in which his affection for his family surged, when his homesickness mounted. And so with greater firmness and consistency he began to try to dissuade his headstrong father from emigrating, and in the course of that effort developed attitudes that would shape his later political career.

Granted that Maryland was unfit for Catholics to live in, where was there a fit place? "The same reasons that make Maryland an uneligible mode," the younger Carroll wrote, "make England equally uneligible: to exchange a bad situation for a worse, or equally bad, wou'd argue want of Judgement." And if the father left Maryland for France, "there you will only exchange religious for civil Tyranny," which of the two was, in his opinion, "the greatest evil. Civil oppression has nothing to console us; religious persecutions are always attended with this consolation at least, of not going unrewarded." (The argument offered a rare instance in which Carroll's Catholicism affected his political argument. The notion that suffering in this world might earn a reward in the next was common to Catholics, but bordered on heresy for most American Protestants.) For all his doubts of yesteryear, Carroll now decided he would "chuse to live under english government rather than under any other: Catholick I mean," he explained, "for I know of no Catholick country where that greatest blessing civil liberty is enjoyed."[78]

Among the English dominions, Maryland has strong advantages. Charles of Annapolis had taken it upon himself to describe that colony for his long-absent son. "Nature has been almost beyond Bounds bountiful to it," he wrote; "the

[77] CCC–CCA, June 14 and November 7, 1758, and December 10, 1759, Mss. 206.
[78] CCC–CCA, January 1, 1761, and February 30, 1760, Mss. 206.

Climate is very good . . . the Soil in General is very fruit-full and yields with very little Labour a plentifull increase of whatever is trusted to it." Cattle and poultry of all sorts multiplied with only moderate care; the vast variety of root crops "made a famine almost impossible." The province's fruits were delicious, and it contained plentiful fowl and game. If its ignorant and malicious people were in any way equal to the country itself, he concluded, "Maryland in time might be in reality what the most pleasant and delightfull Countries are described to have been by the fruitfull fancy of the best poets." The account was picturesque, Charly answered, and "by all accounts your encomiums are not unmerited. How displeasing then must the thought be of Leaving such a charming country to avoid the unjust the malicious prosecutions of an ignorant, base, contemptible rabble." And how unnecessary since its injustice might be blocked by a moderate governor, by the upper house of assembly with its many gentlemen of a "distinterested, enlarged, and noble way of thinking," and by the proprietor, who was not at present disposed to permit further molestation of Catholics. With time, as Maryland's people became "more civilized," he believed that they too might leave behind their "prejudices and animosities." Wealth earned by their own industry might satisfy their avarice or at least moderate their "eager longing after other men's property." And so Catholics could hope one day to enjoy peace and tranquillity in Maryland, although "men's minds and dispositions in that country must undergo a great change, before so favourable a revolution can happen."[79]

Through the pain of separation from family in the name of future gain, through reflection upon the situation of Catholics in the eighteenth-century Atlantic world, Carroll of Carrollton came at a young age to a mature wisdom. The admirer of Voltaire knew from experience as well as literature that there was pain and disappointment in even a best of all possible worlds: "true happiness on earth is not to be met with"; "in all we do there is a mixture of pain and pleasure." In the absence of utopia he cast his lot with Maryland as the best of the imperfect alternatives life presented to him. There he might experience the joys of familial affection, but the future was filled with uncertainty. "I may lead a happy life in my native country," he thought, "tho' the prospect seems unpromising. But as I expect little happiness, so if I meet with difficulties I shall not be disappointed and unprepared."[80]

Charles of Annapolis was of a different frame of mind. He saw life in sharp contrasts, not in shades of gray. But in the end he, too, abandoned all thought of leaving his home, probably not because he was persuaded by Charly's arguments, but because he had come to understand that he, not his opponents, would suffer most from the impulses of his pride and anger. Unlike his own father, Carroll of Annapolis had been born and lived all his adult life in Maryland. Both his friends and his enemies were there; by them he knew himself. To go elsewhere, abandoning a place perfect in all respects but one, would be to make of himself, late in the sixth decade of his life, an alien. He spoke at first of the hard realities of age. "Were I younger," he wrote his son in July 1760, he would definitely quit Maryland, but "at my age . . . a change of Climate would certainly shorten my Days." Still he was selling his property so his son might "the sooner and with more ease and less loss leave it." Three and a half years later his tone was far different. "When my eyes are Closed live where you Please," he wrote Charly, but "I think Maryland more agreable to sollid happyness than any Country I have seen. It is plentifull and the Climate Charming."[81]

His father's willingness to consider his advice and arguments, to leave him critical life choices, was all the more pleasing to the younger Carroll because little tastes of free-

[80] CCC–CCA, February 30, 1760, Mss. 206, October 11, 1761 (from Paris), and March 17, 1762, *MdHM*, XI, 345, 261.
[81] CCA–CCC, July 14, 1760, Mss. 220, and January 9, 1764, *MdHM*, XII, 28.

dom promised to become full drafts. "God be thanked I have been born to an independent fortune," he wrote in 1760, "for I am sure I shou'd never have acquired one by a servile dependence on the great. I have too much pride to cringe and too much sincerity to flatter, both necessary to him whose hopes are centered on Powerfull men." But he had not been clearly born to an independent fortune, had suffered a dependency not wholly free of servility, and his hopes had long centered on a powerful man. Raised under the authority of a strong father, he came to value (like that father) the dignity of independence; but to win it took time, patience, and a measure of its apparent opposite, submission. From his mother's example and from the experience of successfully negotiating his childhood under a strong and demanding father, Carroll of Carrollton learned that temporary surrender need not signal dishonor or defeat. It could instead be a necessary step toward ultimate freedom. The insight would serve him well with a headstrong people. "There is a time," he wrote in 1777, "when it is wisdom to yield to injustice, and to popular frenzies and delusions: many wise and good men have acted so."[82]

In the course of debate with his father, Carroll also made a decision critical to his revolutionary career: that he would live in Maryland. Despite his reservations about government by the people, he was never tempted by the Loyalists' fantasy of England as a home where they could be protected from popular oppression. For Catholics, of course, that prospect was particularly unrealistic (which may be why they, unlike many other minority groups, rallied to the American cause); England's penal laws were still more harsh than those of Maryland. Carroll had, moreover, lived in England. It had been no home to him, and he had had exile enough. Now he would stay in America, as he had decided firmly a decade and a half earlier, knowing there was a price to pay for that decision. He would persist, work to improve the best among flawed alternatives, and not insist upon absolute right in a world where it was not to be found. Just as he had chosen

<hr />

[82] CCC–CCA, January 29, 1760, and November 13, 1777, Mss. 206.

to live in Maryland not because it was perfect but because it was better than England or France, so he overcame his fears for the future of the republic by comparing them to a yet more frightening possibility. In a triumphant United States the rage of party and jarring interests might keep alive civil dissensions until men grew tired of discord and turned (as all history taught) to some strong leader who could end the anarchy by establishing a tyranny like that the Americans had originally fought. But defeat at British hands promised, he decided, a more certain and a worse fate: "we shall become a second Ireland . . . governed by a military force and corrupt and venal governments."[83]

Carroll's arguments during the Legal Tender Act crisis also echoed his words of times gone by. His father's demand that he quit the Maryland senate when the act was passed paralleled Carroll of Annapolis's earlier determination to leave that province after its legislature imposed a double tax on Catholics' land. And once again the son argued that to withdraw would gain nothing, that it would in fact make their situation worse. Evil would be defeated not by those who fled the field, but by those who held their ground to fight another day. Having come to terms with a world marked by the sin of Adam, where there were no great dreams to be dreamed, no great passions to be realized, and never having idealized the people, Carroll escaped the acute disillusionment of revolutionaries who first encountered the tyranny of the majority in the tender acts and other similar legislative enactments of the late 1770s and 1780s. The problem was not new to him, nor was its solution—strengthened checks and balances, by governors and upper houses removed by steps from the democracy itself. And so again the reflections and experiences of times past helped him to persist through the turns of revolutionary politics, displaying a labored equanimity in the face of temporary injustices, working to make not a perfect but a better world. Never expecting much, he won more than he had dared to hope. Within a decade and a half the "favourable revolution" of which he

[83] CCC–CCA, March 15, 1777, Mss. 206.

had dreamed in 1760, by which Catholics would be allowed peace and tranquillity, was durably accomplished in his home province.

Did Carroll join the independence movement to win religious liberty? He suggested as much himself: he had "entered zealously into the Revolution," he wrote in 1827, "to obtain religious, as well as civil liberty." But of the two he had long since ranked civil liberty first; and his arguments of the period before independence, like those of his father and most other contemporary Americans, were concerned primarily with civil liberty. He was no doubt a strong supporter of religious freedom: "I am a warm friend to toleration," he wrote William Graves in 1774. "I execrate the intolerating spirit of the Church of Rome, and of other Churches. . . ." Yet his convictions remained primitive compared to those of men like Isaac Bacchus or James Madison, colonists who took a particular interest in that issue. Carroll criticized efforts to suppress dissenting religions less as interferences with divine truth (for he was willing at least to entertain Graves's notion that all religions were alike to the Creator), or as violations of freedom of thought, than as an example of counterproductive policymaking. "No persecutions have ever been found effectual in suppression of any religious sect," he wrote, "unless such as will totally exterminate it . . . by banishment or by putting to death men women and children." Men might be "laughed or coaxed" out of their opinions, but "force of all others is certainly the most improper argument to convince the mind—with it those against whom it is employed are apt to conclude that their opinions can not be confuted by other arguments." If public offices were confined to members of the established church, that alone might tempt men from other religions. Such measures were, however, more often the product of simple corruption than of creedal convictions. "Designing and selfish men invented religious tests to exclude from posts of profit and trust their weaker or more conscientious fellow-subjects," he argued, "thus to secure to themselves all the emoluments of Government." He once suggested that the laws on religion undermined public tranquillity, that if men of all sects were "allowed . . . to converse freely with each other their aversion from a difference of religious principles would soon wear away."[84] Without more considered convictions on the importance of voluntarism in religious commitments or of freedom of thought from public restraint he could not proceed from a defense of toleration to the more radical separation of church and state, which became the meaning of religious freedom in the course of the revolutionary period.

Nor was Carroll's belief in toleration as broad as it might have been. He called his father's attention to the liberal provisions on religion in Pennsylvania's constitution of September 1776, which declared "that all men have a natural and unalienable right to worship Almighty God according to the dictates of their own consciences and understanding," and assured equal civil rights to all men who acknowledged the "being of a God." But by all appearances Carroll of Carrollton was content with the less inclusive assurances in Maryland's constitution, passed in November 1776, which spoke not of the rights of men but of their duty to worship God in ways acceptable to themselves, and provided that "a declaration of a belief in the Christian religion" might be required for admission to offices of trust or profit.[85] Carroll, in short, favored religious liberty for Catholics in an age when freedom of religion was coming to mean far more than that.

In removing the disabilities imposed on Catholics, however, the Revolution gave the Carrolls, who were so long men without a country, something more valuable than religious freedom alone. It gave them a political home. As they identified with the cause of their country, the resentments of earlier years faded before a new pride clear already in November 1765, when the younger Carroll advised an English friend to sell his estate in the mother country and "purchase lands in this province where liberty will maintain her empire" for ages after it had disappeared from England. His father, too, felt free to associate himself ever more closely

---

[84] CCC–Rev. John Stanford, Doughoregan, October 9, 1827, in Rowland, *Carroll*, II, 358; CCC–Graves, August 14, 1774, *MdHM*, XXXII, 222–23; CCC–Jennings, August 12, 1767, and also October 14, 1766, Mss. 203.1.
[85] Constitutional provisions in Curran, *Catholics in Colonial Law*, pp. 113–14.

with a land he loved, whose growth he had witnessed and in which he had shared. "I am now very near 73," he wrote Graves in 1774; "I have lived Here full 54 years [and] I have not been a Careless observer. Our Increase in People trade agriculture and Arts is almost incredible." He had returned in 1720 from studies abroad in a boat carrying wheat from London to gentlemen's families in Maryland, but now America was "almost . . . the granary of Europe." Then there had been two pairs of cartwheels in the province, which brought the stares and admiration of planters; now there were enough wagons and carriages in the province to equip an army. By 1774 his son's absorption in the extralegal government of the Revolution signaled the end of their forced exclusion from the public sphere, so Carroll of Annapolis could write of his country's strivings for freedom as "our Struggles," and he predicted eventual success.[86] The return of a civil capacity to Catholics in the Maryland constitution of 1776 confirmed a new tolerance begun earlier, in the revolutionary movement. A crisis of legitimacy, the Revolution legitimized the Carrolls, raising them to full-fledged membership in the new republican state.

That victory was, it would seem, most important to Carroll of Annapolis. It was he who insisted that Charly study law so he might better be able to serve in a "publick Character," who refused to consider the civil disabilities imposed upon Catholics as anything but a temporary injustice, whose thirst for participation in the public sphere made him willing even to violate his "virtuous" character by paying a gratuity that his son might enter the bar without taking the required oaths. Carroll of Carrollton had found it far easier to forsake such ambitions and envisage a life without public office. Indeed, he found the private life better suited to his personality and personal preferences, and endured public service from a sense of duty, resenting the "tedious absence" from his "dearest connections" that it demanded—from the domestic life denied him through so much of his earlier life.[87] He may

[86] CCC–Mr. Bradshaw, November 21, 1765, Mss. 203.1; CCA–Graves, December 23, 1768, *MdHM*, XII, 183; November 29, 1774, Mss. 206.
[87] CCC–Molly Carroll, Saratoga, April 15, 1776; and also to CCA, May 24, 1777, Mss. 206.

in fact have entered public life from a long-practiced habit of gratifying his father's wishes. After Carroll of Annapolis died in 1782, the younger Carroll's political career failed to build upon what eminence he had achieved in earlier years. Samuel Adams became governor of Massachusetts, Richard Henry Lee became president of the Continental Congress, and Josiah Bartlett, the son of a shoemaker, became governor of New Hampshire. But Carroll of Carrollton refused to take up a seat in the federal constitutional convention despite his interest and expertise in its work, and resigned his place in the United States Senate when to remain there would have required resigning his place in the more powerful and more convenient Maryland senate.[88] He seems to have had no ambition for higher office: it was from the Maryland upper house that he retired at the age of sixty-three. During the final three decades of his life his contributions to the new nation were from what he once called the private station. Carroll was a founder of the Second Bank of the United States as he had been of the First; and he was probably more confident of the future on July 4, 1828, when he turned the first sod at ceremonies inaugurating the Baltimore and Ohio Railroad, than he had been at the birth of the republic.

Did he ever find the warm family life he sought? The courting of Louisa Baker over, Carroll had returned to Maryland as a bachelor ready to marry but fearful of an institution that might link him for life to "a dull, insipid companion, whose whole conversation is confined to the colours and fashions of her dress and the empty chit chat of the tea table, or to the salting of hogs." Within a year he became engaged to a first cousin, Rachel Cooke, who was, he wrote an English correspondent, in "no ways inferior to Louisa"; but she died before their marriage. Soon he was betrothed once more, again to a cousin, Mary (Molly) Darnall, nineteen years old and the favorite of Charles of Annapolis, in whose home she had been raised for the previous seven years. "She really is a sweet tempered, charming, neat girl" though

---

[88] For the reasons why Carroll refused to join the constitutional convention, see Hoffman, *Spirit of Dissension*, p. 268.

somewhat too young for him, the younger Carroll wrote a friend. To Graves he stressed her cleanliness (a virtue "very often wanting in the fair sex": some men find prostitutes cleaner than their wives, he noted, and he presumed they spoke from experience). And again he protested that "I prefer her . . . to all the women I have ever seen, even to Louisa."[89] At first a light-hearted woman who enjoyed society and the pleasures life afforded, Molly was perhaps ill suited to a man who once described himself as "naturally . . . of a melancholy and contemplative cast." Nor was she the companion of cultivated understanding whom Carroll had hoped to find: "I would write a separate letter to Molly," he told his father from Philadelphia in 1774, "if I had a subject to write on, but not having seen any of the ladies as yet, I want matter for a letter."[90]

The marriage was celebrated in June 1768, and Charles waited impatiently as his wife bore him three daughters in 1769, 1770, and 1772 before producing a son and heir in the year of Lexington and Concord. He adjusted only with difficulty to the role of father and seems to have been, as one biographer said, "something less than the adoring parent" of his young children, most of whom never saw adolescence. Seven babies in all were born to the family, of whom only three reached the age of four.[91]

During these years Charles, who once prescribed company as a remedy for melancholy, fought off his chronic depression by work, for which the work of revolution provided but one source. He absorbed himself "in a variety of employments, business, exercise and study. In short," he wrote in 1772, "I never allow myself time to be idle, . . . and to this perpetual occupation" he ascribed the "equal flow of spirits" so unnatural to his constitution. His wife found her consola-

---

[89] CCC–Bradshaw, November 21, 1765; to Christopher Bird, September 17, 1765; to Jennings, August 12, 1767; and to Graves, August 23 and November 7, 1767, all Mss. 203.1. For CCA's affection for Molly, and his assurances that she was his son's own choice, see his letter to Graves, December 23, 1768, *MdHM*, XII, 178.

[90] CCC–Graves, August 14, 1772, *MdHM*, XXXII, 218; to CCA, September 9, 1774, Mss. 206.

[91] Hanley, *Carroll*, pp. 168–70; genealogical charts in DeVanter, *"Anywhere So Long as There Be Freedom,"* after p. xvi.

tion in opium. In May 1782, she witnessed Charles of Annapolis's fatal fall from the porch of his home, withdrew to her room, and met her own eternity two weeks later. Her husband never remarried. Nor did he find the pride and pleasure in his son that his own father had wished for him. Charles Carroll IV, or Carroll of Homewood, was a spendthrift whose addiction to alcohol caused deep disappointment in his father, who in 1814 wrote that he could no longer sign letters "with the name of an affectionate father" because the course of his son's life "has nearly extinguished my affection."[92]

Carroll of Carrollton spent his old age in the home of his daughter, Mary Caton, three of whose daughters married members of the English aristocracy, becoming the duchess of Leeds, Lady Stafford, and the marchioness of Wellesley when the marquis of Wellesley was the Lord Lieutenant of Ireland. For some the last of these marriages marked a glorious conclusion to the family's odyssey: "Charles Carroll of Carrollton," began a toast of 1827, "in the land from which his grandfather fled in terror, his granddaughter now reigns a queen." Others might find it a strange achievement for a family whose most famous member had signed the Declaration of Independence and opposed the use of titles in the new nation. But it was no stranger, perhaps, than Carroll's own words of 1828, when he replied to a patriotic address from the blacksmiths of Baltimore. Hope for the survival of the republic, he said, rested in the "morality, sobriety and industry of the people, and on no part more than on the mechanics," who made up the greatest part of the country's "useful citizens." Forty-six years earlier he had seen such men as part of the "vulgar at large."[93] The last of the generation of 1776 had lived to join the railroad age, and made some peace with the world of Jackson.

Even in the furthest reaches of his life, however, the past survived within him. As he began his ninth decade, and his

---

[92] CCC–Graves, August 14, 1772, *MdHM*, XXXII, 218; Mason, "Carroll," pp. 27–28; CCC to his son, May 15, 1814, quoted in ibid., p. 30.
[93] Mason, "Carroll," p. 31; toast of July 4, 1827, in Rowland, *Carroll*, II, 352. Address of William Baer on behalf of the blacksmiths of Baltimore, July 4, 1828; Carroll's reply; and CCC–Chase, February 3, 1782, Mss. 206.

sight slowly slipped away, Carroll of Carrollton found pleasure in the conversation of a young Frenchman who could discuss Racine and other French dramatists with him, and who read for him from Molière. Occasionally Carroll would stop him, the visitor recalled, "or ask me to read over again some parts which he had either not well understood, or wished to hear again, the better to enjoy the wit and gaiety of the passage."[94] And so he found final solace and joy in speaking a language he had learned through a time of pain under the demands of an exacting father, and in works which, some three quarters of a century earlier, that father had asked him to lay aside—that he might better master the mysteries of law.

[94] Reminiscences of a French visitor, September 23, 1833, Mss. 206.

CHAPTER SIX

———⋘⋙———

ON FAITH AND
GENERATIONS IN
REVOLUTIONARY
POLITICS

THE REVOLUTION OF 1776 was the work of men who were in many ways astoundingly different from one another. Among Adams, Sears, Young, Lee, and Carroll there were two Anglicans, a Congregationalist, a deist, and a Roman Catholic; a merchant, a doctor, a man best described as a big businessman of the Chesapeake variety (part banker, part landlord, part planter, part manufacturer), and two politicians; a man of undistinguished origins who was upwardly mobile, one of humble birth with more limited mobility, another who was wellborn but hard pressed to maintain his social position, a man of wealth conscious of the precariousness of all American fortunes, and, finally, a patriot who remained steadfastly unconcerned with economic and social status. All were active in mobilizing popular resistance to Britain, but in ways as distinctive as the communities in which they worked. Even when they spoke the same values, their words took on different meanings. "Virtue" to Adams, Young, Lee, and Carroll implied sacrifice and austerity, but allowed Sears to build a fortune while serving his country. Five men, of course, say little about the masses who supported the Revolution. Nor are they in any sense a scientific sample of the Revolution's leadership. But that there were within that handful of colonists preeminent in the American revolutionary movement five such diverse persons suggests that revolution is not so different from the rest of life, where people frequently do the same thing for different reasons.

Still, those who committed themselves to the American cause had much in common; they came from the same place in time, and their beginnings were critical to the politics of their lives. The Old Revolutionaries were a generation of American politicians born in the 1720s and 1730s who reached a natural plateau of power and influence four decades later. Adams (born in 1722), Sears (1729), Young (1731), Lee (1732), and Carroll (1737) were joined by others such as Josiah Bartlett (1729), Sears's colleagues Alexander McDougall (1732) and John Lamb (1735), Philadelphia's Charles Thomson (1729), the Virginians George Mason (1725) and Patrick Henry (1736), North Carolina's Cornelius Harnett (1723), and South Carolina's Christopher Gadsden (1724). Some of these were "new men of the revolution"—that is, they represented social or economic groups that were absorbed into organized politics only in the course of the American Revolution. Sears and Young are examples. They lacked the overriding sense of corporate identity, either with a community or with past and future generations, that was so central to the lives of Adams, Bartlett, Lee, and Carroll. In their search for the individual satisfactions of doing well they suggested a later America. More often the Revolutionaries entered politics under the old colonial system, serving in their provincial assemblies and distinguishing themselves as defenders of legislative prerogatives.[1]

---

[1] Lee had entered the Virginia House of Burgesses in 1758; Samuel Adams and Josiah Bartlett became assembly members in 1765. Harnett served as a justice of the peace for Hanover County and a commissioner of the town of Wilmington before becoming a member of the North Carolina assembly in 1754. On his career, see R. D. W. Connor, *Cornelius Harnett: An Essay in North Carolina History* (Raleigh, N.C., 1909). Gadsden entered the South Carolina assembly in 1757. Like Harnett, who became a prominent spokesman for the provincial legislature in controversies with the Crown, Gadsden so alienated the royal governor that the governor tried to unseat him from the assembly in 1762. Later Gadsden defended assembly prerogatives in the Wilkes fund controversy. See Richard Walsh's

As children of mid-eighteenth-century America, the Old Revolutionaries remained uncomfortable with parties, and indeed with public political division of any sort. Division indicated decay: it proved that the community had failed to unite behind its own best interests, that some of its members had chosen instead the path of selfishness and corruption. The pre-Tammany politics of revolutionary New York, like those of the Boston caucus, sought to win a broad agreement on matters of public policy. Their inherited discomfort with division committed them, in short, to a politics that demanded a particular capacity for patience and persistence. And there were other, more formal political ideas common to Americans of the late colonial period: that the British constitution was uniquely able to protect freedom; that the "balance" of King, Lords, and Commons had to be protected, above all from pretensions to greater power on the part of the Crown; that simple democracy was unstable, leading to anarchy and then military depotism, and could work if at all only in small areas where the people were like one another, and separate interests did not divide man from man.

As they moved from resistance to revolution, the Old Revolutionaries left behind some of these traditional beliefs. Their experiences between 1764 and 1776 led them to decide that the British constitution was not, after all, so splendid a "machine" for the protection of freedom; and the willingness of Americans to obey the elected committees and congresses of the resistance movement gave reason to conclude that government founded on the people alone was a far more practical possibility than established wisdom allowed.[2] In declaring an end to hereditary rule and in founding a re-

---

brief summary of his life in the introduction to *The Writings of Christopher Gadsden* (Columbia, S.C., 1966), esp. pp. xix–xx; and also Walsh, "Christopher Gadsden: Radical or Conservative Revolutionary?" *South Carolina Historical Magazine,* CXIII (1962), 195–203. Uncited biographical material in this chapter is drawn from *The Dictionary of American Biography* (New York, 1928–36).

[2] Pauline Maier, "The Beginnings of American Republicanism, 1765–1776," *The Development of a Revolutionary Mentality; Papers presented at the First* [Library of Congress] *Symposium, May 5 and 6, 1972* (Washington, 1972), pp. 99–117.

public the Americans opened a new era in government. Even the word "revolution" began to take on its modern meaning and imply a major upheaval, a transforming event. In earlier times the word had continued to reflect its origins in astronomy and suggested a return to some earlier state, much as the sun or moon "revolved." Appropriately, colonists had first set out to recapture the "balanced" British constitution of the late seventeenth century. By 1776, however, they instead hoped to found—in the phrase from Virgil added by Charles Thomson to the Great Seal of the United States—a *"novus ordo seclorum,"* a new order of the ages. The success of America's republican experiment was far from certain, and remained so into the nineteenth century. No man living could foresee the consequences of independence, John Adams wrote James Warren in April 1776. "We may please ourselves with the prospect of free and popular governments, but there is great Danger that these Governments will not make Us happy. God grant that they may!"[3]

In the midst of change, some revolutionaries cultivated continuity. For Josiah and Mary Bartlett, the permanent alterations the Revolution brought to them and their provincial world were grafted upon a larger field of stability. Josiah might help design a national government that would determine the happiness of all future generations, but the seasons would come as always, the drought and worms at most a little earlier, a little later; and even the failure of the Revolution would have been, it seemed, but another of the troubles that marked men's existence and for which Providence would again somehow provide. For Samuel Adams above all 1776 represented not a departure from the past but a working out of New England's historic mission, a commitment of America to the familiar ways of his ancestors. To a remarkable extent his admirers from other parts of the colonies agreed. For Thomas Young, for Richard Henry

[3] On Thomson see J. Edwin Hendricks, "Charles Thomson and the Creation of 'A New Order of the Ages,'" in John B. Boles, ed., *America: The Middle Period. Essays in Honor of Bernard Mayo* (Charlottesville, 1973), pp. 1–13. Adams to Warren, April 22, 1776, *Warren-Adams Letters,* I, *1743–1777* (Boston, 1917), 233–34.

Lee, and also for Christopher Gadsden,[4] New England provided a working model for the new republic. There, Lee claimed, the people were wise, frugal, hard-working, free of aristocratic parade. New England's political institutions were more closely tied to its people than were those of other sections, its communities more united behind their common interests. New England was, moreover, as Young emphasized, an open society that offered abundant opportunities to able men of humble birth.

There was a basis for this conception of New England. The prevalence of town meetings, the existence of charter governments in Rhode Island and Connecticut under which all provincial offices were filled through elections, the fact that Massachusetts's upper house was elected by the lower rather than appointed by the Crown (as was normal in royal colonies)—all these made New England's government distinctively dependent upon the people or "republican." Because more important positions were filled by election, the opportunities for political mobility were of course greater in New England than elsewhere. Because its people were mainly of native birth and British origin, and because they had from the settlement years clustered in towns, New England may well have realized a corporate ethic more completely than did other parts of America. Its relative poverty and its Puritan heritage also gave it a sobriety of style that a later age would call "republican simplicity." It was, however, also peculiarly insular, resembling more the world of seventeenth-century covenanters than the pluralistic America of the nineteenth century, which was better prefig-

---

[4] Gadsden's comments in a letter to Samuel Adams, Charleston, April 4, 1779, in Walsh, ed., *Writings of Christopher Gadsden,* p. 163. Gadsden remembered how some members of the Continental Congress had left "no Stone . . . unturned . . . to make us look upon the New England States with a kind of Horror, as artful and designing Men altogether pursuing selfish purpose. How often I stood up in their Defence, and only wish we wou'd imitate instead of abusing them, and thank'd God We had such a systematical Body of Men as an Assylum that honest Men might resort to in the Time of their last Distress, supposing them driven out of their own States. So far from being under any Apprehensions that I bless'd God there was such a People in America."

ured by New York or Pennsylvania. For Richard Henry Lee as for some others, Pennsylvania, in fact, offered an alternative "republican" model for the future, one that took on appeal less for its political institutions than for the opportunities it freely offered to all industrious and able men.

The positive image of New England in the writings of Adams, Lee, Young, and Gadsden had a significance in itself, quite apart from the objective character of the section. The image suggested an openness to change in a republican direction that was characteristic of the Old Revolutionaries as a group. These were popular politicians: the democratic elements of colonial government had sustained them and awoke their support, such that they had every reason to welcome a new order in which all power would come from the people. Confident of their abilities, they endorsed as well the republican notion that rank should follow merit alone, that all advancement founded upon ascription or corruption should be ended with hereditary rule, which had far-reaching implications for American society. The origins of the revolutionaries' democratic inclinations might lie in the accident of birth, as some (like Young or Sears) were born of undistinguished parents and found a natural constituency in the lower orders, or in the accident of place. The remoteness of Lee's home, far from Williamsburg, where what benefits power could offer were dispensed, led him to side with the masses of men who lacked such privilege. Samuel Adams's politics were those of his father and of Boston, but his equalitarianism also had an instinctual quality that was probably his alone. The foundations of republican radicalism might even appear contradictory: Sears and Young favored a meritocracy out of hope, Lee from fear. Charles Carroll of Carrollton remained distinctive among these partisans of revolution in that he had long distrusted the people more than men whose power was inherited or appointive, and accepted neither the image of New England nor its message. Yet he could live in a republican country more easily than in a land where he could neither belong nor be free. An openness to change was not, then, an imperative to change. In no case, with the possible exception of Young, were republican inclinations so strong as to push men toward independence as a first step in the construction of a new order. Their receptivity to republicanism was, however, enough to distinguish the Old Revolutionaries from more moderate Whigs, such as those whose suspicions of New England were so apparent in the First Continental Congress, and even more from the Loyalists whose disdain for a republican future was announced in their condemnations of a living idea they called New England.

The full Loyalist case against New England emerged late, in the formal histories and tracts they wrote after the French alliance had been concluded, but it was apparent earlier in the pamphlets they published before independence. In many details the Loyalists' view of New England agreed with that of their opponents. Thomas Bradbury Chandler and Samuel Seabury traced the American Revolution back to the republican "missions" founded in seventeenth-century New England by Samuel Adams's revered ancestors. And they saw New England as distinctly democratic (that is, ruled by a mob), as equalitarian, as internally united. But what was for the Old Revolutionaries a model for the future became for Loyalists a prescription of disaster. If such a system were established throughout the continent, Americans could look forward to a military dictatorship under some latter-day Oliver Cromwell; they would see their property threatened by agrarian laws for the equalization of wealth; they would find all the land infested with that bigotry which, the Loyalists suggested, lay behind New England's unity. "You are setting up a sort of people for your masters," Chandler warned, ". . . who were always fond of subduing by the iron rod of oppression, all those whose principles or sentiments were different from their own." No denomination of men would enjoy liberty and security "if subjected to the fiery genius of a New England Republican Government."[5]

[5] Mary Beth Norton, The British-Americans; The Loyalist Exiles in England, 1774–1789 (Boston, 1972), esp. pp. 142–45; Thomas Bradbury Chandler, A Friendly Address to All Reasonable Americans, on the Subject of Our Political Confusions (New York, 1774), pp. 29–30 and n, 49–50, 53; Samuel Seabury as A Westchester Farmer, The Congress Canvassed (1774), available in Clarence Vance, ed., Letters of a Westchester Farmer, Publications of the Westchester County Historical Society, VIII (White

These were not the conclusions of men who were Loyalists out of ignorance—like those in backcountry Carolina or in Farmington, Connecticut, who were found "grossly ignorant of the true grounds of the present war with Great Britain" so late as 1777,[6] and whose loyalism therefore demands no labored explanation. Loyalist critics of New England came from the settled areas of the Atlantic seaboard; they were fully aware of those events that led an Adams and a Lee to conclude that America's future within the empire would be like that of the downtrodden Irish. Nor did Loyalist writers differ from revolutionaries in political principle: both were Whigs, ready to defend the contractual nature of government and the people's right of resistance. However much they might later belittle the colonists' grievances, in the mid-1770s few disagreed with Joseph Galloway's acknowledgment that the Americans had much to complain of. Some Loyalists were in fact outspoken in their criticism of British policy.[7] They could (as in New York) work for redress, but backed away from independence and the republican reformation it came to imply.

They often did so, it would seem, for good reason. If the revolutionaries' positions were founded upon popular support, those of Loyalists were instead threatened by the "many." Connecticut's Loyalists, for example, were Anglicans, long protected from the Congregationalist majority by the Crown. Or Loyalists were Crown officials—the one category of colonists most clearly represented among the Crown's supporters far beyond their proportion of the population at large. British office may, moreover, have been particularly important to men like Thomas Hutchinson who lacked the inner certainty Samuel Adams derived from New England's

---

Plains, 1930), 75–76; James Chalmers, *Plain Truth* (1776), available in Merrill Jensen, ed., *Tracts of the American Revolution, 1763–1776* (Indianapolis, 1967), esp. pp. 486–87. See also Carol Berkin, *Jonathan Sewall, Odyssey of an American Loyalist* (New York, 1974), pp. 112–13.

[6] Quoted by John Shy in Stephen G. Kurtz and James H. Hutson, *Essays on the American Revolution* (Chapel Hill, 1973), p. 150.

[7] Mary Beth Norton, "The Loyalist Critique of the Revolution," in *Development of a Revolutionary Mentality*, esp. pp. 129–34; Galloway, *A Candid Examination of the Mutual Claims of Great Britain, and the Colonies* (1775), in Jensen, ed., *Tracts of the American Revolution*, p. 388.

history and Thomas Young received from science. Hutchinson needed, his biographer notes, the carefully calibrated scale provided by an established hierarchical system to measure and know himself. There might even have been a "distinctive Loyalist 'personality,'" marked by a high need for external authority, a fear of autonomy, and a low tolerance for disorder," as Edwin G. Burrows and Michael Wallace have argued. Satisfied with the old order, unwilling or unable to accept "the emotional burdens of freedom," they preferred the comforts of the present or near past to the opportunities of the future. In Massachusetts, moreover, Loyalists seem to have been distinctly older than the revolutionaries. According to William Pencak, the average Bay Colony Loyalist was born in 1715 and so reached the age of sixty-one in the year independence was declared. By contrast, the average Massachusetts revolutionary leader was then forty-seven, having been born in 1729. But age, like office and personality, correlated with political preferences. Loyalists "regarded politics as an administrative activity consisting of public service performed by an elite for the benefit of a deferential populace" and were "overwhelmed" by the revolutionaries' more modern effort to secure power by mobilizing popular support. And so where the revolutionaries loved Boston with its "exciting if undignified town meeting politics," the Loyalists were repelled by that metropolis and the changes it seemed to portend.[8]

The reason some Americans took up their "revolutionary

8 William Nelson, *The American Tory* (Oxford, 1961), pp. 88–91; Otto Zeichner, *Connecticut's Years of Controversy, 1750–1776* (Chapel Hill, 1949), p. 229; Wallace Brown, *The King's Friends; The Composition and Motives of the American Loyalist Claimants* (Providence, 1965), esp. p. 263; Bernard Bailyn, *The Ordeal of Thomas Hutchinson* (Cambridge, 1974), esp. pp. 25–26; Edwin G. Burrows and Michael Wallace, "The American Revolution: The Ideology and Psychology of National Liberation," in *Perspectives in American History*, VI (1972), esp. 295, 298; William Pencak, "The Revolt Against Gerontocracy: Genealogy and the Massachusetts Revolution," *National Genealogical Society Quarterly*, LXVI (1978), esp. 291–95. See also Carol Berkin's discussion of Jonathan Sewall as a "man of little faith" whose "pessimism about reform, . . . cynicism about men's motivations, and . . . total lack of confidence in the masses of men" were widely shared by other office-holding Loyalists, in her *Sewall*, p. 161.

argument" and others remained unconvinced may well therefore lie beyond events and ideology, in the way men viewed a world on the far side of independence, which they agreed by the mid-1770s was prefigured in the republican tendencies of New England's government and society. The dilemma colonists faced was like that of persons offered jobs in cities where they have never before lived. Could they be contented there? How they answer that question may well determine the whole issue, however they later explain their decisions. If they answer it in the affirmative, the prospect of higher pay and rapid advancement elsewhere becomes compelling. If not, they might come to prefer the quieter assurances of familiar working conditions, expect what problems exist to be easily resolved, and disparage what advantages seemed to lie in the alternative declined.

The decision before Americans in the mid-1770s was political, defined for both sides by a shared political tradition. But men responded to issues according to how well they could accept their implications—according to their confidence in or fear of that new, republican "city." All agreed resistance to authority was justified only after all the alternatives were exhausted, but for Loyalists that point never arrived: the colonists never petitioned enough or with language sufficiently respectful to obtain a favorable hearing. Revolutionaries found in their countrymen's strong sense of common plight after Lexington and Concord evidence of a widespread civic commitment that fitted them for republicanism; Loyalists saw instead evidence aplenty of corruption and selfishness, which had through history made republics prey to faction and failure. Thomas Paine argued that foreign nations would come to the Americans' aid once they declared their independence, but the Loyalist James Chalmers wondered how colonists could be so deluded as to expect help from princes whose thrones would be threatened by the example of an American republic.[9] In the Declaration of Independence the Americans indicted Britain in the person of her King for a "long train of abuses and usurpations,

---

[9] Paine, *Common Sense,* and Chalmers, *Plain Truth,* in Jensen, ed., *Tracts of the American Revolution,* pp. 445, 461–62.

pursuing invariably the same object" which indicated "a design to reduce them under absolute despotism." It was therefore the Americans' right and duty to "throw off such government" and to "provide new guards for their future security." But for Loyalists, British oppression, however real, was never so extreme as to dissolve the bonds that bound America to its mother country, and certainly not so extreme as to make preferable a republican future.

The difference between the promoters and opponents of revolution lay, then, in faith, in their different capacities to believe in a possibility. Rather than risk a republic, the Loyalists tried to cling to the comforts of the established order. Too often they lost more than they had anticipated, and found their earlier choices could not be undone. "Sincerely wish I had never left Boston," Hannah Winslow wrote from England in 1779, "but its now t[oo late] and my unhappy fate is fix'd." The roots and pleasures of an earlier life—even the Newton apples and cranberries Jonathan Sewall longed for—took on an importance beyond all else. The "distresses of mind" they daily suffered seemed then a far worse fate than "the comparative trifling conditions of insults, reproaches, and perhaps a dress of tar and feathers."[10] The Loyalist exiles suffered, in short, a fate Carroll had done all possible to avoid.

The faith of the Old Revolutionaries was sometimes strained in the years after 1776, but they were spared the peculiar agony of being lost in place. Josiah Bartlett could return to the New England apple cider for which he had thirsted in Philadelphia, Cornelius Harnett to the source of his pickled oysters, to the vine and fig tree that was, as he once noted, a reality at his North Carolina home, not just the biblical image of the Bartlett sisters. The Revolution threatened them with a different fate—of being stranded in time, marked by their colonial origins and seeming hopelessly old-fashioned in the new-formed world that they had introduced, until they lost credit even for founding the republic to younger men who built upon their achievement.

[10] Winslow and Samuel Curwin quoted in Norton, *British-Americans,* p. 125.

The constitution of 1787 was the work of the Founding Fathers, who were, as the historians Stanley Elkins and Eric McKitrick have noted, the "young men of the Revolution." They were born in the 1740s, particularly the late 1740s, and 1750s. The Pennsylvania Federalist James Wilson was born in 1742, but arrived in America from his native Scotland only in 1765. John Jay was born in 1745, James Madison in 1750/51, Alexander Hamilton in 1757. Elkins and McKitrick argued that such men were shaped by their "close engagement" in the "continental aspect of the Revolution." Having served in the army, the diplomatic corps, or in particularly responsible domestic positions under the Confederation, they naturally became nationalists.[11] Continental service was, however, but part of a more general experience unique to the Founding Fathers' generation: their politics were formed within institutions born of the Revolution. Unlike the Old Revolutionaries, the Founding Fathers served their political apprenticeships within the emergent republican institutions of the resistance movement. James Madison entered politics in his mid-twenties as a member of the revolutionary committee of Orange County, which he represented two years later at the Virginia convention of 1776. John Jay was first elected to office as a member of New York's Committee of Fifty-one in 1774 (age twenty-nine). James Wilson headed the Carlisle, Pennsylvania, committee of correspondence in 1774 at age thirty-two, nine years after his arrival in America. He then went on to Philadelphia as a delegate to the first provincial conference of Pennsylvania. Hamilton arrived at New York in 1772 while still in his teens, and began his public career in the American army.

In 1776, Paine later argued, time had begun anew, freeing men from the past. All the facts relevant to human affairs were in the experience of living men "unmutilated by the contrivance or the errors of tradition." And William Maclay claimed in 1789 that more light had been thrown on the

[11] Elkins and McKitrick, "The Founding Fathers: Young Men of the Revolution," *Political Science Quarterly*, LXXVI (1971), 181–216, esp. 202–06.

subject of government in the previous twenty years than had been done "for generations before."[12] The men best prepared to contribute to the new science of politics were those who grew up with the Revolution. Having served their political apprenticeships in the nascent institutions of a republic, the Founding Fathers found commonplace what had long been considered radical. The truths of traditional politics were for them suspect at best: having absorbed less of the old order, they had less to unlearn. Starting further along in time than the Old Revolutionaries, they found it possible to go further in breaking with the past, making major contributions to republican theory and practice. The Founding Fathers were not as fixated with the dangers of central authority as were their predecessors, who had learned politics combatting the power of royal governors, then went on to fight a King. The Founding Fathers faced instead the new problem of majoritarian tyranny, and could revive magisterial and central power as a check upon the powerful state legislatures of the early republic, understanding always that such power was different in character from what it had been under a crown. The Founding Fathers rejected the axioms of traditional political science: James Madison refuted the notion that popular government could survive only in a small area; James Wilson resolved a longstanding obstacle to the creation of a federal government. The existence of two sovereign legislatures over the same territory, it was long believed, amounted to the creation of a state within a state, an *imperium in imperio,* and so institutionalized civil war. But in the American republic, Wilson insisted, the people were sovereign. And a sovereign people could parcel out responsibility for local and national government rather as a housewife delegates different tasks to her cook and her maid, remaining mistress of the household nonetheless.[13]

[12] Paine, *The Rights of Man* (second part, 1792) in Philip S. Foner, ed., *The Complete Writings of Thomas Paine* (New York, 1969), I, 376; Maclay in Charles A. Beard, ed., *The Journal of William Maclay, United States Senator from Pennsylvania, 1789–1791* (New York, 1927), p. 22.
[13] The fullest discussion of Federalist political science is in Gordon S. Wood, *The Creation of the American Republic, 1776–1787* (Chapel Hill, 1969).

The Founding Fathers were also less concerned with consensus than were their predecessors. Theirs was a new and more familiar style of democratic politics that involved the businesslike jockeying of votes in a quest for electoral victory, not internal unanimity. At this new game of politics they were highly skilled. They succeeded in getting the states to send delegates to the Philadelphia convention of 1787, even to send delegates sympathetic to their nationalist aims. Then they seized the initiative: the Virginia plan set the terms of debate at the convention, which rapidly went far beyond its announced purpose of suggesting amendments to the Confederation; and they devised a strategy by which the constitution would be enacted before its opposition could mobilize.[14]

The Old Revolutionaries took no one position in the debate on the constitution. Many never lived to see the Founding Fathers' work. Young died in 1777, Harnett in 1781 as a result of mistreatment while a prisoner of the British. Both Sears and McDougall died in 1786. It seems likely, given their strong nationalism and association with business (McDougall served as president of the Bank of New York before his death), that they would have been Federalists. Gadsden, Bartlett, and Carroll were known to favor the constitution. But the most outspoken of that generation were on the other side, such that the "men of faith" of 1776 were particularly prominent among what Cecelia Kenyon called the "men of little faith" of 1788.[15] Insofar

[14] Elkins and McKitrick, "The Founding Fathers"; and John Roche, "The Founding Fathers: A Reform Caucus in Action," *American Political Science Review*, LV (1961), 799–816.

[15] Cecelia M. Kenyon, "Men of Little Faith: The Anti-Federalists on the Nature of Representative Government," *William and Mary Quarterly*, 3d Ser., VII (1955), 3–43. The historian Charles Warren noted long ago that "in all the States . . . the leading Anti-Federalists were, as a rule, the older patriots, the men who had been most vigorous in urging independence and in bringing on the War of the Revolution," while its proponents—except for George Washington, Benjamin Franklin, Nathaniel Gorham, and James Wilson—were younger men or persons who had been "somewhat lukewarm toward independence." See Warren's "Elbridge Gerry, James Warren, Mercy Warren and the Ratification of the Federal Constitution," *Proceedings of the Massachusetts Historical Society* for 1930–1932, LXIV (Boston, 1932), 143–64, esp. 145. In his *The Making*

as the "anti-constitutionalists" had an organized base it was in a New York committee chaired by John Lamb, the one-time secretary of the New York Sons of Liberty. The Federal Republican Committee, as it came to be called, tried to organize a correspondence union like those of the period before independence, and contacted persons who had been prominent in the resistance to Britain such as Carroll's onetime ally Samuel Chase, and the Virginians George Mason, Patrick Henry, and Richard Henry Lee. Among the pamphlets it distributed was a tract by the "Columbian Patriot," Mercy Warren (born in 1728), the wife of Plymouth's old patriot James Warren (1726) and herself an active writer for the American cause.[16] The arguments of Warren, Henry, Lee, and other Old Revolutionaries drew heavily upon their experience in late-colonial politics and in the early stages of the Revolution, and assumed emotional depth and moral authority from their authors' association with the independence movement.

Old Revolutionaries who opposed the constitution were nationalists—the United States, after all, had been their creation—and they acknowledged a need to reform the Confederation, much as their Loyalist opponents of earlier days had admitted all was not right in the empire. At most they argued, like Patrick Henry, that the country's problems were less urgent than the Federalists claimed. "It was but yesterday when our enemies marched in triumph through our country," he reminded the Virginia ratifying convention. "Where is the peril now, compared to that?" Richard Henry

---

of the Constitution (Cambridge, 1947), 759 and n, Warren listed ten Anti-Federalists over forty and nine Federalists of a younger age. Jackson Turner Main has contested the point, arguing that "a few selected examples do not prove a point." Warren was, however, writing about the most prominent spokesmen for the two sides, which were by the nature of the case few in number, while Main studied the rank-and-file divisions within the state ratifying conventions. Within those conventions age was not an important political determinant, since, by Main's calculations, the Federalists were on the whole only about two years younger than their antagonists. See Main, *The Anti-Federalists, Critics of the Constitution, 1781–1788* (Chapel Hill, 1961), pp. 259–70.

[16] Lamb papers, New York Historical Society, New York. See also Linda Grant De Pauw, *The Eleventh Pillar: New York and the Federal Constitution* (Ithaca, 1966), pp. 127–29.

Lee was certainly as involved in the "continental aspects" of the Revolution as were the Founding Fathers. He had served as president of the Continental Congress, and knew its problems well. The "present federal system," he wrote on September 5, 1787, less than two weeks before the convention completed its work, was "inefficient and ineffectual" because the states were neglecting their duties to it, and he anticipated without fear a new federal constitution modeled after Britain's, with a bicameral legislature and an executive entrusted with "duration and power." A "departure from Simple Democracy" then seemed to him "indispensibly necessary if any government at all is to exist in N. America." Experience had proved "that our governments have not Tone enough for the unruly passions of men." Samuel Adams also expressed concern over the state of the nation. For want of Congressional power over commerce, foreign treaties, "&c.," he told the Massachusetts ratifying convention, "our friends are grieved, and our enemies insult us. Our ambassador at the court of London is considered as a mere cipher, instead of the representative of the United States." Power to remedy that evil should be given Congress, he urged, "and the remedy applied as soon as possible." There were indeed few, as Mercy Warren noted, who did not "unite in the general wish for the restoration of public faith, the revival of commerce, arts, agriculture, and industry, under a lenient, peaceable and energetick government."[17]

It was the constitution itself that awakened the opposition of such persons. "I have considered the new Constitution,"

[17] Patrick Henry in Jonathan Elliot, ed., *The Debates in the Several State Conventions, on the Adoption of the Federal Constitution* (Washington, 1836), III, 48; Richard Henry Lee to John Adams, New York, September 5, 1787; to Francis Lightfoot Lee, New York, July 14, 1787; and to Thomas Lee Shippen, New York, July 22, 1787, in James C. Ballagh, ed., *The Letters of Richard Henry Lee* (New York, 1914), II, 434, 424, 427; Samuel Adams in Elliot, ed., *Debates,* II, 124; Warren as a "Columbian Patriot," *Observations on the new Constitution and on the Federal and State Conventions* (1788), in Paul L. Ford, ed., *Pamphlets on the Constitution of the United States* (Brooklyn, 1888), p. 7. On Ford's misidentification of the "Columbian Patriot" as Elbridge Gerry and on other misidentifications see Gordon S. Wood, "The Authorship of the *Letters from the Federal Farmer," William and Mary Quarterly,* 3d Ser., XXXI (1974), 299–308; esp. n23.

Richard Henry Lee wrote soon after the federal convention had disbanded, ". . . and I find it impossible . . . to doubt, that in its present State, unamended, the adoption of it will put Civil Liberty and the unhappiness of the people at the mercy of Rulers" who held "great unguarded powers." Samuel Adams also stumbled at the threshold of the new building, as he put it: "I meet with a National Government, instead of a Federal Union of Sovereign States." If ratified the constitution would accomplish what the British had attempted without success; it would destroy the powers of the separate states, drawing all together under "one Legislature, the Powers of which shall extend to every Subject of Legislation," whose laws would be "supreme and controul the whole." The new government could lay and collect taxes, a prerogative the colonists had denied to Parliament; and it could raise and support armies. Nor were those powers sufficiently guarded to prevent the onset of tyranny. "There will be no checks, no real balances, in this government," Patrick Henry claimed. Such a "consolidated government" was "incompatible with the genius of republicanism."[18]

For the Old Revolutionaries who became opponents of the constitution, the Revolution of 1776 clearly meant something far different from what it meant for the Founding Fathers. It had for them inaugurated a new political world, but no new rules of politics. The Revolution had for them instead confirmed and hardened traditional fears of central authority into the "wisdom of '76." For Lee, or Henry, or Lamb, the federal constitution in recreating a dangerous central authority like that of the British would serve to undo the Revolution of 1776, which was in some sense theirs. " 'Tis really astonishing," Richard Henry Lee wrote in 1788, "that the same people, who have just emerged from a long and cruel war in defence of liberty, should agree to fix an elective despotism upon themselves and posterity!" To men weighted down by such past experience, the constitution marked no landmark in political science, no new solu-

[18] Lee to William Shippen, Jr., New York, October 2, 1787, in Ballagh, ed., *Lee Letters*, II, 441; Adams to Lee, Boston, December 3, 1787, in Harry Alonzo Cushing, ed., *The Writings of Samuel Adams* (New York, 1904–08), IV, 324; Henry in Elliot, ed., *Debates*, III, 54, 44.

tions to the problems of government. It was all too familiar. "This Constitution is said to have some beautiful features," Patrick Henry noted, "but when I come to examine those features . . . they appear to me horribly frightful. Among other deformities, it has an awful squinting; it squints toward monarchy." Others agreed the constitution created at least an aristocracy, and in any case contradicted the message of 1776. Institutional checks on power were gone, and the resorts of a people jealous of its freedom would also be yielded up to national officials who would "trample on our fallen liberty." Provision after provision of the proposed constitution was cited as proof.[19]

As it became clear ratification could not be averted, the constitution's opponents sought to amend it in ways that might "restrain from oppression the wicked and tyrannic" without, as Lee put it, interfering with the new government's power of doing good. A bill of rights was essential, and structural changes were also suggested in great abundance and variety. [20] But beyond all such schemes lay a lingering

[19] Lee to John Lamb, Chantilly, June 27, 1788, in Ballagh, ed., *Lee Letters*, II, 475; Henry in Elliot, ed., *Debates*, III, 58, 47–48. Critics complained, for example, that the President was given excessive powers; that he was bound to act with no council in vetoing acts of Congress or pardoning criminals, as were many state governors, while the requirement that he secure the "advice and consent" of the Senate in making treaties or appointing ambassadors and other officers of the United States would serve only to violate the separation of powers. The President could hold office indefinitely, "which by a little well timed bribery, will probably be done," particularly since the electoral college was but an "aristocratic junto, who may easily combine in each State to place at the head of the Union the most convenient instrument for despotic sway" (Warren in Ford, ed., *Pamphlets*, p. 11–12). The small size of the House of Representatives, where there could be no more than one representative for 30,000 Americans, would render "that house of little effect to promote good, or restrain bad government" (Lee in Ballagh, ed., *Lee Letters*, II, 452). Executive and legislative powers were so blended that it would be difficult to know who was responsible—a complaint Paine had made about British government in *Common Sense*. "There is no true responsibility," Henry charged, such that "the preservation of our liberty depends on the single chance of men being virtuous enough to make laws to punish themselves." The people, moreover, could not resist federal oppression since their "only defence, the militia," was "put into the hands of Congress" (Elliot, ed., *Debates*, III, esp. 61, 47–48).

[20] See, for example, Lee to Shippen, New York, October 2, 1787; and his draft of proposed amendments to the constitution, in Ballagh, ed., *Lee Letters*, II, 441 and 442–44n.

doubt that anything more than a league of sovereign states could work over so large an area as the United States. All "reason and experience" argued that a territory including "such a variety of climates, productions, interests, . . . of manners, habits and customs" could not be governed in freedom "unless formed into States sovereign sub modo, and confederated for the common good." No consensus could be won in so varied a nation; and where agreement waned dissonance and tumult would thrive, to be put down as always by force.[21]

The Founding Fathers' political methods were as shocking as their proposal to men who had waited years for the bells of revolution to ring together, for whom patience was the essence of good politics. Why such haste? The constitution, Henry thought, was "as radical as that which separated us from Great Britain," reason enough for care and deliberation. "Take longer time in reckoning things," he advised. The people ought to be "extremely cautious, watchful, jealous" of their liberty lest they lose it; and "if a wrong step be now made, the republic may be lost forever." The proposed constitution had already awakened a new "inflammatory resentment in different parts of the country" and so upset that internal harmony upon which republican rule depended. The existence of pockets of intense opposition to the constitution concerned even those men who spoke its arguments. One-third of the Pennsylvania ratifying convention had opposed the constitution, Samuel Adams noted in 1788. Should there be similarly large dissenting minorities in the other states he feared the consequences. "It is of the greatest importance that *America* should still be united in sentiment." It was in fact "essential that the people should be united in the federal government, to withstand the common enemy, and to preserve their valuable rights and liberties." The Massachusetts ratifying convention should propose a slate of amendments, Adams argued, so later conventions could follow its example ("the resolutions of Massa-

---

[21] Lee to Samuel Adams, New York, August 8, 1789, and also to Patrick Henry, New York, September 14, 1789, in Ballagh, ed., *Lee Letters,* II, 495, 502–03.

chusetts," he fondly noted, "have ever had their influence"),
and so facilitate the adoption of changes and additions to
the constitution that would quiet the minds of its critics.
Lee also hoped amendments would preclude the "perpetual
opposition" of state legislatures that seemed to him otherwise inevitable. Theirs were the traditional politics of consensus, the old quest for unanimity, not the newer majoritarian politics of the constitution's promoters.[22]

When forced by logic to consider why their opponents had
so departed from the wisdom of experience, Anti-Federalist
spokesmen of the old school resorted instinctively to the
charge of corruption. Like the "Court Party" in English
politics, the Federalists were partisans of monarchy, they
were "interested and avaricious adventurers for place, who
. . . prostrated every worthy principle beneath the shrine of
ambition," men who sought "places, Sallery, and pensions
under the New Constitution," unlike the "honest disinterested" men of republican virtue on the other side.[23] At
other times, however, critics of the constitution acknowledged that age separated them from that document's supporters. The constitution emerged, it seemed, in part from
the ignorance of innocents; it was one of "the ideal projects
of *young ambition, . . .* which imagination has painted in
such gawdy colours as to intoxicate the *inexperienced
votary.*" Since leaving the British Empire, America had,
according to Mercy Warren, "in many instances, resembled
the conduct of a restless, vigorous, luxurious youth, prema-
turely emancipated from the authority of a parent, but
without the experience necessary to direct him to act with
dignity or discretion." The young seemed so different from
their elders. They craved all their predecessors had denied
themselves, and so imperiled what the past had achieved. "If
we admit this consolidated government," Henry proclaimed,
"it will be because we like a great, splendid one. Some way
or other we must be a great and mighty empire; we must

---

[22] Henry and Adams in Elliot, ed., *Debates,* III, 44, 46, 21–22; II, 123–
25; Lee to Edmund Pendleton, Chantilly, May 22, 1788, in Ballagh, ed.,
Lee Letters, II, 473.

[23] Warren in Ford, ed., *Pamphlets,* pp. 4–5; Hugh Ledlie to John Lamb,
Hartford, January 15, 1788, Lamb papers.

have an army, and a navy, and a number of things. When the American spirit was in its youth," he recalled, "the language of America was different: liberty, sir, was then the primary object."[24]

That the debate on the constitution was in part a confrontation of generations became clear above all at the Virginia convention, where Henry put on the old man to the point of caricature. Confident that "having lived so long" (some fifty-two years) he had learned all that was worth knowing, Henry, like all men old in spirit, took it upon himself to convey that earned wisdom to the young, who, in the way of the modern young, found him tiresome. After all, the wisdom of Henry's experience seemed to have little to do with the wisdom of theirs. Henry was sarcastic: "I am fearful I have lived long enough to become an old-fashioned fellow," he said. "Perhaps an invincible attachment to the dearest rights of man may, in these refined, enlightened days, be deemed old-fashioned; if so, I am contented to be so." He was pathetic: he could not help thinking the constitution "perilous and destructive . . . Perhaps it may be the result of my age. These may be feelings natural to a man of my years, when the American spirit has left him, and his mental powers, like the members of his body, are decayed." He was perhaps also eloquent and moving—one listener "involuntarily felt his wrists to assure himself that the fetters were not already pressing his flesh." But, as his critics quickly noted, he contradicted himself; he rambled (even Henry admitted his mind had rushed from subject to subject, without order), went on for hours, and drove his more organized opponents to distraction. If the convention continued in this manner, Governor Edmund Randolph noted after Henry's first great speech, "instead of three or six weeks, it will take us six months to decide this question." And then Randolph began his answer: "Mr. Chairman, I am a child of the revolution."[25]

[24] Warren in Ford, ed., *Pamphlets,* pp. 7 (and also p. 5, where she says some proponents of the constitution were "in the arms of infancy" during the struggle with Britain), 22; Henry in Elliot, ed., *Debates,* III, 53.

[25] Ibid., 45, 50, 64–65. Listener's comment quoted in Michael P. Riccards, "The Presidency and the Ratification Controversy," *Presidential Studies Quarterly,* VII (1977), 43.

Edmund Randolph was indeed, like other more prominent supporters of the constitution, a child of the Revolution. Born in 1753, seventeen critical years after Henry, he had joined the American army at Cambridge in 1775, then entered politics as the youngest member of the convention that drafted Virginia's first republican constitution in 1776. He was by then a child of the Revolution in still a further sense, for that event had separated him from his natural parent, the Loyalist John Randolph. No front-line promoter of the constitution, Edmund Randolph served as an active member of the federal convention in 1787, then joined his countryman George Mason in refusing to sign the finished document. Compared to Wilson and Madison, he was a marginal Federalist; but with them he shared faith in the possibility of a free federal republic. His entire political experience had been within institutions answerable to the people; the obsessive fears of Henry and Henry's generation, formed in a world of kings and of governors answerable only to kings, made little sense to him. Henry spoke of the "necessity of being suspicious of those who govern," but Randolph thought this "political jealousy" could be taken too far. "Wisdom shrinks from extremes, and fixes on a medium as her choice." To suggestions that officials under the constitution would take whatever paths toward tyranny were left open to them—that, for example, Congress would remove the right of trial by jury in civil cases because the constitution did not expressly secure that right—Randolph responded simply, "I have no fear on this subject." And was a republican system impractical over an extensive country? Though he was not ready or able, like Madison, to argue the advantages of size, still "extent of country" seemed to Randolph "no bar to the adoption of a good government. No extent on earth seemed to be too great, provided the laws be wisely made and executed." A republic was distinguished from monarchy, he noted, not "by the extent of its boundaries, but by the nature of its principles." Did the "most illustrious and distinguished authorities" argue differently? It made no difference; "that authority has no weight with me till I am convinced." Reason, not "the dignity of names," commanded his assent.[26]

Randolph had come to support the constitution out of a new fear, which he stated in terms that predicted the way Americans of the next century would understand their obligation to preserve the republic. Enough states had already ratified the constitution to put it into effect. As a result, if Virginia refused to ratify, her decision would serve, as Randolph put it, to dissolve the Union; and if the Union was lost, "I fear it will remain so forever." Should the convention have approved the constitution, still another danger remained—that a dissident minority headed by Henry would stage a "secession" within Virginia. "Such an idea of refusing to submit to the decision of the majority is destructive of every republican principle," Randolph argued; it would "kindle a civil war, and reduce every thing to anarchy and confusion." Unanimity was no longer expected; but the submission of defeated minorities was essential to the new politics born of the Revolution and practiced by its children.[27]

If Randolph's fears looked to the future, the arguments of Old Revolutionaries who joined him in supporting the constitution remained firmly rooted in an earlier time. Christopher Gadsden understood and accepted the fact that the new federal government drew its power from the people, not the states; he thought its component parts provided "sufficient and wholesome checks on each other," and in general found every essential of republican government "well secured" in the constitution. Yet he continued to think in terms not of executive, legislative, and judiciary, but of President, Senators, and Representatives, much as the British constitution had been divided into King, Lords, and Commons. And he favored the constitution with the spirit of an old partisan of independence, hopeful that the strong government it created would undercut his countrymen's "pernissious partiality to the British trade."[28]

---

[26] Randolph in Elliot, ed., *Debates*, III, 70, 68, 84–85.
[27] Ibid., esp. 85–86 (and see also 652), 597.
[28] Gadsden as "A Steady and Open Republican," in Paul L. Ford, ed., *Essays on the Constitution of the United States* (Brooklyn, 1892), esp.

John Adams—who was born with the older generation of
revolutionaries in 1735—could never understand the federal
character of American national government. For him the
institutions of the United States were necessarily "wholly
national" (or consolidated, as the Anti-Federalists said) because sovereignty was to him, as it had been to the defenders
of parliamentary supremacy, in the legislature and indivis-
ible. That, he claimed, was the lesson of "history and experience." Nor could he any more than Gadsden break with
the old idea that the critical components of any constitutional order were social: conflict was for him always between
the few and the many. He was "obsessed with aristocracy"
even when it had become a "superannuated idea" and remained, as Gordon Wood observes, "so wrapped up in the
traditional categories of political theory" that he could never
grasp how his countrymen had succeeded in making all parts
of government, executive as well as legislative, representative
of the people.[29]

Samuel Adams did better. When in 1790 cousin John confessed confusion over the very meaning of the word "republic," and suggested that it implied a government in which
the people had "an essential share in the sovereignty," Samuel
corrected him. "Is not the *whole* sovereignity, my friend,
essentially in the people? . . . *We, the people,* is the stile
of the federal Constitution," he noted. "They adopted it; and,
conformably to it, they delegate the exercise of the Powers
of Government to particular persons, who, after short inter-
vals, resign their Powers to the People, and they will re-elect
them, or appoint others, as they think fit."[30] Far less a
scholar than John, but far better a democrat, Samuel could
understand the popular foundations of Federalist political
science, and share the Founding Fathers' faith in the possibility of a nationwide republic. Yet for younger Americans

p. 413 (Ford misidentified the author as Charles Pinckney); and also
Gadsden to Thomas Jefferson, Charleston, October 29, 1787, in Walsh,
ed., *Writings of Christopher Gadsden,* pp. 245–47.

[29] Wood, *Creation of the American Republic,* pp. 580–87.

[30] Samuel to John Adams, Boston, November 25, 1790, in Cushing, ed.,
Writings of Samuel Adams, IV, 344–45.

it was he who became the very incarnation of an anachronism—walking about in a three-cornered hat long after they had gone out of style, rambling on about the importance of New England's ancestors in a modern nation that could not have cared less.

His fate was at least a common one. The symbol of resistance and revolution in a new nation that required order and submission, the advocate of sacrifice and "virtue" in a world that had become more tolerant of private indulgence, Adams, like others of his generation, had also lived through a transformation in attitudes toward age that would spread through much of the western world but first appeared in America.[31] In establishing a republic, the Americans cut themselves off from the wisdom of the past and so, it seems, undermined the rank and respect that had traditionally been accorded the old. The future lay not with those obsessed by their colonial ancestors like Adams, but with the Thomas Youngs who saw in the unthinking veneration of forefathers a commitment to error, with those who, like Paine, found the past as outmoded as the almanacs of yesteryear and could delight in the thought that all history before 1776 had become irrelevant to the concerns of mankind. Reverence for the past and for the wisdom of age did not, of course, disappear all at once. The federal constitution's demands for more advanced ages and longer terms of residency in the nation's highest officials betrayed a continuing recognition that accumulated experience is of importance to government. Yet it was but a short step from Young or Paine to Henry David Thoreau's assertion in the 1840s that the old had nothing of importance to teach the young.[32] Having lived their youth in a time when age was respected, the Revolutionaries of 1776 became old just as their countrymen were coming to prefer the young. They might instinctively—like Patrick Henry—grasp on age to enhance their authority, but

[31] See David Hackett Fischer, *Growing Old in America* (New York, 1977), esp. p. 108. Fischer does not, however, include the American Revolution among the causes of the transformation in attitudes toward age. See pp. 77, 112.
[32] Thoreau cited in ibid., pp. 113, 115–16.

without effect; at best they might become, like Carroll in his dotage, living, empty symbols of independence and the new order's beginning.

Always, however, the Old Revolutionaries' fate was tied to the magnitude of their achievement. The creation of the republic was an advance in the eighteenth-century science of politics which, like the great revolutions in natural science, divided in a decisive way the wisdom of the past from that of the future and so of necessity divided the old from the young. Those who ushered in the Revolution of 1776 were revolutionaries in the fullest sense of that term; their achievement was fundamental to the reformation of American society and government in ways that undercut its originators, in the manner of revolutions. But one revolution is enough in any lifetime. The Revolution of 1787 lay beyond the Old Revolutionaries' capacity for innovation and very often for understanding. They had moved forward, but were also held back by their beginnings. Their successors could proceed further in developing the republic—but again only so far, for reasons that were for once not of place or of time but common to the lot of man. Even revolutionaries, the greatest of human innovators, can depart from the world that fostered them only within measure.

NOTES TO THE INTRODUCTION

1. This summary draws particularly upon the writings of Gordon S. Wood and Joyce Oldham Appleby. Among Wood's publications relevant to the social meaning of the Revolution are his book, *The Creation of the American Republic, 1776–1787* (Chapel Hill, 1969), parts of the general and unit introductions in Wood, ed., *The Rising Glory of America, 1760–1820* (New York, 1971), and "Interests and Disinterestedness in the Making of the Constitution," in Richard Beeman et al., eds., *Beyond Confederation: Origins of the Constitution and American National Identity* (Chapel Hill and London, 1987), 69–109. Among Appleby's writings, see particularly "The Social Origins of American Revolutionary Ideology," *Journal of American History*, LXIV (1978), 935–58, and also *Capitalism and a New Social Order: The Republican Vision of the 1790s* (New York and London, 1984). For Pocock's views, see especially "Civic Humanism and Its Role in Anglo-American Thought," in Pocock, *Politics, Language and Time* (New York, 1971), pp. 80–103, and *The Machiavellian Moment: Florentine Political Thought and the Atlantic Republican Tradition* (Princeton, 1975).

Wood and Appleby have provoked statements of both support and criticism, evidence of which is scattered through journals such as the *William and Mary Quarterly (WMQ)* and the *American Historical Review*. Some historians, while accepting the essentially conservative interpretation of 1776, have altered the interpretation in significant ways. See, for example, Joseph J. Ellis, *After the Revolution: Profiles of Early American Culture* (New York, 1979). Although Ellis agrees that the Revolution was dominated by the "nostalgic, backward-looking ideology" of civic humanism, he also sees liberal ideas embedded in that event. Far from distinguishing groups of people from each other, those two political "creeds" warred even within individuals (esp. pp. 34–36). Isaac Kramnick makes much the same point in "The 'Great National Discussion': The Discourse of Politics in 1787," *WMQ*, 3d Ser., XLV (1988), 3–32. Younger scholars have also tried valiantly to understand their subjects within the classical republican/liberal paradigm. One good example is Steven Watts, *The Republic Reborn: War and the Making of Liberal America, 1790–1820* (Baltimore and London, 1987).

2. Gadsden as "A Steady and Open Republican," May 6, 1784, in Richard Walsh, ed., *The Writings of Christopher Gadsden* (Columbia, S.C., 1966), p. 206, and Pauline Maier, "The Charleston Mob and the Evolution of Popular Politics in Revolutionary South Carolina, 1765–1784," *Perspectives in American History*, IV (1972), 173–96, esp. 186–91; Appleby, "Social Origins of American Revolutionary Ideology," 953–55. Lee also attacked Bernard Mandeville's *Fable of the Bees* (1714) for identifying the pursuit of self-interest with the public good. Here, as elsewhere, Lee's views were extraor-

dinarily complex and even contradictory. Note, however, that Appleby distinguishes Mandeville from earlier and more egalitarian "liberal" writers, whose views would seem to have been more congenial to Americans: Appleby, *Economic Thought and Ideology in Seventeenth-Century England* (Princeton, 1978), pp. 287–88.

3. It is worth noting, moreover, that the conception of virtue in *Cato's Letters* sometimes lacked the connotations of personal sacrifice that historians (including myself, in this book) have often associated with it. Instead virtue became, as it would become increasingly for Americans in the 1780s, the pursuit of a man's "true interest," which necessarily coincided with the public interest. That "true interest" was different from the pursuit of "present Benefit, without considering how it will affect their general Interest," by which men brought "lasting Misery upon themselves." And "true interest," again, had material implications: "every Man's private Advantage," "Cato" said, "is so much wrapt up in the Publick Felicity, that by every Step which he takes to depreciate his Country's Happiness, he undermines and destroys his own: when the Publick is secure, and Trade and Commerce flourish, every Man who has Property, or the Means of acquiring Property, will feel the blessed Effects of such a Circumstance of affairs; all the Commodities which he has to dispose of will find a ready Vent, and at a Good Price; his Inheritance will encrease every Day in Value; he is encouraged, and finds it his Interest, to build, and improve his Lands, cultivate new Trades, and promote new Manufactures," so more people would be employed and enabled to live in plenty, marry, and have children. Even the "Poor and Helpless" would "have their Share in the general Felicity, arising from the Superfluities and Charity of the Rich."

The letters were, of course, written within the social context of early eighteenth-century England, and include statements such as that only "a very small part of Mankind have Capacities large enough to judge of the Whole of Things." In revolutionary America, however, the emphasis on "true Interest," or what we would call enlightened self-interest, supported arguments for a more general diffusion of knowledge through the population so the masses would see how their private interests and the public interest coincided. The citations are from [Trenchard and Gordon,] *Cato's Letters. Essays on Liberty, Civil and Religious, and Other Important Subjects,* four volumes bound in two (New York, 1971; a reprinting of the 6th edition, London 1755), II (original Vol. III), pp. 192–94.

INDEX

Judith (Judith Gordon), 161
Judkins, 142

Kalm, Peter, 116
Kenyon, Cecelia, 282
Kim, Sung Bok, 117 *n.*
King's County, Ireland, 205

Lamb, Anthony, 69
Lamb, John: background, 68–9;
    meets Congressional delegates,
    84; mentioned, 83, 100; an Old
    Revolutionary, 270; opposes
    federal constitution, 283, 285;
    and politics, 71–2, 73, 82 *n.*, 203;
    presides at public meeting, 83;
    skills, 70; writes broadsides
    against British soldiers, 74
Lancaster, Pa., 121
Laty, Michael, 201
Laurens, Henry, 183–4
Lecky, William, 47
Lee, Arthur: and Samuel Adams,
    23, 24–5; and Silas Deane, 183;
    in England, 179, 192, 197; in
    father's will, 167; mentioned,
    213; seeks offices, 194; and
    slavery, 189
Lee, Charles, 195
Lee, Gen. Charles, 88–9, 89 *n.*
Lee, Francis Lightfoot, 167
Lee, Hannah Ludwell (Mrs.
    Thomas Lee), 166–7
Lee, Hannah Ludwell (Mrs.
    William Lee), 173
Lee, Ludwell, 170
Lee, Philip Ludwell, 167, 174
Lee, Richard ("the emigrant"),
    166, 175
Lee, Richard Henry: accusations
    against, 195; and Samuel
    Adams, 44, 46, 182, 199;
    alienation from Virginia, xviii,
    188–92; and American
    interdependence, 179–80, 192;
    ancestry, 164, 166–7, 185;
    appearance, 165; austerity of,
    170–1; basis of his political
    commitment, 185–200; birth and
    childhood, 166–7; and Charles
    Carroll of Carrollton, 223;
    children, 170; conservatism of,
    180, 183–4, 187; on constitutions:

U.S., 283–5, 286, Virginia, 180–
    1, 191; contradictions, 193–5,
    197; and democracy, 181–4;
    disillusionment with Britain,
    178–80, 186; economic thought,
    186–7, 190; education of, 175;
    elitism, 182–3; family life, 192;
    financial state, 113, 167–8, 170–
    4, 176, 194; founds cooperative
    store, 172; on the French
    Revolution, 184–5; on
    government, 181; guilt, 196–
    7; and independence, American,
    180, 185, 197; mentioned, 209,
    210, 216, 276; and New
    England, 165–6, 199–200, 272–3,
    274; an Old Revolutionary, xvii–
    xviii, 269, 270; organizes
    demonstrations, 177–8, 196–7;
    political career, 175–6, 185, 203,
    265, 270 *n.*, 274; politics of, 165,
    177–85; on politics, 176;
    portraits, xv, 204; on property
    rights, 186; radicalism of, 199–
    200; and religion, 185, 200; and
    republicanism, 187–8, 274; seeks
    British appointments, 176, 194,
    194–5 *n.*; on slavery, 188–91,
    193–4, 195, 196, 197; on the
    South, 193; and virtue, 177, 178–
    9, 197–200, 212, 269; a Whig,
    185
Lee, Robert E., 198–9
Lee, Thomas ("the empire
    builder"), 166, 167, 171, 175
Lee, Thomas, 170
Lee, Thomas Ludwell, 167
Lee, William: and Deane-Lee
    controversy, 183–4; in father's
    will, 167; and R. H. Lee, 173,
    176, 192; and London politics,
    179, 197; mentioned, 213; and
    trade, 186, 193; and virtue, 179,
    198
Leedstown, Va., 178 *n.*
Leonard, Daniel, 13
*Letters from a Farmer in
    Pennsylvania* (Dickinson), 214
Lexington, Mass.: battle at, 26, 278
liberty: economic implications, 98–
    100, 186
Liberty Hall, 193
liberty pole, 74, 75, 77